"一带一路"共建国家航运从业人员培训系列教材

本书由辽宁省大连海事大学教育发展基金会和大连泛和集团支持出版

U0586023

港口物流实务

Practical Operation of Port Logistics

（汉英对照）

主 编 / 陈 康 曲晨蕊

主 审 / 孙家康

大连海事大学出版社

DALIAN MARITIME UNIVERSITY PRESS

图书在版编目（CIP）数据

港口物流实务 = Practical Operation of Port
Logistics：汉英对照 / 陈康，曲晨蕊主编. — 大连 ：
大连海事大学出版社，2024.12
　　"一带一路"共建国家航运从业人员培训系列教材
　　ISBN 978-7-5632-4490-4

　　Ⅰ.①港…　Ⅱ.①陈…②曲…　Ⅲ.①港口—物流管
理—高等学校—教材—汉、英　Ⅳ.①U695.2

中国国家版本馆 CIP 数据核字（2023）第 245695 号

大连海事大学出版社出版

地址：大连市黄浦路523号　邮编：116026　电话：0411-84729665（营销部）　84729480（总编室）
http://press.dlmu.edu.cn　E-mail：dmupress@ dlmu.edu.cn

大连天骄彩色印刷有限公司印装　　　　　大连海事大学出版社发行
2024 年 12 月第 1 版　　　　　　　　　2024 年 12 月第 1 次印刷
幅面尺寸：184 mm×260 mm　　　　　　印张：15.5
字数：360 千　　　　　　　　　　　　印数：1～1700 册

出版人：刘明凯

责任编辑：王　琴　　　　　　　　　　责任校对：高　颖
封面设计：解瑶瑶　　　　　　　　　　版式设计：解瑶瑶

ISBN 978-7-5632-4490-4　　　　定价：43.00 元

"一带一路"共建国家
航运从业人员培训系列教材

编委会

总序

  习近平总书记指出，航运业是国际贸易发展的重要保障，也是世界各国人民友好往来的重要纽带。2013年秋，习近平总书记提出了共建丝绸之路经济带和21世纪海上丝绸之路重大倡议。在"一带一路"建设中，海运发挥着先导性、战略性作用，它不仅是21世纪海上丝绸之路的主要运输方式，而且对丝绸之路经济带的形成和发展起着重要的支持和推动作用。

  中华人民共和国成立后，我国海运业经过了70多年的发展建设，逐步发展壮大。我国已经成为名副其实的海运大国，正向着海运强国的建设目标迈进。目前，我国海运连接度世界领先，航线网络遍布全球，海运服务能力位居世界前列，海运船队运力规模居世界第二，沿海港口规模和吞吐量稳居世界第一。作为海运业最活跃、最关键、最重要的因素，涉海类专门人才发挥着不可替代的作用，是重要的战略资源。职业素养过硬、业务能力扎实、管理水平高超、心理素质良好的高素质从业人员，在推动海运业发展建设中发挥着关键作用。近年来，世界各国特别是"一带一路"共建国家对涉海类专门人才的需求越来越大，加强相关人才培训培养的需要也越来越迫切。交通运输部党组书记、部长李小鹏在出席2023年中国航海日主论坛的致辞中强调：习近平总书记高度重视交通运输事业发展，多次到港口、航运等交通运输一线视察并做出一系列重要指示，为推进交通运输和航运发展指明了前进方向、提供了根本遵循。我们要坚持交通天下，打造开放航运。要推进与"一带一路"共建国家和地区基础设施"硬联通"和规则标准"软联通"，提升国际运输便利化水平。

  在此背景下，校友江四元先生建议，由大连海事大学组织力量，专门编写一套面向"一带一路"共建国家航运从业人员培训系列教材，学校慨然应允。一方面，国际合作与人文交流是海事教育的重要职能之一，是实现海事行业科技发展和人才培养以及不同文化交汇融合的有效途径。另一方面，作为我国高等航海教育的引领者和国际海事教育发展的推动者，大连海事大学是我国最早开展境外实质性办学的高校，早在2007年就在斯里兰卡建立了海外校区，实现了海事教育的首次输出；目前学校的留学生群体中，"一带一路"共建国家生源占比超90%。综上，大连海事大学具备开展此项工作的基础和条件。

  为提高教材编纂质量，学校专门成立了教材编委会，组织校内外权威专家学者和行业企事业单位精英，围绕航运管理、金融、保险、法律、经纪、船舶经营管理、海事行政管理等领域开展研究，力求保证教材的时代性、创新性、系统性、权威性和指导性。为提高教材的适用性和可读性，本系列教材采用中英文对照的方式进行编写，同时辅之以大量实际案例和生动故事，便于国内外读者的理解和思考。我相信，这套教材一定会成为国家对外开放合作的优秀作品。

大连海事大学原党委书记、校长

2023年9月28日

前言

经过三十余年的发展,我国港口规模稳居世界第一,港口作业效率位居世界前列,港口设施全球领先,港口已经成为交通强国与海洋强国的重要支撑。随着港口作业模式不断优化,以及物联网、大数据、云计算、人工智能和移动互联网等新兴信息技术的快速发展,港口码头专业化、现代化水平显著提升,夯实了我国的港口大国地位。目前,我国已构成"布局合理、层次分明、功能齐全"的港口格局,初步形成环渤海、长三角、东南沿海、珠三角和西南沿海五大港口群,港口物流对畅通国际贸易和国际物流通道发挥了重要作用。

本书面向港口物流全过程中的实际问题,将实务操作与实际案例相结合,系统介绍了港口物流的基本运作流程、技术和方法,主要内容包括:港口物流概述、港口物流设施与设备、港口物流运作流程与管理、港口物流发展新技术、港口物流发展政策与措施。本书可作为高等院校物流管理专业、交通运输专业和其他经济管理类专业师生的参考用书,也可作为港航物流领域从业人员和其他对港口物流感兴趣人员进行阅读和学习的重要资料。

本书编写分工如下:曾庆成、曲晨蕊编写第 1 章;马千里编写第 2 章;陈康、陈苏敏编写第 3 章;王泽浩编写第 4 章;曲晨蕊编写第 5 章。管理科学与工程博士研究生王泽浩、陈苏敏和硕士研究生李姗、王茹梦、崔耀桦、周嘉欣、王振霞等参与了本书的英文翻译工作。陈康对全书进行校对、统稿。孙家康担任本书主审,并对书稿进行最终审定。

本书在编写过程中参阅了大量的文献资料,主要参考资料已列在书后。在此,谨向国内外作者表示由衷感谢。鉴于港口物流领域的快速发展,对该领域的认识和研究还在持续深入。

受编者水平所限,书中不妥之处在所难免,希望专家学者和广大读者提出宝贵意见。

编　者

2023 年 8 月 1 日

目录

第1章 港口物流概述
Chapter 1 | Overview of Port Logistics

◆ 1.1 港口的产生与发展
1.1 Generation and Development of Ports

1.1.1 港口的概念与分类
1.1.1 Concept and Category of Ports

港口是供船舶进出、停泊、靠泊,旅客集散,货物装卸、驳运、储存的地方,它具有相应的码头设施,由一定范围的水域和陆域组成。港口可以由一个或者多个港区组成(参见《中华人民共和国港口法》)。按照不同标准,港口可以划分为不同的种类,如表1.1所示。

表 1.1 港口的分类

分类依据	类别
规模	特大型港口、大型港口、中型港口、小型港口
用途	商港、工业港、渔港、军港
位置	海港、河口港、河港、湖港
地位	干线港、支线港、喂给港

A port refers to an area of a specific range of water and land with corresponding terminal facilities, where for ships to enter and leave, berth and moor, for passengers to collect and distribute, and for cargos to be transferred by barged and stored. The area comprises one or more harbor areas(as see "The Port Act of the People's Republic of China"). As shown in Table 1.1, ports are divided into different categories, according to various taxonomy.

Table 1.1　Category of ports

Taxonomy	Category
Scale	Extra-large-sized port, Large-sized port, Medium-sized port, Small-sized port
Function	Commercial port, Industrial port, Fishing port, Naval port
Location	Sea port, Estuary port, River port, Lake port
Status	Hub port, Spoke port, Feeder port

1.1.2　海上运输及港口发展
1.1.2　Maritime Transport and Port Development

全球产业分工与国际贸易的发展影响着海运格局的变化。20 世纪 80 年代以来,全球制造业逐步向亚太地区,尤其是向中国转移,国际航运重心也由西欧地区、北美地区向亚太地区转移。表 1.2 显示了全球集装箱港口吞吐量排名。2022 年全球十大集装箱港口中,中国占据 7 席,已成为全球港口大国。

表 1.2　全球集装箱港口吞吐量排名

排名	1998 年	2008 年	2018 年	2022 年
1	新加坡港	新加坡港	上海港	上海港
2	香港港	上海港	新加坡港	新加坡港
3	高雄港	香港港	宁波舟山港	宁波舟山港
4	鹿特丹港	深圳港	深圳港	深圳港
5	釜山港	釜山港	广州港	青岛港
6	长滩港	迪拜港	釜山港	广州港
7	汉堡港	广州港	香港港	釜山港
8	洛杉矶港	宁波舟山港	青岛港	天津港
9	安特卫普港	鹿特丹港	天津港	香港港
10	上海港	青岛港	迪拜港	鹿特丹港

The global industrial division of labor and international trade development have been affecting the changes in the pattern of the maritime transport. Since the 1980s, the global manufacturing industry has gradually shifted to the Asia-Pacific region, especially to China. The international shipping center has also shifted from Western Europe and North America to the Asia-Pacific region. Global container port throughput ranking is shown in Table 1.2. In 2022, China holds seven seats in the list of top ten container ports in the world and has gradually become a global port power.

Table 1.2　Global container port throughput ranking

Ranking	1998	2008	2018	2022
1	Singapore Port	Singapore Port	Shanghai Port	Shanghai Port
2	Hong Kong Port	Shanghai Port	Singapore Port	Singapore Port
3	Kaohsiung Port	Hong Kong Port	Ningbo-Zhoushan Port	Ningbo-Zhoushan Port
4	Rotterdam Port	Shenzhen Port	Shenzhen Port	Shenzhen Port
5	Busan Port	Busan Port	Guangzhou Port	Qingdao Port
6	Long Beach Port	Dubai Port	Busan Port	Guangzhou Port
7	Hamburg Port	Guangzhou Port	Hong Kong Port	Busan Port
8	Los Angeles Port	Ningbo-Zhoushan Port	Qingdao Port	Tianjin Port
9	Antwerp Port	Rotterdam Port	Tianjin Port	Hong Kong Port
10	Shanghai Port	Qingdao Port	Dubai Port	Rotterdam Port

1.1.3　港口功能演变与拓展
1.1.3　Function Evolution and Expansion of Ports

港口最早定义为水陆交界处适于船舶装卸货物的地点。随着社会经济以及全球化的发展,港口功能逐步拓展。1992 年,联合国贸易与发展会议针对"港口营销和第三代港口"的讨论中,将港口的发展进程划分为三个阶段。1999 年,联合国贸发会提出了第四代港口的概念。港口功能也随着港口代际更替而演变。

Ports were first defined as locations at the junction of water and land where ships load and unload cargos. The functions of ports have gradually expanded with the development of social economy and globalization. In 1992, port development has gone through three stages in the discussion on "Port Marketing and Third Generation Port", which was launched by UNCTAD (United Nations Conference on Trade and Development). Moreover, the concept of the fourth-generation port was introduced by UNCTAD in 1999. The functions have also evolved with inter-generational changes of ports.

第一代港口定位为"运输枢纽",主要提供船舶挂靠、货物装卸、转运以及仓储等基础服务,完成货物在海运与其他运输方式之间的换装。

The first-generation port was positioned as a "transport hub", which mainly provided essential services such as ship docking, cargo handling, transhipment, warehousing and so on. Cargos could be reloaded between maritime transport and other transport modes at the port.

第二代港口定位为"运输、工业和商业服务中心"。港口与所在城市的经济相互依赖,工业逐步向港区集聚,出现了临港工业区、物流园区等。港口服务既包括船舶靠泊、货物装卸、仓储服务等基础服务,也包括换装货物、货物加工等增值服务,港口的综合服务功能逐步增强。

The second-generation port was positioned as a "transport, industrial, and commercial service center". The port and the economy of the port city are interdependent, and the port-centered industrial zone and logistics park were set up with industries gradually converging towards the port area. The comprehensive service functions of ports have been gradually enhanced, apart from the essential services (ship berthing, loading and unloading, warehousing services and so on) and value-added services (transhipment of cargo and processing of goods).

第三代港口定位为"国际物流中心"。港口为国际贸易提供物流平台,服务于船公司、托运人、货运代理等。服务范围既包括船舶挂靠、货物装卸、转运以及仓储等基础服务,又进一步向陆向物流服务延伸,形成以港口为中心的物流服务链。港口与所在城市的关系更加密切,港城一体化不断发展。

The third-generation port was positioned as an "international logistics center". Ports provide a logistics platform for international trade, serving shipping companies, consignors, freight forwarders and so on. The scope of services not only includes essential services such as ship docking, cargo handling, transhipment, warehousing. But also further extends to land-based logistics services, forming a port-centric logistics service chain has. The port has closer relations with the city where it is located, and the port-city integration has been promoted.

第四代港口被定义为"综合中心",是资源配置的枢纽,港口功能涵盖仓储、集散、信息传输和增值服务。港口经济与内陆腹地城市经济融合,港口之间的竞争逐渐转变为以港口为核心的物流服务链之间的竞争。

The fourth-generation port was defined as a "comprehensive center", a hub for resource allocation. Port functions include warehousing, cargo distribution, information transmission, and value-added services. With the economic integration of the port and the in land hinterland cities, the competition between ports has gradually transformed into the competition between port-centric logistics service chains.

◆ 1.2 港口物流的内涵与发展
1.2 Connotation and Development of Port Logistics

1.2.1 港口物流的概念与基本特征
1.2.1 Concept and Basic Characteristics of Port Logistics

（1）港口物流的概念
（1）Concept of Port Logistics
物流是货物从供应地向接收地的实体流动中,根据实际需要,将运输、储存、装卸、搬运、包装、流通加工、配送和信息处理等功能有机结合起来,以实现用户要求的过程(中国的物流术语标准)。

Logistics is the process of the physical flow of goods from the supply place of supply to the place of reception. According to actual needs, the functions of transportation, storage, loading and unloading, handling, packaging, circulation processing, distribution and information processing are organically combined to achieve the user-requirements (China's logistics terminology standards).

港口物流是以港口口岸为核心,针对用户的实际需求,借助先进的技术和完备的设施,将运输、储存、装卸、搬运、包装、流通加工、配送、信息处理、报关报检、其他配套增值服务等多个物流环节进行整合,以提供集多功能于一体的综合物流服务或物流解决方案的过程。港口物流系统的运作成本与效率是港口带动口岸城市及腹地经济发展的决定性因素。此外,全球物流网络,是通过船舶在港口间的海上运营,由各个口岸物流系统构建、扩展起来的,对推动全球经济一体化越来越重要。而且,建设高效、经济的口岸物流系统,不仅是提升港口竞争力的需要,也是港口城市及腹地经济发展的客观需求。

Port logistics, an integrated logistic service or logistics solution centered around the port, aiming to fulfill the practical requirements of users. The whole process integrates multiple logistics functions by advanced technology and comprehensive facilities, including transportation, storage, loading and unloading, handling, packaging, circulation processing, distribution, information processing, customs declaration and inspection, as well as other supporting value-added services. The operation cost and efficiency of the port logistics system are determining factors to promote the economic development of port cities and hinterland. Besides, the global logistics network is constructed and expanded by port logistics systems through the maritime operations of ships between ports. It is playing an increasingly important role in promoting global economic integration. Furthermore, the construction of an efficient and economical port logistics system is not only the needs to enhance the competitiveness of the port, but also meet the objective demand of the economic development of port cities and hinterland.

(2)基本特征

(2)Basic Characteristics

港口物流的特征可以总结为:

The characteristics of port logistics can be summarized as:

①港口物流具有集散效应

①Port Logistics Has Distribution Effects

围绕港口货物装卸与转运,集聚船公司、陆运物流公司、船舶燃料公司、船舶修理公司、货运代理公司等,产生了以物流增值为主的物流园区和物流中心,集聚了航运保险、航运金融、船舶租赁、航运法律等高端航运服务业。

Around the loading, unloading and handling of port goods, the logistics parks and logistics centers have gathered shipping companies, land logistics companies, fuel companies, ship repairing companies, freight forwarder companies and so on, which mainly focus on value-added logistics activities. Shipping insurance, shipping finance, ship leasing, and shipping laws and other high-end shipping services, are also provided in the logistics parks and logistics centers.

②港口物流具有整合效应

②Port Logistics Has Integration Effects

港口依托腹地运输、拆拼箱、包装、库存管理等增值服务,将多个环节的功能进行整合,充分发挥国际化、规模化、系统化优势,以提供物流解决方案、满足全球经济一体化的需求,通过多环节协同运作以形成高度整合的供应链关系,进而提高物流综合效率。

In order to meet the needs of global economic integration, port logistics should be international, large-scale and systematic. Furthermore, the port provides logistics solutions by relying on value-added services such as hinterland transportation, vanning and devanning, packaging, and inventory management. Through coordinated operations, the port logistics forms a highly integrated supply chain relationship and improves logistics efficiency.

③港口物流具有供应链属性

③Port Logistics Has Supply Chain Attributes

第四代港口强调港口是供应链中的一部分,通过延伸港口物流服务功能来提供物流金融、供应链金融,以发挥港口在供应链中的作用,进而提升港口综合竞争力。

The fourth-generation port emphasizes that the port is part of the supply chain. By extending the port logistics service function, ports provide logistics finance and supply chain finance, give play to the role of port in the supply chain, and enhance overall competitiveness of the port.

1.2.2　港口物流的形成与发展
1.2.2　Formation and Development of Port Logistics

在工业制造中,为消除库存积压、减少资源浪费,准时制生产方式应运而生,即在需要的时间和需要的地点,按照需要的数量,生产所需的产品。准时制生产方式是以订单驱动,将"供-产-销"多环节紧密衔接起来,以实现柔性制造、控制生产成本,对原材料及产成品的物流链也提出了更高要求。同时,经济全球化的发展也进一步推动了国际物流的快速发展。国际物流具有跨区域与复杂性的特征,而传统的运输服务只针对单一环节,已经无法满足客户日益增长的物流需求。作为海、陆运输的转运节点,港口是国际物流活动的主要集散节点。港口功能由装卸、仓储功能沿物流链上、下游进行拓展,以提供更多物流增值服务,如转运、配送、加工、仓储等。港口从单一的运输枢纽节点向国际物流中心转变。

As for industrial manufacturing, Just-In-Time(JIT) is a way to eliminate inventory backlog and reduce waste of resources, i.e., to produce the required products at the required time and place, in the required quantity. Just-In-Time production mode is order-driven and closely connects "supply-production-marketing" stages to achieve flexible manufacturing and control production costs, which also puts forward higher requirements on the logistics chain of raw materials and finished products. Meanwhile, with the development of economic globalization, international logistics has developed rapidly. Due to the cross-regional and complex characteristics of international logistics, the traditional single-link transportation service has been unable to meet the increasing logistics needs of customers. As transit nodes between marine and land transportation, ports are the primary distribution nodes for international logistics activities. Port functions are expanded along the upstream and downstream of the logistics chain by loading and unloading, warehousing to provide more logistics value-added services, such as transfer, distribution, processing, warehousing and so on. The port has transformed from a single transport hub node to an international logistics center.

在港口竞争日益激烈、客户需求日趋多样化的背景下,港口物流具有国际化、多功能化、标准化、信息化与智能化的发展趋势。

Under the background of increasingly fierce competition in ports and increasingly diversified customer needs, port logistics has a development trend of internationalization, multi-functionalization, standardization, informatization and intelligence.

(1) 国际化
(1) Internationalization

在贸易全球化发展的进程中,货物的生产地与消费地往往归属不同的国家或地区,因而驱动了国际物流服务需求的产生。

In the process of globalization of trade, the place of production and consumption of goods often belongs to different countries or regions, and it also drives the demand for international logistics services.

(2) 多功能化
(2) Multi-functionalization

港口物流集装卸、仓储等基础功能和配套的物流增值服务于一体,能够满足个性化的客户需求,提供综合物流服务。

In order to meet the personalized needs of customers, the integrated logistics service is provided based on basic functions (loading and unloading, warehousing, etc.) and value-added services.

(3) 标准化
(3) Standardization

基于标准化的运输单元,针对运输设备、港口装备及其他基础设施构建标准化体系,简化多环节之间的货物流动,降低货损概率,进而提升港口物流效率。

Based on standardized transportation units, a standardized system is established for transportation equipment, port equipment and other infrastructure to simplify the flow of goods between multiple links, reduce the probability of cargo damage, and improve port logistics efficiency.

（4）信息化与智能化
（4）Informatization and Intelligence

物联网、大数据、云计算、人工智能等新兴信息技术发展,为港口自动化与智能化发展奠定了基础。以港口信息化、数字化为基础,搭建港口物流服务平台,提供由数据驱动的港口决策支持,是港口发展的主要方向。

The development of emerging information technologies, such as the Internet of Things, big data, cloud computing and artificial intelligence, has laid a foundation for the development of port automation and intelligence. Based on port informatization and digitalization, it is the main direction of port development to build port logistics service platform in order to provide operational decision support driven by data.

1.2.3 港口物流的功能
1.2.3 Functions of Port Logistics

港口物流的功能主要包括运输功能,装卸搬运功能,仓储功能,加工、包装、分拣功能,货物配载功能和信息处理功能,如图 1.1 所示。

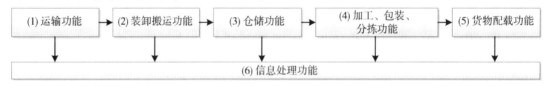

图 1.1 港口物流的功能

The functions of port logistics mainly include transport function, loading, unloading and handling functions, warehousing function, processing, packaging, and sorting functions, cargo stowage function and information processing function, as shown in Figure 1.1.

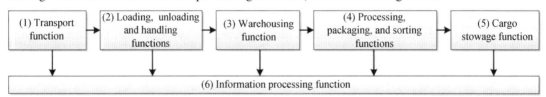

Figure 1.1　Functions of port logistics

（1）运输功能
（1）Transport Function

运输是港口物流服务的主要功能。港口作为多种运输方式的交叉节点,集公路、铁路、水路于一体,既辐射内陆腹地,又与海运网络相连接,可以完成货物在不同运输方式之间的转运。

Transport is the primary function of port logistics services. As a transit node of various modes of transportation, the port integrates roads, railways and waterways, which not only radiates inland hinterland, but also connects with maritime network, and can complete the transfer of goods between different modes of transportation within the port.

（2）装卸搬运功能
（2）Loading, Unloading and Handling Functions

装卸搬运是港口物流的基本功能,包括码头前沿的装卸作业、码头前沿与堆场之间的搬运作业、堆场的堆码拆垛和分拣理货作业、铁路列车和集卡的装卸作业等。

Loading, unloading and handling are the essential functions of port logistics, including loading and unloading operations at the quayside of the port, handling operations between the quayside and the yard, stacking and tallying operations at the yard, and loading and unloading operations of trains and trucks.

（3）仓储功能
（3）Warehousing Function

货物在不同运输方式间进行转换的过程中会产生临时库存,港口对在港区内进行转运的货物提供集拼箱、拆箱、查验、临时存储和保管服务。

When the goods are transferred between different modes of transportation, there will be temporary inventory. The port provides consolidation, unpacking, inspection, temporary storage and safekeeping services for the goods transferred in the port area.

（4）加工、包装、分拣功能
（4）Processing, Packaging, Sorting Functions

加工、包装、分拣功能包括给货物粘贴标签、零部件组装、商品包装和运输包装作业等,并能在货物合理存放的基础上进行快速分类。

Processing, packaging, sorting functions include the operations such as the labelling of goods, assembly of parts, product packaging and transportation packaging. And the goods can be quickly classified based on proper storage.

（5）货物配载功能
（5）Cargo Stowage Function

对进行装船的货物进行合理配载,以保证运输的安全性。

Reasonably stow the cargo for shipment to ensure the safety of transportation.

（6）信息处理功能
（6）Information Processing Function

利用港口的信息资源、通信设施和智能装备,对到港船舶、集卡和货物的物流、贸易、金

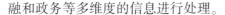

融和政务等多维度的信息进行处理。

Utilize the port's information resources, communication facilities and intelligent equipment to process multi-dimensional information such as logistics, trade, finance, and government affairs of arriving ships, trucks and cargo.

◈ 1.3 现代物流业与港口发展
1.3 Modern Logistics and Port Development

1.3.1 港口与区域经济
1.3.1 Port and Regional Economy

港口物流与区域经济的发展相互依存、相互促进。一方面,港口发展依托港口所在的区域,区域经济的发展能够大力推动港口功能的转变和改善;另一方面,借助港口及其物流系统的优势,可以提升区域的资本吸引力。

Port logistics and the development of the regional economy are interactive. On the one hand, the development of a port is inseparable from the region where it is located. The development of the regional economy can promote the transformation and improvement of port functions. On the other hand, regional capital attractiveness can be enhanced with the advantages of the port and its logistics system.

（1）港口物流对区域经济发展的作用
（1）Role of Port Logistics to Regional Economic Development

港口是全球物流网络系统建设的基础,港口物流的发展显著提高了运输的便利性。整合区域内部资源,吸引临港产业集聚,升级产业结构,优化产业布局,可以形成规模经济效应,从而带动区域经济的迅速发展。

Ports are the foundation of the construction of a global logistics network system. The development of port logistics has significantly improved the convenience of transportation. The rapid development of regional economy comes from the scale economy effect by integrating regional resources, attracting port-centered industries, upgrading industrial structure, and optimizing industrial layout.

（2）区域经济增长对港口发展的促进作用
（2）Promoting Effect of Regional Economic Growth on Port Development

最初作为海陆运输方式交互的运输枢纽中心,港口与城市相互独立。港口城市的经济发展逐步带动腹地货物运输需求的增长,进而推动了港口的发展,港口功能也从单一的运输、存储功能向综合的港口物流服务转变。

Initially, as the transport hub center for interaction between land and sea transportation modes, the port and the city were independent of each other. The economic development of port city gradually drives the growth of the transport demand in the hinterland, and then promotes the development of the port. The port function has also changed from a single function of transport and storage to a comprehensive port logistics service.

1.3.2 港口与城市互动
1.3.2 Interaction Between Port and City

(1) 港口对城市的作用
(1) Role of Ports for Cities

港口是城市的重要基础设施,对提高城市可达性、降低运输成本和提升城市功能至关重要。同时,港口发展有助于吸引产业在沿海城市集聚,促进城市临港产业、航运服务业发展,港口功能和港口规模的提升能够带动城市综合竞争力的提高。

Ports are critical infrastructures of the city, which play an essential role in improving urban accessibility, reducing transport costs and improving port city functions. At the same time, the development of the port will help promote the industrial agglomeration in the port city, promote the development of the port-centered industry and shipping service industry, and the improvement of port function and port scale can enhance the comprehensive competitiveness of the city.

(2) 城市对港口的作用
(2) Role of Cities for Ports

港口城市有充足的港口建设所需的自然资源和人力资源,同时当地政府能够提供优惠政策支撑港口的发展。港口城市也是港口的直接经济腹地,其发展有助于经济腹地范围的扩张,加强港口的货源支持,从而推动港口转型和对外开放升级。

The sufficient natural and human resources of port cities are required for port construction. In the meanwhile, local government would also provide preferential policies to support port development. The port city is also the direct economic hinterland of the port. The port city's development will lead to the expansion of the hinterland area, drive the growth of freight demand in the hinterland, which will, in turn, promote the functional transformation and opening-up and upgrading of the port.

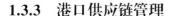
1.3.3　港口供应链管理
1.3.3　Port Supply Chain Management

（1）港口供应链管理的概念
（1）Concept of Port Supply Chain Management

港口供应链是以港口企业为基础,将与港口物流相关的上、下游企业(内陆集疏运企业、仓储企业、货运代理公司、船务代理公司、报关公司等)、服务商(航运金融公司、保险公司、法律公司)、客户(货主公司、航运公司)连接成一个整体,将港口物流服务作为产品销售给客户的功能性网链结构。

The port supply chain is based on port enterprises. It integrates upstream and downstream enterprises related to port logistics (inland collection and distribution enterprises, storage enterprises, freight forwarding companies, shipping agency companies, customs declaration companies and so on) , service providers (shipping finance companies, insurance companies, legal companies) , customers (consignor companies, shipping companies) as a whole. The port supply chain is a functional network chain structure that sells port logistics services as products to customers.

港口供应链管理就是对港口供应链中的物流、信息流、资金流、商流进行管理,包括货物、信息、资金在供应链中每个节点的流转和处理。通过合作机制、决策机制、激励机制等,港口物流供应链的整体竞争力和整体效益得到增强和提升。

Port supply chain management manages cargo flow, information flow, capital flow and business flow in the port supply chain, including the circulation and processing of goods, information and capital at each node in the supply chain. The overall competitiveness and efficiency of the port logistics supply chain are enhanced through cooperation mechanisms, decision-making mechanisms, incentive mechanisms and so on.

（2）港口供应链管理的意义
（2）Significance of Port Supply Chain Management

港口供应链的有效管理可以缩短货物在运输节点上的中转时间,及时转换包装方式,并促进港口及相关物流资源的有效配置和利用,加快信息在供应链中各节点之间的流转速度,形成高质量、快反应、低成本的港口物流体系,提高运输效率和质量。一方面,对运输需求方提供更加精准和有效的一体化服务,能够提高客户的满意度。另一方面,日益增长的货运需求可以吸引更多的相关服务企业进驻,从而形成更为完善的多式联运网络。

The effective management of the port supply chain can shorten the transit time of goods at the transport nodes, change the packaging method in time and promote the effective allocation and utilization of related logistics resources. It can also accelerate the flow of information between nodes in the supply chain. A high-quality, fast-response and low-cost port logistics system would improve transport efficiency and quality. On the one hand, it provides more accurate and effective integrated services to the transport demanders and improves customer satisfaction. On the other hand, more and more relevant service enterprises are attracted to settle in, because of the increasing transport demand. Therefore, a more comprehensive multimodal transport network could be formed.

◆ 1.4 世界典型港口物流的发展状况
1.4 Development Status of Global Typical Port Logistics

1.4.1 全球港口物流的基本情况
1.4.1 Basic Situation of Global Port Logistics

港口已经完成了由"运输枢纽中心"向"国际物流中心"的转变,港口基础设施日趋完善,临港产业不断发展,为客户提供多样化、综合性的物流增值服务。港口物流也逐步从单环节的优化向全供应链的多环节的协调优化转变,全球港口物流的发展具有以下趋势:

The port has completed the transformation from a "Transport Hub Center" to an "International Logistics Center". The port infrastructures are becoming more and more perfect, and the port centered industry is constantly developing, which can provide customers with diversified and comprehensive logistics value-added services. Port logistics is also gradually changing from a single link optimization to a multi-link coordination optimization of the entire supply chain. The development of global port logistics has the following trends:

(1)港口物流专业化
(1) Specialization of Port Logistics

结合自然条件与腹地货源特点,港口建设不同用途的专业化码头,制定装卸、运输、仓储、配送等服务标准,力争实现港口物流系统内多环节之间的无缝衔接,大幅提升港口物流整体效率,进而形成竞争优势。

With the combination of natural conditions and the characteristics of the hinterland, the port builds specialized terminals for different uses and formulates technical standards for services such as loading and unloading, transport, warehousing, distribution. The port is also committed to the seamless connection of multiple links in the port logistics system to improve the overall efficiency of port logistics. A competitive advantage could be formed ultimately.

（2）港口物流柔性化
（2）Flexibility of Port Logistics

由于港口间竞争日趋激烈和客户需求日趋多样，港口物流企业通过提升对客户需求的响应速度，延伸服务范围，以期为不同区域、不同货种、不同规模的客户提供柔性化的服务和定制化的物流方案。

Because of the intense competition between ports and the diversified customer demands, port logistics companies in order to provide flexible services and customized logistics solutions to customers in different regions, different cargo types and different sizes. For example, port logistics companies and extend the scope of services by improving the response speed to customer needs.

（3）港口物流合作化
（3）Cooperation of Port Logistics

港口物流企业之间的单一竞争已经演变成港口供应链之间的竞争，任一环节的低效率均会对整个港口供应链产生负面影响。因此，港口物流服务系统中的协调合作是必然趋势。通过港口与腹地、港口之间、港航企业间的多种合作模式建立的港口物流战略联盟，可以整合资源，以达到港口物流系统整体最优的目标。

The competition between port logistics companies has evolved into the competition between port supply chains. The inefficiency of any link will have a negative impact on the entire port supply chain. Therefore, coordination and cooperation in the port logistics service system is an inevitable trend. It is necessary to establish a port logistics strategic alliance based on different cooperation modes, such as the cooperation between the port and the hinterland, the cooperation among ports, and the cooperation between the port and shipping companies. The resource integration and the overall optimization of port logistics systems could be achieved.

（4）港口物流绿色化
（4）Green of Port Logistics

随着环保压力的增大，绿色港口建设越来越受到重视。构建节能和低碳的港口物流体系，合理利用有限的资源并降低能耗和污染，解决港口物流发展与环境保护的冲突，是实现港口物流可持续发展的关键。

With increased environmental protection pressure, green port construction has received more and more attention. Building an energy-efficient and low-carbon port logistics system, making reasonable using of limited resources, reducing energy consumption and pollution, alleviating the contradiction between port logistics development and environmental protection have become essential themes for sustainable development of port logistics.

（5）港口物流智能化
（5）Intelligence of Port Logistics

随着物联网、云计算、大数据等新兴信息技术的发展，港口物流的可视化、智能化和自动化快速发展。自动化码头建设步伐不断加快,智慧港口得到了全世界的重视,智能化成为提升港口竞争力的重要手段。

With the development of emerging information technologies such as the Internet of Things, cloud computing, and big data, port logistics has begun to develop rapidly toward visualization, intelligence and automation. The pace of automated terminal construction has been accelerating, smart ports have received worldwide attention, and intelligence has become an essential means to enhance port competitiveness.

1.4.2　中国港口布局与港口物流发展
1.4.2　China's Port Layout and Port Logistics Development

（1）中国港口基本布局
（1）Basic Layout of Chinese Ports

在经济全球化背景下,世界港口物流的发展重心逐步向亚洲转移,中国成为最重要的港口国家,目前在区域分布上形成了环渤海、长三角、东南沿海、珠三角、西南沿海等五大港口群体,在主要货类上形成煤炭运输系统、石油运输系统、铁矿石运输系统、集装箱运输系统、粮食运输系统、商品汽车运输及物流系统、陆岛滚装运输系统及旅客运输系统等八大运输系统在内的布局。港口群的腹地特征和物流结构如下:

In the context of economic globalization, the focus of the development of global port logistics has gradually shifted to Asia, and China has become the most significant port country. At present, there are five major port cluster: the Bohai Rim, the Yangtze River Delta, the southeast coast, the Pearl River Delta and the southwest coast. The spatial layout of eight transportation systems has been formed, including coal transportation system, petroleum transportation system, iron ore transportation system, containers transportation system, food transportation system, commercial vehicles transportation and logistics system, land island ro-ro transportation system and passenger transportation system. The hinterland characteristics and logistics structure of the port cluster are as follows:

①环渤海港口群
①Bohai Rim Port Cluster

环渤海港口群涵盖辽宁沿海港口群、津冀沿海港口群和山东沿海港口群。其中辽宁沿海港口群以大连港和营口港为主,锦州港、丹东港等港为辅,服务范围辐射东北三省及内蒙古东部地区。津冀沿海港口群包括天津港、秦皇岛港、唐山港、黄骅港等,服务范围为京津、华北及其西向延伸的部分地区。山东沿海港口群以青岛港、烟台港、日照港为主,为山东半岛及其西向延伸部分地区提供服务。环渤海港口群主要布局煤炭、石油、天然气、铁矿石和粮食等大宗散货以及集装箱运输、旅客运输等。辽宁、津冀沿海港口群布局商品汽车中转储运,辽宁、山东沿海港口群布局陆岛滚装。

Bohai Rim port cluster consists of Liaoning coastal port cluster, Tianjin-Hebei coastal port group and Shandong coastal port cluster. Liaoning coastal port cluster is mainly supported by Dalian and Yingkou ports, supplemented by Jinzhou and Dandong ports. The service scope covers the three provinces in the northeast of China and eastern Inner Mongolia. Tianjin-Hebei coastal port cluster includes Tianjin Port, Qinhuangdao Port, Tangshan Port, Huanghua Port and so on, and serves Beijing, Tianjin, North China and its westward extension. Shandong coastal port cluster are mainly Qingdao Port, Yantai Port and Rizhao Port, serving the Shandong Peninsula and its westward extension. The main cargo types are bulk cargo such as coal, petroleum, liquefied natural gas, iron ore, and grain, container transport, passenger transport in Bohai Rim port cluster. The commercial vehicle transport is also included in Liaoning coastal port cluster and Tianjin-Hebei coastal port cluster, and land island ro-ro transport coastal port cluster is included in Liaoning and Shandong coastal port cluster.

②长三角港口群

②Yangtze River Delta Port Cluster

上海港、宁波舟山港、连云港港等主要港口充分发挥带动作用,温州港、南京港、镇江港、南通港、苏州港等沿海和长江下游港口等辅以支持,形成了服务于长三角区域的港口集群。按货物种类划分,集装箱运输系统以上海港、宁波舟山港、苏州港为干线港,以连云港港、嘉兴港、温州港、台州港等港口为支线港。进口石油与天然气中转储运系统依托上海港、南通港、宁波舟山港以及南京港等港口。进口铁矿石中转运输系统则主要以宁波舟山港和连云港港为主,煤炭和原油运输以连云港港为主,粮食运输以上海港、南通港、连云港港、舟山港和嘉兴港等港口为主。

Shanghai Port, Ningbo-Zhoushan Port, Lianyungang Port are the primary ports we should give full play to the leading role, supported by the coastal ports and the ports in the lower reaches of Yangtze River, such as Wenzhou Port, Nanjing Port, Zhenjiang Port, Nantong Port, Suzhou Port and so on. As a result, a port cluster serving the Yangtze River Delta region is formed. In terms of cargo types, the container transport system takes Shanghai Port, Ningbo-Zhoushan Port, and Suzhou Port as the trunk ports, and Lianyungang Port, Jiaxing Port, Wenzhou Port and Taizhou Port as the feeder ports. The imported petroleum and natural gas transportation rely on Shanghai Port, Nantong Port, Ningbo-Zhoushan Port and Nanjing Port. The imported iron ore transportation system is mainly based on Ningbo-Zhoushan Port and Lianyungang Port. The coal and crude oil is transported through Lianyungang Port, and grain transportation is mainly based in Shanghai Port, Nantong Port, Lianyungang Port, Zhoushan Port and Jiaxing Port.

③东南沿海港口群

③Southeast Coastal Port Cluster

东南沿海港口群由厦门港、福州港、泉州港、莆田港、漳州港等港口构成,为福建、江西等内陆区域提供运输保障。集装箱运输系统由厦门港(作为干线港)和福州港、泉州港、莆田港等港口(作为支线港)共同构成。泉州港以石油和天然气运输为主,福州港、厦门港及莆田港等港口则以粮食运输为主。

Southeast coastal port cluster includes Xiamen Port, Fuzhou Port, Quanzhou Port, Putian Port, Zhangzhou Port and so on, providing transportation guarantee for Fujian and Jiangxi and other inland region. The container transport system is composed of Xiamen Port (as the trunk port), and Fuzhou Port, Quanzhou Port, Putian Port (as the feeder ports). Quanzhou Port is dominated by petroleum and natural gas transport, while Fuzhou Port, Xiamen Port and Putian Port are dominated by grain transport.

④珠三角港口群

④Pearl River Delta Port Cluster

珠三角港口群包括香港港、广州港、深圳港、珠海港、汕头港、惠州港等港口,为中国华南和西南局部地区提供服务。集装箱运输系统以香港港、深圳港与广州港作为干线港,汕头港、惠州港、虎门港、珠海港、中山港、阳江港、茂名港等港口作为支线港。广州港布局石油、天然气、铁矿石、粮食和商品汽车。深圳港布局石油、天然气和粮食,珠海港、惠州港、茂名港、虎门港是构成石油和天然气运输系统的重要港口。

Pearl river delta port cluster includes Hongkong Port, Guangzhou Port, Shenzhen Port, Zhuhai Port, Shantou Port, Huizhou Port and so on, mainly serving South China and Southwest China. The container transport system takes Hongkong Port, Shenzhen Port and Guangzhou Port as the trunk ports and Shantou Port, Huizhou Port, Humen Port, Zhuhai Port, Zhongshan Port, Yangjiang Port, Maoming Port, as the feeder ports. Guangzhou Port is dominated by petroleum, natural gas, iron ore, grain, and vehicles. Shenzhen Port serves for petroleum, natural gas and grain transport. Zhuhai Port, Huizhou Port, Maoming Port and Humen Port are also main ports for petroleum and natural gas transportation.

⑤西南沿海港口群

⑤Southwest Coastal Port Cluster

西南沿海港口群主要由湛江港、防城港、海口港、北海港、钦州港、洋浦港、三亚港等港口构成,侧重服务于西部地区和海南省。集装箱运输系统以湛江港、防城港、海口港作为干线港口,以北海港、钦州港、洋浦港、三亚港等港口作为支线港口。石油与天然气运输系统由湛江港、海口港、洋浦港、广西沿海港口等组成。铁矿石和粮食等大宗散货运输系统由湛江港、防城港等港口组成。

Southwest coastal port cluster includes Zhanjiang Port, Fangcheng Port, Haikou Port, Beihai Port, Qinzhou Port, Yangpu Port, Sanya Port and so on, serving Western China and Hainan province. The container transport system takes Zhanjiang Port, Fangcheng Port, Haikou Port as the trunk ports and Beihai Port, Qinzhou Port, Yangpu Port, Sanya Port, as the feeder ports. The petroleum and natural gas transport system consists of Zhanjiang Port, Haikou Port, Yangpu Port, and Guangxi coastal ports. Bulk cargo transport system, such as iron ore and grain, is made up of Zhanjiang Port and Fangcheng Port.

(2)中国港口物流发展情况

(2)Development of Port Logistics in China

中国港口物流发展现状可以总结为:

The development of port logistics in China can be summarized as：

①构建了完善的港口基础设施体系：

①Establishing a well-developed port infrastructure system：

经过几十年的发展,中国逐步构筑了完善的港口基础设施体系,港口吞吐能力基本满足货物需求,港口基础设施水平快速提升,港口作业效率位居世界前列。尤其是近年来先后投产了多个自动化码头,港口自动化与智能化水平快速提升。

After decades of development, a well-developed port infrastructure system has gradually been built in China. The throughput capacity of ports has basically met the transport demand, the level of port infrastructure has been rapidly improved, and the port operation efficiency ranks among the top in the world. Especially in recent years, many automated terminals have been put into production, and the level of port automation and intelligence has increased rapidly.

②港口功能逐步完善,港口物流模式创新速度加快:中国港口物流功能的不断延伸,使传统的货物装卸完成了向多层次综合物流服务体系的转变,从而形成了多层次服务体系。港口发展从以硬件设施建设为主,向软硬并重、改善软环境转变,从要素投入驱动向创新驱动转变。

② Port functions are gradually improved, and the innovation speed of port logistics mode is accelerating. Because of the continuous extension of China's port logistics functions, a multi-level service system has been formed after the transformation from traditional cargo handling to comprehensive logistics services. The development of ports has shifted from focusing on the construction of hardware facilities to focusing on both hardware facilities and improving soft environment. It has also shifted from input factor-driven development to innovation-driven development.

③港口发展政策不断创新:中国逐步探索适应各港口实际情况的港口管理模式,建立了较完善的港口管理体系,实施了建立保税物流园区、保税港、自由贸易试验区等促进港口发展的政策。同时,开始了自由贸易港建设的探索。

③The port development policy has been continuously innovated. China has gradually explored various port management modes adapted to the actual conditions of different ports. A more comprehensive port management system has been established. Policies are implemented to promote port development, such as building bonded logistics parks, bonded ports, and free trade pilot zones. At the same time, the exploration of the construction of a free trade port began.

④港口资源整合不断加快,港口布局逐渐完善:港口间的整合联盟成为热点,先后成立了浙江港口集团、辽宁港口集团和山东港口集团等,以省为单位整合港口资源,港口竞争力被大大提升。同时,航运企业也参与到港口资源整合中,如招商集团整合大连港、营口港和辽宁省的其他港口,成立了辽宁港口集团有限公司。

④ The integration of port resources is accelerating, and the port layout becomes gradually perfect. The integration alliance between ports has become a hot spot. Zhejiang Port Group, Liaoning Port Group and Shandong Port Group have been established based on the integration of port resources in provinces. The competitiveness of these port groups have been significantly improved. At the same time, shipping companies are also participating in the integration of port resources. For example, China Merchants Group integrated Dalian Port, Yingkou Port and other ports in Liaoning province to establish Liaoning Port Group.

第2章 港口物流设施与设备

Chapter 2 | Port Logistics Infrastructure and Equipment

港口物流基础设施与设备是现代港口物流活动的物质基础,主要包括港口设施与设备、港口物流园区、港口物流联运设施及港口物流信息系统。

Port logistics infrastructure and equipment are the material basis of modern port logistics activities, mainly including port facilities and equipment, port logistics park, port logistics intermodal facilities and port logistics information system.

◈ 2.1 港口设施与设备

2.1 Port Facilities and Equipment

港口由港界范围内的相关设施构成,港界是构成港口的水陆两部分区域与水陆外围区域的分界。与物流活动相关的港口基础设施主要包括码头前沿作业区、存储作业区、道路、关检设施、管网、集疏运通道等陆域设施,以及船舶进出港航道、制动水域、回旋水域、港池、码头前沿水域以及锚地等水域设施(详见表2.1)。

表 2.1　港口物流基础设施

水域设施	船舶进出港航道、制动水域、回旋水域、港池、码头前沿水域以及锚地
陆域设施	装卸作业设施：泊位、堆场、仓库、道路、站场等
	辅助作业设施：车库、变电站、修理厂、通信设施、消防站、给排水设施等
	货物处理设施：起重、传输和管路等设施设备
外堤设施	防波堤、护岸等

The port consists of relevant facilities within the port boundary, and the port boundary is the boundary between the land and water areas that make up the port and the peripheral area of those two areas. The port infrastructure related to logistics activities mainly includes land facilities such as wharf front operation area, wharf storage operation area, roads, customs inspection facilities, pipe network, collection and distribution channel, as well as water facilities such as ship access channel, brake water area, turning basin, harbor basin, quayside of the port water area and anchorage area(see Table 2.1 for details).

Table 2.1　Port logistics infrastructure

Water facilities	Ship access channel, brake water area, turning basin, harbor basin, quayside of the port water area and anchorage area
Land facilities	Loading and unloading facilities: berth, storage yard, warehouse, road, station, etc.
	Auxiliary operation facilities: garage, substation, repair shop, communication facilities, fire station, water supply and drainage facilities, etc.
	Cargo handling facilities: lifting, transmission, pipeline and other facilities and equipment
External levee facilities	Breakwater, revetment, etc.

2.1.1　水域设施
2.1.1　Water Facilities

（1）航道
（1）Port Channel

航道是水域中满足船舶进出港时安全航行要求的通道。船舶进出港口必须按照设置的航行标志航行，遵守航行规则，以免发生海上事故。大连港普湾港区公用航道平面布置示意图如图 2.1 所示。

Port channel is a channel in the water area to meet the requirements of safe navigation when ships enter and leave the port. Ships entering or leaving the port must navigate according to the set navigation marks and abide by the navigation rules so as to avoid maritime accidents. The layout schematic diagram of the public channel in the Puwan port area of Dalian Port is shown in Figure 2.1.

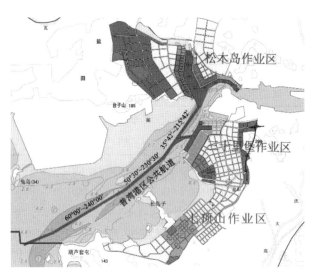

图 2.1 大连港普湾港区公用航道平面布置示意图

（图片来源：大连市交通运输局.）

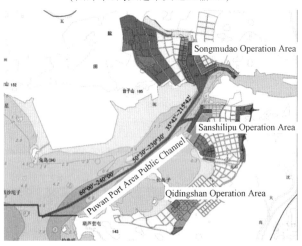

Figure 2.1 The layout schematic diagram of the public channel in the Puwan port area of Dalian Port

航道需拥有足够的水深和宽度,一般设在天然水深良好、泥沙回淤量小、受横风流和冰凌等因素影响较小的水域中,航道中线应与水流的方向一致或接近,以便船舶安全进出港。在港口货物吞吐量增加和船舶大型化的发展趋势和背景下,航道成为限制港口效率和通过能力的重要影响因素之一。

The channel must have sufficient water depth and width, which is generally located in the water area with good natural water depth, small amount of sediment back silting and little influence by cross wind current, ice and other factors. The center line of the channel should be consistent with or close to the direction of water flow so as to facilitate the safe entry and exit of ships. Under the development trend and background of increasing cargo throughput and large-scale ships, the channel has become one of the critical factors limiting port efficiency and throughput.

按照形成原因,航道分为天然航道和人工航道。大多数情况下,港口自然水深不能满足船舶航行所需的深度等要求,需人工进行疏浚和整治。按照使用性质,航道分为专用航道和公用航道。专用航道是指由水利电力、水产、林业、军事等部门和其他机构自行建设和使用的航道。公用航道是指由国家各级专业航道管理机构进行管理(养护)、供社会船舶使用的航道。

According to the formation reason, the channel is divided into natural channel and artificial channel. In most cases, the natural water depth of the port cannot meet the requirements of the depth for the ship navigation, and manual dredging and remediation are required. According to the nature of use, the channel is divided into special channel and public channel. Special channels refer to channels built and used by departments of water conservancy, aquatic products, forestry, military and other departments and institutions. Public channels refer to channels constructed and maintained by professional management agencies at all levels, which are used by social ships.

(2)锚地及回旋水域
(2) Anchorage Area and Turning Basin

具有天然掩护或人工掩护条件,供船舶停泊及进行水上装卸作业的特定区域称为锚地。锚地按所处位置可分为港外锚地和港内锚地,一般以防波堤为界。港外锚地供船舶候潮、待泊、联检及避风使用,也可进行水上装卸作业;港内锚地供待泊或水上装卸作业使用。

Anchorage area refers to the specific area with natural or artificial cover conditions for ships to berth and carries out water loading and unloading operations. Anchorage area can be divided into anchorage outside the port and anchorage inside the port according to its location. Generally, the breakwater is used as the boundary. The anchorage outside the port is for ships waiting for tide and for berthing, joint inspection and wind shelter, sometimes water loading and unloading operations are also carried out in this area; The anchorage inside the port is used for berthing or water loading and unloading operations.

船舶的回旋水域是指船舶靠离泊位时掉头或转向所需的水域。回旋水域可占用航行水域,但当航道上船舶进出频繁时,会影响港口运营效率。回旋水域的大小与船舶尺度、掉头方向、水流和风速风向等因素相关。

Turning basin refers to the water area required for turning around of the ships to berthing and unberthing. The turning basin can occupy the navigation water area, but when the ships are in and out of the channel frequently, it will affect the port operation efficiency. The size of the turning basin is related to the size of the ship, turnaround direction, water current, wind speed and direction.

(3)港池
(3) Harbor Basin

港池指供船舶靠泊、系缆和装卸作业使用的,与码头直接相连的水域。对于突堤式码头,码头从岸边伸入水域中,突堤与突堤之间的水域即为港池;对于顺岸式码头,码头前沿供船舶靠离泊作业所占用的水域即为港池,一般不可占用主航道。

Harbor basin refers to the water area directly connected with the wharf for ship's berthing, mooring, and loading and unloading operations. For the jetty-type wharf, the wharf extends from the shore into the water, and the water area between two jetties is the harbor basin; For the on-shore-type wharf, quayside of the port water area ships to berthing and unberthing is the harbor basin, and the main channel is generally not occupied.

2.1.2 陆域设施
2.1.2 Land Facilities

码头是船舶停靠和货物装卸的场所。港口陆域和水域的交界线称为港口前沿线或港口岸线,是港口生产活动的核心区域。针对不同货物种类,港口设置了与其装卸、储存和运输相适应的码头类型,主要包括集装箱码头、液体散货码头、干散货码头、件杂货码头和滚装码头。

A terminal is a place where ships dock and cargo is loaded and unloaded. The boundary between the land and water area of the port is called the front line of the port or the port shoreline, which is the core area of production activities of the port. According to different types of cargo, the port has set up the types of terminals suitable for loading and unloading, storage and transportation, mainly including container terminals, liquid bulk terminals, dry bulk terminals, general cargo terminals and ro-ro terminals.

（1）集装箱码头
（1）Container Terminal

专业化集装箱码头采用封闭式管理方式,要求在设施布置上实现与周围其他作业区的隔离。图 2.2 是集装箱码头装卸作业及水平运输流程示意图。集装箱码头装卸作业地带主要包括:码头前沿作业地带、码头堆场、拆装箱库和货运站、大门、港内道路、通道和调度管理中心等。一般情况下,码头前沿作业地带至码头堆场无其他固定设施,特殊情况下布置有变电所。大门及检查桥通常是港区与外界的唯一通道,调度管理中心集中设置在大门的一侧,大门外与交通干道的连接段应留有一定的缓冲空间,以便集卡进入大门前临时等待。拆装箱库设于大门的一侧,靠近堆场一侧为待处理集装箱的停放区,另一侧为汽车或铁路的装卸线。集装箱码头的主要技术参数可参考表 2.2。

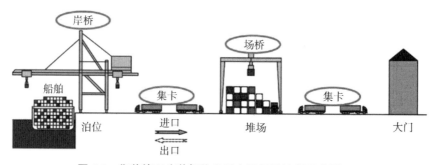

图 2.2　集装箱码头装卸作业及水平运输流程示意图

表 2.2　集装箱码头的主要技术参数

设计船型		主要技术参数					所属港口类型
		码头尺度			装卸桥配备数量（台/泊位）	泊位通过能力（TEU/年）	
吨级 DWT（万 t）	载箱量（TEU）	泊位平均长度(m)	码头前沿水深(m)	陆域纵深(m)			
1	≤1 050	161	9.0	≤400	2	25 万	喂给港
2	1 900	210	11.6	400~500	2~3	25 万~30 万	支线港
3	3 500	281	13.2	500~600	3~4	30 万~50 万	支线港
5	5 650	333	14.3	600~700	4	50 万~80 万	干线港
7	6 630	340	15.4	700~800	4		
10	9 500	386	16.0	800~900	4~5		
15	12 500	438	18.2	~1 000	5	80 万~100 万	干线港
20	18 000	440	23.1	~1 000	5~6		

Specialized container terminals adopt closed management mode, which requires the layout of facilities to realize isolation from other surrounding operation areas. Figure 2.2 is a schematic diagram of the loading and unloading operation and horizontal transportation process of container terminal. The loading and unloading area of container terminal mainly includes: the quayside operation area of the port, the terminal yard, the container depot and freight station, the gate, the road in the port, the passage and the dispatching management center, etc. There are no other fixed facilities from the quayside operation area of the port to the container yard in general, and the substation is arranged in special cases. The gate and inspection bridge are usually the only access between the port area and the outside. The dispatching management center is set on one side of the gate. There should be a certain buffer space for the connection section between the gate and the main traffic road, so that the truck can wait temporarily before entering the gate. The container depots are set on one side of the gate, and the area near the yard is the storage area for the containers to be processed, and the loading and unloading line of the automobile or railway is on the other side. Refer to Table 2.2 for the main technical parameters of container terminal.

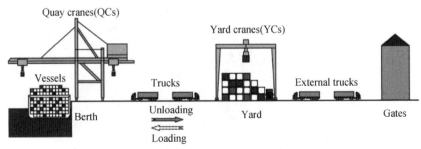

Figure 2.2　Schematic diagram of the loading and unloading operation and horizontal transportation process of container terminal

Table 2.2　Main technical parameters of container terminal

Design ship form		Main technical parameters					Port type
		Dock scale			Number of quay crane (per berth)	Berth capacity (TEU/year)	
DWT (×10,000 t)	Carrying capacity (TEU)	Average length of berth(m)	Water depth at quayside of the port(m)	Land depth(m)			
1	≤1,050	161	9.0	≤400	2	250,000	Feeding port
2	1,900	210	11.6	400~500	2~3	250,000~300,000	Feeder port
3	3,500	281	13.2	500~600	3~4	300,000~500,000	Feeder port
5	5,650	333	14.3	600~700	4	500,000~800,000	Trunk port
7	6,630	340	15.4	700~800	4		
10	9,500	386	16.0	800~900	4~5		
15	12,500	438	18.2	~1,000	5	800,000~1,000,000	Trunk port
20	18,000	440	23.1	~1,000	5~6		

　　另外,集装箱码头还需根据港区规模及地形条件,在紧邻装卸作业地带和港区大门处设置辅助生产设施,如维修车间和集装箱冲洗场地;在码头区以外布置生活区,避免与码头生产作业相互干扰。大连港大窑湾港区顺岸式码头是典型的现代化集装箱专用码头,其陆域设施布置效果如图 2.3 所示。

In addition, according to the scale and terrain conditions of the port area, auxiliary production facilities, such as maintenance workshop and container washing site, shall be set up in the area adjacent to the loading and unloading operation area and the port gate; Living area shall be arranged outside the port area to avoid mutual interference with the production operation of the port. The coastal wharf of Dayaowan Port Area of Dalian Port is a typical modern container terminal, and its layout of land facilities is shown in Figure 2.3.

图 2.3　大连港大窑湾港区集装箱专用码头陆域设施布置效果图

Figure 2.3　The layout of land facilities of container terminal in Dayaowan Port Area of Dalian Port

专业化集装箱码头前沿船舶装卸作业机型均采用集装箱装卸桥(岸桥),堆场作业设备主要包括轮胎式龙门吊(RTG)、轨道式龙门吊(RMG)、跨运车、集装箱叉车等,水平运输多采用集装箱卡车等。

Container loading and unloading crane (quay crane) is adopted for quayside of the port loading and unloading operation of the specialized container terminal. The yard operation equipment mainly includes RTG,RMG,straddle carrier,container forklift,etc. The horizontal transportation adopts container trucks,etc.

以高度发展的现代机械、信息科技为基础和以"高效、可靠、绿色"为目标的自动化集装箱码头成为未来港口建设及改造的发展方向。自动化集装箱码头的发展历程基本可分为以下几个阶段:第一代以1993年投入运营的荷兰鹿特丹港ECT码头为代表;第二代以2002年投入运营的德国汉堡港CTA码头为代表;第三代以2008年投入运营的荷兰鹿特丹港Euromax码头为代表。中国厦门远海自动化码头(2016年投产)深度融合人工智能和系统工程理论等先进科技,是中国首个自主研发的全智能和零排放的全自动化集装箱码头。2017年上海港洋山四期码头全面启用,成为世界规模最大、设备最先进且具有自主知识产权的全自动化集装箱码头。之后,青岛新前湾、天津港、广州南沙四期的自动化集装箱码头相继启用,自动化码头已经成为港口领域的热点和趋势。截至2021年,全球有30多个自动化码头投产,10余个自动化码头正在建设中。

Based on the highly developed modern machinery and information technology,and with the goal of "high efficiency,reliability and green",the automated container terminal will become the key direction of future port construction and transformation. The development process of the automated container terminal can be divided into the following generations:The first generation is represented by the ECT terminal in Rotterdam Port, the Netherlands, which was put into operation in 1993;The second generation is represented by the CTA terminal in Hamburg Port, Germany,which was put into operation in 2002;The third generation is represented by Euromax terminal in Rotterdam Port,the Netherlands,which was put into operation in 2008. China's Xiamen Yuanhai automated terminal(put into operation in 2016), which profoundly integrates advanced technologies such as artificial intelligence and system engineering theory,is the first fully automated container terminal with full intelligence and zero emissions developed independently in China. In 2017, the Yangshan Phase Ⅳ terminal of Shanghai Port was put into operation, which became the world's largest and most advanced fully automated container terminal with independent intellectual property rights. After that,the automated container terminals of Qingdao Xinqianwan,Tianjin Port,and Guangzhou Nansha Phase Ⅳ were opened one after another,and automated terminals have become a hot spot and trend in the port field. By 2021,more than 30 automated terminals have been put into production worldwide,and more than 10 automated terminals are under construction.

一般情况下,自动化集装箱码头与传统集装箱码头的区别在于自动化码头采用了自动化设备完成集装箱作业。此外,自动化码头的岸侧与自动化堆场间的水平运输采用无人驾驶的自动导引运输车(AGV),在AGV运行区域地面上埋设磁钉。AGV凭借自身的感应天

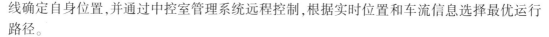

线确定自身位置,并通过中控室管理系统远程控制,根据实时位置和车流信息选择最优运行路径。

In general, the difference between an automated container terminal and a traditional container terminal is that the automated terminal uses automated equipment to complete container operations. In addition, the horizontal transportation between the quayside of the automated terminal and the automated storage yard uses an unmanned automated guided vehicle(AGV), and magnetic nails are embedded on the ground of the AGV operating area. The AGV determines its position with its own inductive antenna, and is controlled remotely by the central control room management system to select the optimal operation according to the real-time location and traffic flow information.

然而,自动化码头的作业效率远未达到预期水平,并且低于传统码头,这种情况制约了自动化码头的快速发展。仅部分自动化码头作业效率达到传统码头作业水平,如青岛新前湾区。因此,一些行业从业者和研究人员正在研究提高自动化码头作业效率的方法:完善关键环节的优化算法,如 AGVs 分配与路径优化算法、场桥与岸桥调度优化等;开发与完善设备控制系统(ECS)与码头操作系统(TOS);创新码头工艺与设备自动化技术,如集装箱旋锁自动拆装技术、轨道吊辅助自动抓箱技术等;分析研发设备数据与智能决策技术等。

However, the operating efficiency of automated terminals is far from reaching the expected level and is lower than that of traditional terminals, which restricts the rapid development of automated terminals. Only some automated terminals have reached the level of traditional terminal operations, such as Qingdao Xinqianwan area. Therefore, some industry practitioners and researchers are studying ways to improve the efficiency of automated terminal operations: improve the optimization algorithms of key links, such as AGVs allocation and route optimization algorithms, yard crane and quay crane scheduling optimization, etc.; develop and improve equipment control systems(ECS) and terminal operating system(TOS); innovative terminal technology and equipment automation technology, such as container twist lock automatic disassembly and assembly technology, track crane auxiliary automatic container grab technology, etc.; analyse the R&D equipment data and intelligent decision-making technology.

(2)液体散货码头
(2)Liquid Bulk Terminal

液体散货码头陆域由码头、储存区及辅建区三部分组成,通常采取远离城市的封闭式布置,且与其他货物码头保持一定安全距离,储存区与辅建区相对分离。码头平面布置需考虑火灾等级和危险性,以及装卸工艺及地形条件。液体散货码头平面布置如图 2.4 所示。

The land area of liquid bulk terminal is composed of three parts: wharf, storage area and auxiliary construction area, which are usually arranged in a closed way far away from the city, and keep a certain safe distance from other cargo terminals. The storage area and auxiliary construction area are relatively separated. The terminal layout needs to consider the fire levels and hazards, loading and unloading technology, and terrain conditions. The layout of liquid bulk terminal is shown in Figure 2.4.

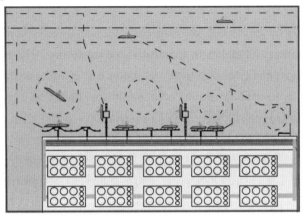

图 2.4 液体散货码头平面布置图

Figure 2.4 The layout of liquid bulk terminal

①原油码头

①Crude Oil Terminal

由于航行于国际航线的原油船吨位较大、吃水较深,从安全考虑,一般原油码头都是天然水深较大的新辟作业区,远离城市区和其他港区。大连港大孤山港区位于大窑湾西南侧,是一个现代化深水油港,水域面积 180 km²,陆域面积 1.57 km²,目前拥有 45 万吨级和 30 万吨级两个大型原油码头,年通过能力为 7 285 万吨,港区内有国家石油战略储备库,配套的输油管道连接至大连石化和西太石化。

Crude oil ships sailing on international routes have large tonnage and deep draught. For safety reasons, generally crude oil terminals are new operation areas with large natural water depths, far away from urban areas and other ports. Dagushan port area of Dalian Port is located in the southwest of Dayaowan, which is a modern deep-water oil port, with a water area of 180 square kilometers and a land area of 1.57 square kilometers. At present, it has two large crude oil terminals of 450,000 tons and 300,000 tons, with an annual throughput of 72.85 million tons. There are national petroleum strategic reserves in the port area, and supporting oil pipelines to Dalian Petrochemical and West Pacific Petrochemical.

原油船的船岸间装卸通过设在码头上的输油臂或软管完成,装卸系统泊稳要求较低,原油码头多为开敞式布置,包括单点系泊式和固定码头式两种。罐区是原油码头陆域布置的主要部分,其位置应便于陆上输油管线及原油码头管线的引入,以减少能源消耗。

The ship-to-shore loading and unloading of crude oil tankers is completed by the oil transfer arm or hose set on the wharf, and the loading and unloading system has low requirements for berthing stability. Most crude oil wharves are open layouts, including single point mooring type and fixed wharf type. The tank farm is the main part of the land layout of the crude oil terminal, and its location should be convenient for the introduction of the land crude oil pipeline and the oil terminal pipeline, so as to reduce energy consumption.

专业化炼油厂所在港区往往同时布置原油进口码头以及成品油出运码头,港区陆域设

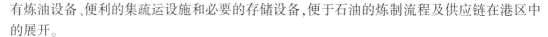

有炼油设备、便利的集疏运设施和必要的存储设备,便于石油的炼制流程及供应链在港区中的展开。

The port area where specialized refineries are located is often equipped with crude oil import terminal and product oil shipment terminal at the same time. The land area of the port is equipped with refining equipment, convenient collection and distribution facilities, and necessary storage equipment, so as to facilitate the oil refining process and supply chain in the port area.

②液化石油气(LPG)和液化天然气(LNG)专用码头

②Special Terminal for LPG and LNG

液化石油气(LPG)和液化天然气(LNG)属危险品,极易挥发和引起爆炸,因而需要设专用码头,布置在城市年常风向的下风侧,且应与其他码头保持足够的安全距离。码头的安全设施和规范操作至关重要。

LPG and LNG are dangerous goods, which are very easy to volatile and cause explosions. Therefore, it is necessary to set up a special terminal, which is located in the downwind side of the city's annual direction of prevailing wind, and keep enough safe distance from other terminals. The safety facilities and standardized operation of the terminal are very important.

液化石油气和液化天然气码头的陆域组成与原油码头类似,可采用陆上布置或离岸布置,从安全和土地利用的角度考虑,最好采用离岸方式。码头操作平台至接收站储罐的净距不应小于150 m。码头陆域有球形罐罐区和主要生产设施。此外,港区还布有液化气放散装置、干粉罐室、干粉罐塔、消防水炮以及码头前水幕等消防工程。

The composition of LPG and LNG terminals on land is similar to that of crude oil terminals, which can be arranged on land or offshore. From the perspective of safety and land use, offshore is the best way. The net distance from the wharf operation platform to the receiving station tank shall not be less than 150 m. There are spherical tank farms and main production facilities on the terminal land. In addition, the port area is also equipped with liquefied gas emission device, dry powder tank room, dry powder tank tower, fire water monitor and water curtain in front of the wharf.

大连液化天然气接收站位于大连大孤山半岛,占地面积21.6公顷,不但具有卸船、储存、汽化、外输和液化天然气槽车装车等功能,而且是国内第一个具有装船能力的液化天然气接收站。

Dalian LNG terminal is located in the Dagushan peninsula of Dalian, covering an area of 21.6 hectares. It not only has the functions of unloading, storage, gasification, export and LNG tank car loading, but also is the first LNG terminal with loading capacity in China.

(3)干散货码头

(3) Dry Bulk Terminal

专业化干散货码头主要包括煤炭矿石码头和散粮码头,前沿作业较为单一。它采用连续作业设备或门机进行水平或垂直作业,并允许较长的输送距离。库场至码头之间的距离不受严格限制。

The specialized dry bulk terminal mainly includes coal ore terminal and bulk grain terminal. The frontier operation is relatively simple. The continuous operation equipment or gantry crane is used for horizontal or vertical operation, allowing a long transportation distance. The distance between the warehouse and the wharf is not strictly limited.

干散货码头陆域组成主要包括:码头前沿作业地带、储存库场、装卸车设施、辅助设施及管理区。其陆域布置与货物种类、工艺方案和地形条件密切相关。

The land area of dry bulk terminal mainly includes: the quayside operation area of the port, storage warehouse, loading and unloading facilities, auxiliary facilities and management area. The layout of land area is closely related to the type of goods, process plan and terrain conditions.

干散货码头的堆场容量计算方法与件杂货相同。通常,大型干散货码头的堆场容量可按与码头能力的比值确定,外贸码头不应大于10%,内贸码头不应大于7%。

For dry bulk terminal, the calculation method of storage yard capacity is the same as that of general cargo. Generally, the storage yard capacity of a large dry bulk cargo terminal can be determined by the ratio of the capacity of the terminal. The foreign trade terminal shall not be more than 10%, and the domestic trade terminal shall not be more than 7%.

煤炭、矿石及其他大宗散货库(场)面积应根据年货运量、货物特性、品种、机械类型和工艺布置等因素确定。

The area of coal, ore and other bulk warehouses (yards) shall be determined according to the annual freight volume, cargo characteristics, varieties, machinery types, layout and other factors.

(4)件/多用途杂货码头
(4)General/Multi-purpose Cargo Terminal

件杂货码头由数个泊位(一般为3~8个)组成一个作业区,其陆域布置形式基本定型。件杂货码头生产区纵深不宜小于250 m,可分为三个相关部分:

The general cargo terminal consists of several berths (generally 3~8) to form a working area, and its land layout is basically finalized. The depth of the production area of the general cargo terminal should not be less than 250 m, which can be divided into three related parts:

①码头前沿作业地带
①The Quayside Operation Aera of the Port

码头前沿作业地带范围为码头前沿至前方库场,包括前沿通道和门机、货物接卸场地以及库场前道路,总宽度为40~50 m,具体根据地形条件及工艺布置做适当调整。码头前沿的装卸船作业可选用门机或船上吊机,考虑到对流动机械的干扰,码头前沿通常不设铁路。

The range of the quayside operation area of the port is from the quayside to the front warehouse, including the quayside passage and gantry crane, cargo unloading yard and the front road of the warehouse, with a total width of 40~50 m, which shall be adjusted according to the terrain conditions and process layout. Gantry cranes or ship cranes can be selected for the loading and unloading operation of the quayside of the wharf. Considering the interference to the mobile ma-

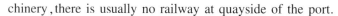
chinery, there is usually no railway at quayside of the port.

②前方库场

②Front Warehouse

前方库场包括库场及铁路或公路装卸作业带。前方库场设在码头前沿旁,供进港货物暂时存放和出港货物在装船前临时集中之用,以缩短货物的搬运距离,加快装卸船速度。前方库场的容量应能接卸对应泊位设计船型的载货量,在布置上应尽可能与泊位对应。前方库场的总宽度由库场宽度、铁路作业站台宽度和铁路装卸线占用宽度构成。

The front warehouse includes warehouse and loading and unloading operation zone of railway or highway. The front warehouse is set beside quayside of the port for temporary storage of inbound goods and temporary concentration of outbound goods before shipment, so as to shorten the handling distance of goods and speed up the loading and unloading of ships. The capacity of the front warehouse shall be able to receive and unload the cargo of the designed ship type, and the layout shall correspond with the berth as far as possible. The total width of the front warehouse is composed of the width of the warehouse, the width of the railway operation platform and the width of the railway loading and unloading line.

③后方库场

③Rear Warehouse

通常情况下,后方库场一般紧邻前方库场布置,供货物集疏运的周转之用,也应满足设计船型的一次载货量需要。后方库场同样需要装卸车作为其配套,可选择布置铁路及道路。

Generally, the rear warehouse is arranged close to the front warehouse, and the turnover of goods collection and distribution shall also meet the demand for primary cargo capacity of the design ship type. The rear warehouse also needs loading and unloading cranes as its supporting facilities, and railway and road can be arranged.

由于车、船载货量相差较大,必须设置具有合适容量的缓冲存储区,以加快车船周转。此外,进出口货物种类繁多、到发地各异,在库场内需分类和核查,并履行必要的验关和发货手续。因此,码头上的库场对加快车船周转和提高港口的通过能力非常重要。

Due to the significant difference in cargo capacity between vehicles and ships, a buffer storage area with appropriate capacity must be set up to speed up the turnover of vehicles and ships. In addition, there are various types of import and export goods and different places of arrival and departure, which need to be classified and verified in the warehouse, and necessary customs clearance and delivery procedures shall be performed. Therefore, the warehouse in the terminal is very important to speed up the turnover of vehicles and ships and improve the port capacity.

随着传统的多甲板杂货船运力逐渐减少,件杂货码头逐渐向多用途杂货码头转变。多用途杂货码头与件杂货码头的区别主要有两点:

a.多用途码头停靠货船装载货物的类型较多,包括集装箱、各类包装形式的件杂货和部分散货等,装卸设备配套能力更强;

b.由于集装箱等货物占用场地较大,多用途码头陆域纵深更大,以适应多类型货物存储。

With the gradual reduction of the traditional multi deck cargo ship capacity, the general cargo terminal is gradually changing to the multi-purpose cargo terminal. There are two main differences between multi-purpose cargo terminal and general cargo terminal:

a. There are many types of cargo loaded by multi-purpose cargo ships, including containers, various packaging forms of general cargo and some bulk cargo, and the handling equipment supporting capacity is stronger;

b. Due to the large space occupied by containers and other cargo, the land depth of multi-purpose terminal is larger, so as to adapt to the storage of multi-type cargo.

（5）滚装码头
（5）Ro-Ro Terminal

滚装码头一般分为平行式和突堤式两种布置形式。跳板作为滚装码头的主要接卸设施,主要分为直跳板、斜跳板和中跳板三类。

Ro-Ro terminal is generally divided into parallel type and jetty type. As the main loading and unloading facilities of ro-ro terminal, springboard is mainly divided into three categories: straight springboard, inclined springboard and midship springboard.

按照装卸货物的种类差异,滚装码头可分为客货滚装码头、货物滚装码头和汽车滚装码头,其陆域组成如下:

According to the different types of loading and unloading goods, ro-ro terminals can be divided into passenger and cargo ro-ro terminals, cargo ro-ro terminals and automobile ro-ro terminals. The land composition is as follows:

①客货滚装码头:站前广场、候船建筑物、汽车待渡场、货物堆场、生产和辅助生产设施、辅助生活设施等;

①Passenger and cargo ro-ro terminal: station square, ship waiting building, car waiting yard, cargo yard, production and auxiliary production facilities, auxiliary living facilities, etc.;

②货物滚装码头:货物堆场、汽车待渡场、生产和辅助生产设施、辅助生活设施等;

②Cargo ro-ro terminal: cargo yard, car waiting yard, production and auxiliary production facilities, auxiliary living facilities, etc.;

③汽车滚装码头:汽车停放场、汽车接收检查区、汽车卸货检查区、生产和辅助生产设施、辅助生活设施等;

③Automobile ro-ro terminal: car parking lot, car receiving inspection area, car unloading inspection area, production and auxiliary production facilities, auxiliary living facilities, etc.;

客货滚装码头陆域布置原则为便于滚装车辆的集散和乘客上下船,堆场上一般不需要大型装卸设备,堆场分区清晰,延伸服务发达。

The principle of land layout of passenger and cargo ro-ro terminal is to facilitate the collection and distribution of vehicles and the embarking and disembarking of passengers. Generally, there is no need for large-scale loading and unloading equipment in the storage yard. The storage yard has clear division and developed extension services.

◆ 2.2 港口物流园区
2.2 Port Logistics Park

物流园区是指以物流中心、配送中心、运输枢纽设施等适应城市物流管理与运作需要的物流设施为基础的城市物流功能区,同时,也是满足城市居民消费、就近生产、区域生产组织所需要的企业生产和经营活动等的经济功能区。

The logistics park refers to an urban logistics functional area based on logistics facilities that meet the needs of urban logistics management and operation, such as logistics centers, distribution centers, and transport hub facilities. At the same time, it is also an economical functional area that meets the needs of urban residents' consumption, nearby production, and regional production organizations for corporate production and business activities.

2.2.1 港口物流园区的概念与功能
2.2.1 Concept and Functions of Port Logistics Park

(1) 港口物流园区的定义
(1) Definition of Port Logistics Park

基于物流园区的概念,借鉴港口物流特征和国内外港口物流园区规划和建设经验,港口物流园区的基本概念如下:港口物流园区是指以港口为依托,由多个港航相关物流组织设施和专业化物流企业构成,具有装卸、仓储、运输和加工等基本功能及相配套的信息、金融、咨询和维修等综合服务功能的现代化物流组织和经济运行区域,是发挥综合协调和基础作用的物流设施的区域集合体,是大规模和集约化物流设施的集中地和物流网络中的水陆交汇点陆侧后方区域。

Based on the concept of logistics park, referring to the characteristics of port logistics and the planning and construction experience of port logistics park at home and abroad, the basic concept of port logistics park is proposed: port logistics park is based on the port and is composed of multiple ports and shipping-related logistics organization facilities and specialized logistics enterprises. It is a modern logistics organization and economic operation area with basic functions such as loading and unloading, warehousing, transportation and processing, and the service functions such as information, finance, consulting and maintenance. It is a regional collection of logistics facilities that play a comprehensive coordination and basic role. It is a concentrated area of large-scale and intensive logistics facilities and the land-side rear area of the water and land junction in the logistics network.

（2）港口物流园区的特征

（2）Characteristics of Port Logistics Park

①集群化

①Clustering

物流园区的空间形态围绕港口物流集聚发展，有利于城市物流布局和体系的合理规划，有利于物流资源的整合与优势互补，可全面刺激并拉动区域和城市经济发展。同一有限区域内存在的具有差异化功能的港航物流企业，集中为港口及航运物流服务，这样就减少了物流的中间环节，有效提高了物流服务的效率和速度，提升了客户所需的物流服务水平。

The spatial form of the logistics park revolves around the development of port logistics, which is conducive to the rational planning of urban logistics layout and system, the integration of logistics resources and complementary advantages, so as to stimulate and promote regional and urban economic development comprehensively. Port and shipping logistics companies with differentiated functions in the same limited area concentrate on providing port and shipping logistics services, which reduces the intermediate links of logistics, effectively improves the efficiency and speed of logistics services, and improves the level of logistics services required by customers.

②信息化

②Informatization

现代物流的信息化，以信息数据库、货物代码、数字平台与资源、港航信息标准化为代表，在航运及集疏运网络合理化与系统化的基础上，使整个港口物流系统实现了运营管理的信息化和电子化，从而使港口物流园区进入以信息网络技术和电子商务为代表的信息化阶段。

The informatization of modern logistics is represented by information databases, cargo codes, digital platforms and resources, and port and shipping information standardization. On the basis of the rationalization and systemization of shipping and collection and distribution networks, the entire port logistics system has realized the informatization and electronization of operation and management, so that the port logistics park has entered the informatization stage represented by information network technology and e-commerce.

③协同化

③Synergy

现代港口物流园区包括装卸、仓储、包装、运输、流通加工等环节，各环节具有各自的工艺流程和设施设备，各环节高效协同运行，最终实现港口物流业务从收取、存储、分拣到运输等服务的高效和顺畅。

The modern port logistics park includes loading and unloading, warehousing, packaging, transportation, circulation processing and other links. Each link has its technological process and facilities, and each link operates efficiently and collaboratively. Finally, the port logistics business will be efficient and smooth from collection, storage, sorting to transportation.

④一体化

④Integration

与港口物流相关的不同职能部门之间或不同企业之间通过合作可实现提高物流效率和降低物流成本的目的。作为一条环环相扣的供应链，港口物流系统应运用现代管理思想与管理手段，有效提高流通效率，实施全流程、一体化的运营管理，最终获取良好的综合效益。

Cooperation between different functional departments related to port logistics or different enterprises can achieve the purpose of improving logistics efficiency and reducing logistics costs. As an interlocking supply chain, the port logistics system should use modern management ideas and management methods to effectively improve circulation efficiency, implement full-process, integrated operation management, and ultimately obtain good comprehensive benefits.

（3）港口物流园区的功能
（3）Functions of Port Logistics Park

港口物流园区属于枢纽型综合物流园区，具备港口枢纽功能，能够推动区域社会经济发展，其应具备以下功能：

The port logistics park is a hub-type comprehensive logistics park with port hub function, which can promote regional social and economic development. It should have the following functions：

①物流服务组织与管理功能

①Logistics Service Organization and Management Function

港口物流园区的核心功能是物流服务组织与管理功能，即应具备物流活动的基本功能，包括运输、装卸、仓储、流通加工、配送及搬运等。

The core function of port logistics park is logistics service organization and management function, that is, it should have the essential functions of logistics activities, including transportation, loading and unloading, storage, circulation processing, distribution and handling, etc.

②物流配套服务功能

②Logistics Supporting Service Function

港口物流园区除了提供物流服务的核心功能外，还具备如货运代理、报关、信息服务、金融保险服务等相应的物流配套服务功能。

In addition to providing the core function of logistics services, the port logistics park should also have corresponding logistics supporting services functions, such as freight forwarding, customs declaration, information service, financial and insurance service, etc.

③经济开发和城市建设功能

③Economic Development and Urban Construction Function

港口物流园区自身就是临港产业开发和城市建设的一部分，主要包括物流基础设施项目、商业交易平台的开发功能，改善城市环境和提升城市形象的城市建设功能等。

The port logistics park itself is a part of the port industry development and urban construction, which mainly includes the development functions of logistics infrastructure projects and commercial trading platforms, and the construction functions of improving the urban environment and promoting the city's image.

④保税功能

④Bonded Function

根据港口物流园区进出口货物物流服务的需求状况,在港口物流园区设立海关监管区或保税仓库,配备完善的口岸功能,以实现与主要口岸的互联互通,提高区域进出口物流运行的效率和运作水平。它主要包括保税仓储和商品展示等贸易服务功能;国际转口贸易功能;出口加工功能。

According to the demand of import and export goods logistics service in the port logistics park, the customs supervision zone or bonded warehouse shall be set up in the port logistics park, equipped with perfect port functions, to realize the interconnection with the main ports, and improve the operation efficiency and operation level of regional import and export logistics. It mainly includes trade service functions such as bonded warehousing and commodity display; international entrepot trade functions; export processing functions.

⑤电子物流功能

⑤Electronic Logistics Function

基于互联网技术支持,港口物流园区的信息平台搭建,实现企业内部、企业与供应商、企业与消费者、企业与政府部门之间的联系和服务,包括实时配送线路规划、在线物流调度、货物实时检查和查询等电子物流功能。同时,通过电子口岸建设,电子报关、异地报关可以得到有效实现,货物通关效率也能得到提高。

Based on Internet technical support, the port logistics park establish the information platform to realize the connection and services between the inner-enterprise, the enterprise and the supplier, the enterprise and the consumer, the enterprise and the government department, including the electronic logistics functions such as real-time distribution route planning, online logistics scheduling, and cargo real-time inspection and query, etc. At the same time, through the construction of electronic ports, electronic customs declaration and off-site customs declaration can be effectively realized, and the efficiency of customs clearance of goods can be improved.

2.2.2　港口物流园区的发展模式
2.2.2　Development Modes of Port Logistics Park

港口物流的发展模式主要包括以下几类:

The development modes of port logistics mainly include the following:

（1）经济开发区模式
（1）Economic Development Zone Mode

此模式是将物流园区作为经济开发区、高新技术开发区或工业开发区的项目进行有组织的开发和建设,是在特定的开发规划的指导、相关政策的引导和专门开发部门的组织下进行的经济开发项目。

This mode is to develop and construct the logistics park as a project similar to economic development zone, high-tech development zone or industrial development zone. It is an economic development project under the organization of specific development planning, policies and special development departments.

（2）主体企业引导模式
（2）Main Enterprise Guidance Mode

在区域宏观政策的引导下,在相关产业供应链管理中具有优势的企业主动率先开发建设并入驻园区,逐步实现港航物流产业的集聚。进而,依托港航物流环境进行发展的工商业企业再逐渐加入,物流园区的队伍建设和配套设施得到不断完善。

Under the guidance of macro policy, enterprises with advantages in related industry supply chain management take the initiative to develop and construct and settle in the park, which gradually realize the agglomeration of the port and shipping logistics industry. Furthermore, industrial and commercial enterprises that rely on the port and shipping logistics environment for development gradually join in, and the team construction and supporting facilities of the logistics park are constantly improved.

（3）工业地产商模式
（3）Industrial Real Estate Business Mode

此模式将物流园区作为工业地产项目,并给予开发者适宜的土地政策、税收政策和市政配套政策。在这些政策的支持下,工业地产商主持进行物流园区道路、仓库基础设施及基础性装备的投资和建设,再以租赁、转让或合资、合作的方式进行物流园区的经营和管理。此外,政府也可进行物流园区相关基础设施的投资、建设,然后委托给物流管理企业,在优惠政策的框架下进行经营管理。

This mode takes the logistics park as an industrial real estate project by giving developers appropriate land policies, tax policies and municipal supporting policies. With the support of these policies, the industrial real estate business will preside over the investment and construction of the roads, warehouses infrastructure and infrastructure equipment of the logistics park, and then operate and manage the logistics park by means of leasing, transfer, joint venture or cooperation. In addition, the government can also invest and build the infrastructure related to the logistics park, and then entrust it to logistics management companies to conduct operations and management under the framework of preferential policies.

（4）综合运作模式
（4）Integrated Operation Mode

此模式是指对上述几类模式进行综合应用的物流园区开发模式。港航物流园区项目一般具有开发规模大和经营范围广的特点,需要土地、税收等政策上的大力扶持和投资方面的有力支持,要求具备较强的园区经营运作能力。因此,单纯采用某一种开发模式,很难开发建设一个完整的港航物流园区,应综合使用经济开发区模式、主体企业引导模式、工业地产商模式等多种模式发展港航物流园区。

This mode refers to a logistics park development mode that comprehensively applies the types mentioned above of models. Port and shipping logistics park projects generally have the characteristics of large-scale development and wide-ranging business scope. They require strong support in policies such as land, taxation, and investment, and require strong park operation capabilities. Therefore, it is difficult to develop and construct a complete port and shipping logistics park simply by adopting a certain mode. The port and shipping logistics park should be developed using multiple modes such as economic development zone mode, main enterprise guidance mode, and industrial real estate business mode.

2.2.3 国内外物流园区的发展情况分析
2.2.3 Analysis on the Development of Domestic and International Logistics Park

物流园区的组织形式和概念起源于日本,之后在欧美得到了较快发展。物流园区给物流企业与其所在腹地城市带来了较大的经济和社会效益,从而引起广泛关注。我国于 20 世纪末和 21 世纪初开始开发物流园区,在 2005 年左右渐入建设高潮并持续发展。

The organization form and concept of logistics park originated in Japan, and then developed rapidly in Europe and America. The logistics park has brought great economic and social benefits to the logistics enterprises and their hinterland cities, which has aroused widespread concern. China began to develop logistics parks at the end of the 20th century and the beginning of the 21st century, and gradually entered the construction climax around 2005, and continued to develop.

(1)国外物流园区
(1) International Logistics Park

东京是日本物流园区的诞生地,当时东京与周边城市间存在着大量各类货物的进出需求。为了解决商流与物流混成一体、交通混杂拥堵、城市功能日益低下的问题,自 1965 年起,日本政府通过将流通功能从市中心分离出去的方法,在政府计划中规定并募集资金。在东京近郊的东、西、南、北四个方向建设了和平岛、葛西、阪桥与足立四个物流园区,并相应配套建立了商务交易大楼、大型仓库群与公路货物集散中心等设施。大型物流园区通过逐步完善各项基础设施、配套服务设施以及各种优惠政策,吸引了物流企业在此聚集,改善了城市环境,提升了城市的综合竞争力。

Tokyo was the birthplace of Japanese logistics parks, when there was a lot of goods in and out of Tokyo and the surrounding cities. In order to solve the situation of mixed traffic congestion and increasingly low urban function caused by the integration of business flow and logistics, the Japanese government adopted the method of separating the circulation function from the city center, which was regulated by the government plan and raised funds to build Heping Island, Gexi, Banqiao and Zuli four logistics parks respectively in the east, south, west and north of the outskirts of Tokyo, and correspondingly set up logistics facilities such as business transaction building, large warehouse group and highway cargo distribution center from 1965. Through gradually supporting and improving various infrastructure, service facilities and providing various preferential policies, large-scale logistics parks are attracting logistics enterprises to gather here, so that they can improve the urban environment and enhance the comprehensive competitiveness of the city.

德国从 1980 年开始,在全国范围内规划建设 40 座物流园区。在此过程中,政府负责监督物流园区建设,规范物流园区准入条件,积极吸引国内大中型企业与国际性物流企业进驻各物流园区。在较大经济区建设联运站的基础上,以货物的快速直达运输为目的,德国将建成的物流中心逐渐转变为物流园区,其中不来梅物流园区和纽伦堡物流园区最为著名。

Since 1980, Germany has planned to build 40 logistics parks in the whole country. In this process, the government is supervising the construction of logistics park, standardizing the access conditions of logistics parks, and actively attracting large and medium-sized domestic enterprises and international logistics enterprises to enter the logistics park. In order to realize the fast and direct transportation of goods, Germany has gradually transformed the established logistics centers into logistics parks based on the construction of intermodal stations in larger economic zones, among which the Bremen Logistics Park and the Nuremberg Logistics Park are the most famous.

荷兰看准鹿特丹港在欧洲独一无二的地理位置与特点,通过政府投资和特殊政策扶持,如兴建部分公共配套设施、利用税收杠杆给予减免税优惠等,不断完善适应物流发展的软硬件环境,推进海港、公路、铁路与相关信息技术等各类基础设施建设,催生出了荷兰著名的鹿特丹港口物流园区。荷兰凭借着其优越的交通区位优势,目前总计规划建设了 14 个物流园区。

In view of the unique geographical location and characteristics of the Port of Rotterdam in Europe, the Netherlands has continuously improved the hardware and software environment suitable for logistics development through government investment and special policy support, such as the construction of some public supporting facilities, the use of tax leverage to grant tax reduction and exemption concessions, and promoted the construction of various infrastructure facilities such as seaports, roads, railways and related information technology, which is giving birth to the famous Rotterdam Port Logistics Park in the Netherlands.

为满足制造商、货运代理、贸易公司、运输与专业仓储公司的需求,新加坡政府沿南部海岸线规划建设了若干物流园区。比如,裕廊港建造了 255 000 m^2 的普通物流仓库、近 4 500 m^2 的空调仓库以及可以堆放超过 4 000 TEU 的集装箱堆场,可进行货物的集散、仓储、包装、装配、贴签等增值服务。

Singapore has many logistics parks along its southern coastline to meet the needs of manufactures, freight forwarders, trading companies, transportation and specialized warehousing companies. For example, Jurong Port in Singapore has a general logistics warehouse of 255,000 square meters, an air-conditioned warehouse of 4,500 square meters, and a container yard that can stack more than 4,000 TEU. The value-added services mainly include goods distribution, storage, packaging, assembly, labeling, etc.

（2）国内物流园区
（2）Domestic Logistics Park

香港港是世界上最繁忙的港口物流中心之一,拥有优良的港口基础设施和物流配套设施,运行效率处于全球先进水平行列。其物流园区依托于中国内地,面向东南亚,连接欧美,为占港口吞吐量八成以上货物的转口贸易提供服务。香港港通过完善专业化管理技术与信息技术手段,建立虚拟供应链控制平台,依靠完善的金融保险服务以及高效的通关水平,不断扩大市场覆盖面。

Hong Kong Port is one of the busiest port logistics centers in the world. It has excellent port infrastructure and logistics supporting facilities, and its operation and conversion efficiency are also at the world's advanced level. Relying on Chinese mainland, facing Southeast Asia, connecting Europe and America, Hong Kong Port Logistics Park focuses on providing logistics services for entrepot trade accounting for more than 80% of port throughput. By improving professional management technology and information technology, Hong Kong Port has gradually become a virtual supply chain control center. Relying on its perfect financial and insurance services and efficient customs clearance level, the market coverage of its port logistics industry has been expanding.

上海洋山深水港物流园区是洋山深水港建设中重要的组成部分,是上海建设国际集装箱枢纽港和国际航运中心的重要依托。洋山深水港物流园区具备仓储、加工、运输、保税、临港工业、分拨、增值和贸易等综合功能,园区包括八大功能区域:港口辅助作业区、口岸查验区、国际保税物流区、铁路集装箱换装区、内河集装箱换装区、危险区仓储区、综合管理服务区和临港保税仓储区等。

As an indispensable part of Yangshan deep water port construction, Shanghai Yangshan deep water port logistics park is an important support for Shanghai to build an international container hub port and an international shipping center. Yangshan deep water port logistics park has comprehensive functions of warehousing, processing, transportation, bonded, port industry, distribution, value-added and international trade. The park includes eight functional areas: port auxiliary operation area, port inspection area, international bonded logistics area, railway container loading area, inland container loading area, dangerous area storage area, comprehensive management service area and port bonded storage area, etc.

大连大窑湾保税港区已发展成为全国最大的冷链物流基地及第二大冷鲜货物进口口岸,在国家新一轮振兴东北老工业基地战略和辽宁沿海经济带建设等政策的推动下,目前已形成规模化、集约化的冷链物流园区,是国内著名的集专业冷藏船泊位、集装箱码头、保税港和冷库群于一体的区域性专业化冷链物流中心。

Dalian Dayaowan Bonded Port Area has developed into the country's largest cold chain logistics base and the second largest import port of cold and fresh goods. Driven by the new national strategy of revitalizing the old industrial base in Northeast China and the construction of Liaoning coastal economic belt, a large-scale and intensive cold chain logistics park has been formed. It is a well-known regional professional cold chain logistics center integrating professional refrigerated ship berths, container terminals, bonded ports and cold storage groups in China.

2.3 港口物流联运设施
2.3 Port Logistics Intermodal Facilities

港口集疏运体系是连接水路运输与其他运输方式的平台和纽带,是进行全链条一体化运输组织的关键。港口物流联运设施的完善及高效运行,能有效缓和由于船舶随时到港、货流不均衡等不确定性引起的压船压货,也可减小货物集散对码头仓库造成的仓储压力。集疏运体系能力的不断增强也会在一定程度上弥补港口其他系统的不足乃至扩大港口腹地半径,从而促进港口发挥最大的潜力。

Port collection and distribution system is the platform and link to connect waterway transportation and other modes of transportation, and the key to the integrated transportation organization. The perfect and efficient operation of port logistics intermodal transportation facilities can alleviate the phenomenon of ship pressure caused by the uneven arrival of ships at any time and unbalanced cargo flow, and can also reduce the storage pressure caused by cargo collection and distribution on the terminal warehouse. The continuous enhancement of the capacity of the collection and distribution system will make up for the deficiencies of other port systems and even expand the port hinterland radius, thereby promoting the port to maximize its potential.

2.3.1 港口集疏运的概念
2.3.1 Concept of Port Collection and Distribution

以港区内码头前沿为界,腹地的货物通过公路、铁路、水路等方式运至码头堆场待运,此为集运,通过各种方式将货物运离码头,则为疏运。外贸船舶从国外港口装运货物到港与内贸船舶从本地区其他港口装运货物来港并无本质区别,只不过外贸船舶是从海上腹地来港,而内贸船从陆上腹地来港,都属于集运。而外贸船舶装运货物离港和内贸船舶装货离港,属于疏运。

Taking quayside of the port in the port area as the boundary, the goods in the hinterland of the port are transported to the wharf yard by road, railway, waterway and other means for transportation, which is called collection transportation. Transporting goods out of the terminal through various means is distribution. There is no essential difference between foreign trade ships' shipment of goods from foreign ports to domestic ports and domestic trade ships' shipment of goods from other domestic ports. The only difference is that foreign trade ships come from the hinterland at sea, while domestic ships come from the hinterland on land, all belonging to the collection transportation. The departure of foreign trade ships and domestic ships with cargo are classified as distribution.

因此,集疏运是整个港口的生产过程,包括内陆运输、港口装卸和堆存、海上运输,港口是整个集疏运网络的一个节点。

Therefore, collection and distribution is the production process of the entire port, including inland transportation, port loading and unloading, storage, and maritime transportation. The port is a node of the entire collection and distribution network.

港口集疏运输体系中,各港口与腹地运输联系的规模、方向、运距及货物结构决定了集疏运线路数量、运输方式构成和地理分布等。一般来说,大型或较大型港口的集疏运系统,均应因地制宜地向多通路、多方向与多种运输方式方向发展。

In the port collection and distribution transportation system, the scale, direction, distance and cargo structure of the transportation links between the ports and the hinterland transportation determine the number of collection and distribution lines, the composition of transportation methods, and the geographical distribution. Generally, the collection and distribution system of large or larger scale ports should develop in the direction of multiple channels, multiple directions and multiple modes of transportation in accordance with local conditions.

2.3.2 港口集疏运体系的构成
2.3.2 Composition of Port Collection and Distribution System

港口集疏运体系主要包含港口码头、港口腹地、集疏运方式和设施等。

Port collection and distribution system mainly includes port terminal, the hinterland of the port, collection and distribution mode and facilities.

(1)港口码头
(1)Port Terminal
港口码头是货物在水路运输系统与陆路运输系统间转换的接口。根据其运营组织特点,港口一般分为枢纽港、干线港和支线港。港口类型差异决定了港口码头设施设备规模、吞吐量和腹地范围,体现了集疏运的规模。

The port terminal is the interface for cargo conversion between the water transportation system and the land transportation system. According to the characteristics of port operation organization, ports can be generally divided into hub ports, trunk ports and feeder ports. The difference of port types determines the scale of port terminal facilities and equipment, port throughput and hinterland range, and also reflects the scale of collection and distribution.

（2）港口腹地
（2）The Hinterland of the Port

港口腹地是指港口的客货集散所涉及的地区。港口功能、规模和服务水平，以及港口所在城市的经济社会发展水平，影响了港口对其腹地的辐射范围。港口腹地范围大小及港口腹地经济社会发展水平，特别是外向型经济的发达程度，关系到港口货源、港口腹地货物的流向，并直接影响腹地集疏运量和港口吞吐量的规模。

The hinterland of the port refers to the area involved in the collection and distribution of passengers and cargo in the port. The function, scale and service level of the port, as well as the economic and social development level of the city where the port is located, affect the radiation range of the port to its hinterland. The size of port hinterland and the level of economic and technological development of port hinterland, especially the development of export-oriented economy, are related to the source of port goods, the flow direction of port hinterland goods, and directly affect collection and distribution volume and the scale of port throughput in hinterland.

（3）集疏运方式和设施
（3）Collection and Distribution Mode and Facilities

连接港口与腹地的集疏运线包括公路运输线、铁路运输线和沿海（内河）航线以及与集疏运线相连接的内陆国际货运站、中转站等。

The collection and distribution lines connecting ports and hinterland include highway transportation line, railway transportation line and coastal (inland) routes, as well as inland international freight stations and transfer stations connected with the collection and distribution lines.

铁路运输具有运量大、速度快、连续性强、时刻准、运输成本低、受自然条件影响小等技术特性，适合大宗货物运输。水运的技术经济特点为线路投资少、运载量大、运输成本低，但运输速度慢，受自然环境限制大，并因水运网络的地理分布，灵活性差，最适于大型笨重、大宗货物或时限要求不高的长距离运输。公路运输具有直达性，有门对门的特点。公路运输的直达性可转换为三个效益：距离差效益——公路运输的路线选择较多，使运距少于铁路及水运；时间差效益——公路运输的送达速度快于铁路和水路运输，增加经济效益；质量差效益——汽车直达运输通常只需一装一卸，更易保持货物原始状态。公路运输机动灵活，运载工具体形小且操作方便，对各种自然条件有较强的适应性，但具有运载量小、劳动生产率低、运输成本高等缺点。铁路站点和水运码头的点线式布局决定了铁路网和水运网的密度远小于公路网密度，使得铁路和水路运输除其运输过程以外的客货集散，大部分都运用公路运输完成。

Railway transportation has the technical characteristics of large capacity, fast speed, strong continuity, accurate time, low transportation cost and little impact by natural conditions. It is suitable for bulk cargo transportation with large volumes and heavy quality. The technical and economic characteristics of water transportation are less line investment, large transportation volume and low transportation cost, but the transportation speed is slow, limited by natural environment. Moreover, because of the geographical distribution of the water transportation network, the flexibility is poor, and it is most suitable for large and heavy, bulky goods or long-distance transportation with a low time limit. Highway transportation has the characteristics of direct access and door-to-door. The direct transportation of highway can be converted into three benefits: distance difference benefit—road transportation has more route options, making the distance less than railway and water transportation; time difference benefit—road transportation has a faster delivery speed than rail and water transportation, increasing economy benefit; poor quality benefit—direct car transportation usually only requires one loading and one unloading, which makes it easier to maintain the original condition of the damaged goods. Road transportation is flexible, small in shape and easy to operate, and has strong adaptability to various natural conditions. But the transportation volume is small, the labor productivity is low, and the transportation cost is high. The point-and-line layout of railway stations and water transport terminals determines that the density of the railway network and water transport network is much smaller than that of the road network, so that most of the passenger and cargo collection and distribution of railway and water transport, except for its transportation process, are completed by road transport.

综合各运输方式的比较优势,多式联运成为发展趋势,在我国发展不断深入,运行质量逐渐提升,综合效益初步显现。2016 年以来,国家发展改革委、交通运输部、铁路总公司等部门从多个政策方面推动多式联运发展,先后印发《"十三五"铁路集装箱多式联运发展规划》《中欧班列建设发展规划(2016—2020 年)》《"十三五"长江经济带港口多式联运建设实施方案》《推进物流大通道建设行动计划(2016—2020 年)》《"十三五"港口集疏运系统建设方案》等文件。其中,铁水联运发展势头强劲,营口港、青岛港集装箱铁水联运量超过 70 万 TEU/年,宁波舟山港、青岛港集装箱铁水联运量增速超过 50%。

Combined with the comparative advantages of various modes of transportation, multimodal transport has become a trend of development. With the continuous development in China, the operation quality has been gradually improved, and the comprehensive benefits have initially emerged. Since 2016, the National Development and Reform Commission, the Ministry of Transport, the Railway Corporation and other departments have promoted the development of multimodal transport from various policy aspects, successively printing and distributing "the 13th Five Year Plan for the Development of Railway Container Multimodal Transport", "the Construction and Development Plan for China Europe Train(2016－2020)", "the Implementation Plan for the Construction of Port Multimodal Transport in the 13th Five Year Plan for the Yangtze River Economic Belt", "Promote the Logistics Chase Road Construction Action Plan(2016－2020)", and "the 13th Five Year Plan for Port Collection and Distribution System Construction", etc. Among

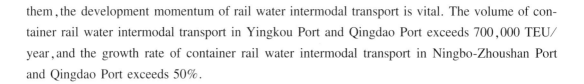

them, the development momentum of rail water intermodal transport is vital. The volume of container rail water intermodal transport in Yingkou Port and Qingdao Port exceeds 700,000 TEU/year, and the growth rate of container rail water intermodal transport in Ningbo-Zhoushan Port and Qingdao Port exceeds 50%.

2.3.3　港口集疏运网络的节点
2.3.3　Node of Port Collection and Distribution Network

集疏运节点是集疏运网络中连接集疏运线路的转换交接处,集疏运活动在线路和节点上进行。在线路上的活动主要包括集货运输和干线运输等。节点是组织和联系集疏运线路上活动的关键,直接影响集疏运线路上的运行效率。

The collection and distribution node is the junction of the collection and distribution lines in the collection and distribution network. All collection and distribution activities are carried out on the lines and nodes. The main activities carried out on the line are transportation, including cargo collection transportation, trunk transportation, etc. Nodes are the key to organizing and connecting activities on the collection and distribution lines, and directly affect the operating efficiency of the collection and distribution lines.

集疏运节点在集疏运网络中除执行一般的装卸职能外在集疏运体系中具有以下功能:

In addition to general loading and unloading functions in the collection and distribution network, the collection and distribution nodes have the following functions in the collection and distribution system:

(1)衔接功能
(1) Connection Function

集疏运节点将各集疏运线路联结成一个整体,使多个线路贯通。在集疏运体系未成网络前,不同线路的衔接存在阻碍,集疏运节点利用各种技术的管理方法可以有效地起到衔接作用,将阻碍中断转化为畅通无阻。

The collection and distribution nodes connect the collection and distribution lines into a whole, so that multiple lines are connected. Before the collection and distribution system has become a network, there are obstacles to the connection of different lines. The management methods of the collection and distribution nodes using various technologies can effectively play a role in the connection and turn the obstacles into unimpeded connections.

(2)信息功能
(2) Information Function

集疏运节点是集疏运体系中信息传递、收集、处理、发送的集中地,在集疏运体系中起着举足轻重的作用。

The collection and distribution node is the centralized place for the information transmission, collection, processing and transmission, which plays a significant role in the collection and distribution system.

（3）管理功能
(3) Management Function

集疏运体系的管理设施和指挥中枢通常集中设置于集疏运节点上，多数集疏运节点是集指挥调度、信息传递和货物处理为一体的物流综合管理设施，影响整个集疏运体系的运转有序化和正常化。

The management facilities and command organizations of the collection and distribution system are often set in the collection and distribution nodes. Most of the collection and distribution nodes are integrated logistics facilities that integrate command and dispatch, information transmission, and cargo handling, which affect the ordering and normalization of the entire collection and distribution system.

各种交通方式在港口相互衔接，形成具备集中与疏散港口吞吐货物服务的集疏运系统。集疏运体系为旅客和货物完成全程运输提供重要基础设施和衔接场所，实现物理和逻辑上的"零距离换乘""无缝连接"，是交通运输适应于各类运输枢纽发展的体现，连接港口与广大腹地，是港口赖以存在与发展的主要外部条件。任何现代化港口必须拥有完善与畅通的集疏运系统，才能成为综合交通运输网中重要的水陆交通枢纽。

All kinds of traffic modes are connected with the port, forming a collection and distribution system of cargo handling service in the centralized and evacuation port. The collection and distribution system is to provide important infrastructure and connecting place for passengers and goods to complete the whole process of transportation, to provide convenient and logical "zero distance transfer" "seamless connection", to meet the development requirements of transportation for various transport hubs, to connect the port and the vast hinterland, and to provide the main external conditions for the existence and development of the port. Any modern port must have a perfect and smooth collection and distribution system to become an important water and land transport hub in the comprehensive transportation network.

2.3.4 港口集疏运系统基础设施
2.3.4 Infrastructure of Port Collection and Distribution System

港口对其周边的集疏运网络畅通度要求较高，而港口及其集疏运交通运输网又必须与城市交通乃至区域交通相互协调，所以集疏运系统的基础设施适合由政府统一规划布局。

The port has a high demand for the smoothness of its surrounding collection and distribution network, and the port and the transportation network near the port must coordinate with the urban traffic and even the regional traffic, so the infrastructure of the collection and distribution link is

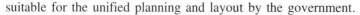

suitable for the unified planning and layout by the government.

改建与完善集疏运系统的基础设施,不断发展内陆集疏运网络,提高从港口向内陆疏运、从内陆向港口集运程度,有利于促进港口集疏运高效、高速、安全地开展,进而促进物流、信息流、资金流向港口集中,为建设现代物流产业基地提供强有力的支持,主要包括:

The reconstruction and improvement of the infrastructure in the collection and distribution system, the continuous development of the inland collection and distribution network, and the improvement of the degree of the collection and distribution from the port to the inland and from the inland to the port are conducive to the efficient, high-speed and safe development of the collection and distribution, thus promoting the concentration of logistics, information flow and capital flow to the port, and providing strong support for the goal of building a modern logistics industrial base, mainly include:

(1) 码头后方堆场

(1) Rear Yard

在原有面积的基础之上,结合进出口、中转等货物类型、货流量、货物持有人等信息,改进现有堆存方式,提高码头货物堆存的科学性,提升堆存能力,提高货物周转率。同时,与从事站场行业的其他单位和个人合资,组建码头以外的延续堆场(后方堆场),以解决堆场货物堆存高峰时期堆存能力不足的问题,同时,也履行站场的功能,为码头提供新的赢利方向。

On the basis of the original area, combined with the information of import and export, transit and other cargo types, cargo flow, cargo holders, etc., improve the existing stacking mode, scientificity of cargo storage, the stacking capacity and the turnover rate. At the same time, the joint venture with other units and individuals engaged in the station and yard industry will be carried out to establish a continuous yard (rear yard) outside the terminal to solve the problem of insufficient stacking capacity at the peak of the yard. Meanwhile, the function of the station and yard will also be performed to provide a new profit direction for the terminal.

(2) 中转场站

(2) Transit Station

目前,中转场站存在数量多,布局分散,能力过剩,缺少规模经营,远离港口等问题。短途运输增加的同时也会带来交通问题,易对港口内陆的集疏运不利,难以支撑港口物流的发展。因此,加速中转站建设、实现码头向内陆的延伸十分必要。内陆中转站作为港口物流内陆的集散点,不仅可以集中附近的出口货物装箱发往港口出口,也可以对进口货物在内地进行中转运输。科学和合理地规划站场布局应遵循以下原则:

At present, there are many problems in transit stations, such as large numbers, scattered layout, excess capacity, lack of scale operation, far away from the ports, etc. The increase of short-distance transportation will also bring traffic problems, which is not conducive to the collection and distribution of inland ports, and does not play a supporting role in the development of port logistics. Therefore, it is necessary to speed up the construction of transfer station and realize the extension of wharf to inland. As the inland distribution center of port logistics, the inland transfer station can not only pack and send the nearby export goods to the port for export, but also transit the import goods in inland areas. Scientific and reasonable planning of station layout should follow the following principles：

①调整码头操作业务与拆装箱业务的分离,以确保码头操作高效化。

①Adjust the separation of terminal operation business and port unpacking business to ensure efficient terminal operation.

②调整港区内的场站布局,加速集疏运多种方式的衔接。

②Adjust the layout of stations in the port area and strengthen the connection of various modes of collection and distribution.

③发展物流中心型综合站场,提高站场的经营档次,增强竞争力,吸引货源,使站场的服务上档次、提水平,推进综合物流服务业的快速发展。

③ Develop the logistics center type comprehensive station and yard, improve the management level of the station and yard, enhance the competitiveness, attract the source of goods, make the service of the station and yard up to the grade and level, and promote the rapid development of the comprehensive logistics service industry.

（3）线路设施
（3）Line Facilities

鉴于港口集疏运系统通过铁路运输的比例较低,为充分发挥铁路运输的优势,港方应加强与铁路部门的合作与联系,开拓内陆铁路中转场站,特别是集装箱中转站,建立以铁路为主干线,辅以公路运输支线,实现"门到门"的运输服务。

In view of the low proportion of port collection and distribution completed by railway, in order to give full play to the advantages of railway transportation, the port side should strengthen the contact with the railway department and open up transit stations in inland railway, especially container transit stations, establish the main railway line supplemented by road branch transportation, and realize the "door-to-door" transportation service.

（4）配套设备
（4）Affiliated Equipment

推进港口集疏运设施机械化、智能化、自动化、大型化、环保化发展趋势,完善港口集疏运装卸搬运设施、设备的配备,可为港口物流发展服务。

Promote the development trend of mechanization, intelligence, automation, large-scale and environmental protection of port collection and distribution facilities, and improve the equipment of port collection and distribution facilities and equipment, which can serve the development of port logistics.

◆ 2.4 港口物流信息系统
2.4 Port Logistics Information System

作为水陆交通运输的枢纽,港口企业在物流系统中发挥着举足轻重的作用。港口企业物流服务效率低下,将制约物流周转速度,成为物流顺畅运行的瓶颈。因此,运用现代物流及供应链管理的思想来指导港口企业的运作势在必行。

As the hub of land and water transportation, port enterprises play an important role in the logistics system. If the logistics service efficiency of port enterprises is low, it will restrict the speed of logistics turnover and become a bottleneck for the smooth operation of logistics. Therefore, it is necessary to guide the operation of port enterprises with the ideas of modern logistics and supply chain management.

由于港口物流运作的过程总伴有各种错综复杂的数据与信息流,因此,亟须一个符合港口功能需求的物流信息系统,以提高港口物流系统运作效率,集中处理物流网络中各节点间的信息流交换。

Because the process of port logistics is always accompanied by a variety of complex data and information flows, in order to improve the operation efficiency of port logistics system, it is necessary to have a logistics information system that meets the functional requirements of the port, and to focus on the information flow exchange between the nodes in the logistics network.

2.4.1 港口物流信息系统概述
2.4.1 Overview of Port Logistics Information System

港口物流信息是指在港口物流活动进行中产生及使用的必要信息,是港口物流活动内容、形式、过程以及发展变化的总体反映,也是港口相关物流活动中传递与交换数字、条件、消息、图表的总称。物流信息在港口物流运作中发挥着业务控制、市场交易、工作协调和战略决策等四大功能。

Port logistics information refers to the necessary information generated and used in the process of port logistics activities. It is the overall reflection of the content, form, process and development of port logistics activities. It is also the general term of transferring and exchanging numbers, conditions, messages and charts in port related logistics activities. Logistics information plays four functions in port logistics activities: business control, market transaction, work coordination and strategic decision-making.

港口物流系统信息一般由内部和外部信息构成,具有信息量大、分布广、动态性强、信息种类多等特征。港口物流系统内部信息是伴随着港口物流活动而产生的信息,包括货物装卸作业信息、仓储信息、车船运输信息和物流管理信息;物流系统外部信息是提供给港口物流活动使用的信息,包括供货人信息、承运人信息、船货运代理信息、合同信息、市场信息、口岸单位信息、金融保险信息、政策信息,港口相关企业信息及其他物流有关的信息。

The information of port logistics system is generally composed of internal and external information, which has the characteristics of a large amount of information, wide distribution, substantial dynamic, many kinds of information. The internal information of the port logistics system is the information accompanying the port logistics activities, including cargo loading and unloading operation information, cargo storage information, vehicle and ship transportation information and logistics management information. The external information of the logistics system is the information provided to the port logistics activities, including the supplier information, carrier information, shipping agent information, contract information, marketing information, port unit information, financial and insurance information, policy information, and information from port related enterprises and other logistics related information.

港口物流信息系统一般是由硬件、软件、数据库和人员等基本要素组成的人机系统,其以电子计算机为基本处理手段,以现代通信设备为基本传输工具,以优化人机系统为目标,具有预测、控制、交易、决策和战略管理等功能,能为港口相关部门和企业提供管理决策信息服务和自动操作控制。港口物流信息系统具有信息集合性、可得性、适应性、准确性、及时性、共享性等特点。

Port logistics information system is a man-machine system composed of hardware, software, database and personnel. It takes electronic computer as the basic information processing means, modern communication equipment as the basic transmission tool, human-machine system optimization as the goal, has the functions of prediction, control, transaction, decision-making and strategic management, and can provide the relevant departments and enterprises of the port with management decision-making information service and automatic operation control. Port logistics information system has the characteristics of information collection, availability, adaptability, accuracy, timeliness and sharing, etc.

（1）港口物流信息系统的基本组成

（1）The Basic Composition of Port Logistics Information System

对于港口企业而言,货物实际流动过程较为简单,如图 2.5 所示。但随货物而流动的物流信息十分复杂。实际上,港口物流信息管理水平已成为港口物流效率提升的关键。一个合适的港口物流信息系统可以使港口物流运作更加流畅、便捷,并减少货物的冗余移动,最终提高港口企业的核心竞争力。

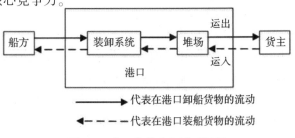

图 2.5 港口货物实际流动过程

For port enterprises, the actual flow process of goods is relatively simple, as shown in Figure 2.5. However, the information that flows with the goods is very complex. In fact, the level of port logistics information management has become the key to the efficiency of port logistics. A suitable port logistics information system can make the port's cargo flow more smooth and simple, minimize the redundant movement of cargo, and ultimately improve the core competitiveness of port enterprises.

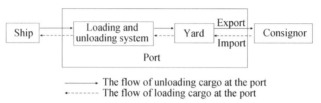

The flow of unloading cargo at the port
The flow of loading cargo at the port

Figure 2.5 Actual flow process of goods

根据港口企业对于信息的特殊要求,一个功能良好的港口物流信息系统应包括以下三个子系统。

According to the special requirements of port enterprises for information, a well-functioning port logistics information system should include the following three subsystems.

①客户服务子系统。其功能包括:

①Customer service subsystem. Its functions include:

a. 信息发布,例如港口企业新闻通告和报价。

a. Information release, such as port enterprise news announcement and quotation.

b. 用户综合物流委托,包括对客户委托的审核、实施各种运输方式及仓储委托的具体操作流程。

b. The user's integrated logistics delegation, including the review of the customer entrustment, the implementation of various transportation methods and the specific operation process of warehousing entrustment.

c. 响应查询,如账单查询,货物在途状态查询,客户对货物的库存状态的查询,客户对统计历史和当前发生的财务数据的查询。

c. Response queries, such as bill queries, goods in transit status queries, customer queries on goods inventory status, customer queries on statistical history and current financial data.

d. 物流配套服务,可提供报关、保险、银行结算及其他配套增值服务。

d. Logistics supporting services, which can provide customs declaration, insurance, bank settlement and other supporting value-added services.

e. 提供对联盟的特殊信息服务,如接收和查询合作方的业务需求或任务下达指令、联盟方的账单查询指令,可按多种条件统计和查询与合作方发生的应收明细及账单等。

e. Special information services for the alliance, such as receiving and querying the business needs or tasks of partners to give instructions, billing query instructions of alliance parties, and statistics and inquiries about the receivable details and bills with the partners according to a variety of conditions.

②码头操作管理子系统。其功能包括：

②Terminal operation management subsystem. Its functions include：

a. 堆场计划和操作系统。

a. Yard planning and operation system.

b. 船舶计划和操作系统。

b. Ship planning and operation system.

c. 货运站箱管系统,包括入库盘点、出库盘点等。

c. Cargo terminal box management system, including warehousing inventory, outbound inventory, etc.

d. 进出口作业管理,包括根据客户不同的委托情况,进行内部作业计划、调度和分工。

d. Import and export operation management, including internal operation planning, scheduling and division of labor according to different entrustment situations of customers.

③信息管理分析子系统。其功能包括：

③Information management analysis subsystem. Its functions include：

a. 接收、录入并管理跟踪信息。

a. Receiving, inputting and managing the tracking information.

b. 对自己承接的业务进行相应信息(如相关单据、EDI 报文等)的接收(或录入)、存储和管理。

b. Receive (or input), store and manage the corresponding information (such as relevant documents, EDI messages, etc.) of the business undertaken by the company.

c. 对系统所接收到的各种与业务相关的信息数据进行分析,并为决策层提供决策依据。

c. Analyze all kinds of business-related information data received by the system, and provide a decision-making basis for the decision-making level.

d. 对客户基本资料信息的收集和管理,包括对客户、联盟伙伴的各种档案资料的录入和管理。

d. The collection and management of basic customer information, including the input and management of various archives of customers and alliance partners.

e. 结合决策准则,能识别需要做出决策的"异常情况"并提醒相关计划或管理人员。

e. Combine decision-making criteria, which can identify "abnormal situations" that need to make decisions and remind relevant plans or managers.

（2）港口物流信息系统的基本结构
（2）The Basic Structure of Port Logistics Information System

从港口企业微观角度分析,一般情况下港口物流信息系统的内容应该与物流管理相对应,结构上分为四个层次,如图 2.6 所示。

From the micro perspective of port enterprises, in general, the content of port logistics information system should correspond to the logistics management, and the structure is divided into four levels, as shown in Figure 2.6.

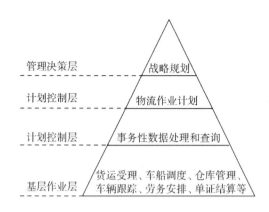

图 2.6　港口物流信息系统的结构

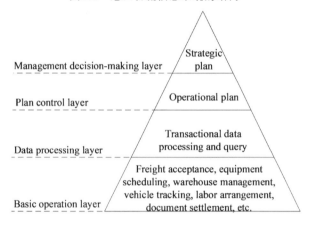

Figure 2.6　Structure of port logistics information system

①基层作业层：将收集、加工的信息以数据库的形式加以存储。

①Basic operation layer：store the collected and processed information in the form of a database.

②数据处理层：对合同、报表和票据等业务表现方式进行处理。

②Data processing layer：processes business performance methods such as contracts, reports, and bills.

③计划控制层：建立作业计划、路线选择、控制评价等模型，检测系统运行状况。

③Plan control layer：establish operation plan, route selection, control evaluation and other models to detect the operation status of the system.

④管理决策层：建立物流系统决策模型，辅助管理人员制订物流计划。

④ Management decision-making layer：establish the decision-making model of logistics system, assist the management personnel to make logistics planning.

与此相对应，完善的港口物流信息系统应为港口提供物流运作协同平台、信息共享平台和决策支持平台，港口物流信息系统的功能结构如图 2.7 所示。

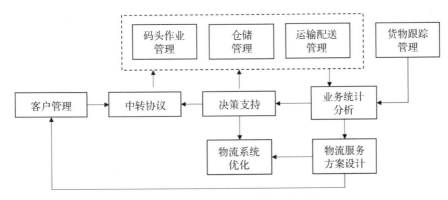

图 2.7 港口物流信息系统的功能结构

Correspondingly, the perfect port logistics information system should provide the port with a logistics operation cooperation platform, information sharing platform and decision support platform. The functional structure of the port logistics information system is shown in Figure 2.7.

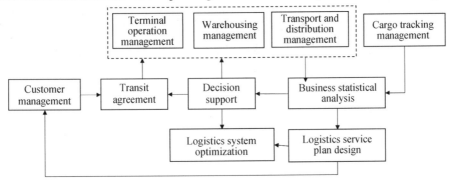

Figure 2.7 The functional structure of port logistics information system

2.4.2 港口物流信息管理平台
2.4.2 Port Logistics Information Management Platform

伴随经济全球化、信息化和网络化发展,港口作为多种运输方式的交汇点,在综合运输体系中发挥着越来越重要的作用。现代物流理念的普及以及实践要求,使得现代港口从交通枢纽转变为内涵更广、层次更高的综合物流体系的中心环节,其功能正朝着提供全方位的增值服务方向发展。发展现代物流已成为港口经济新的增长点,给港口带来了更大的发展空间。为了适应现代物流市场的发展,拓展和完善港口服务功能,世界上许多国家都十分重视港口现代物流系统的建设。

With the development of economic globalization, information and network, as the intersection of various modes of transportation, ports play an increasingly important role in the comprehensive transportation system. With the popularization of modern logistics concept and the requirement of modern logistics practice, the modern port has been transformed from a transportation hub into a central link of comprehensive logistics operation with broader connotation and higher level. Its function is also developing towards providing all-round value-added services. The development of modern logistics has become a new growth point of port economy, which has brought greater development space to the port. In order to adapt to the development of modern logistics market, expand and improve the port service function, many countries in the world attach great importance to the construction of port modern logistics systems.

港口综合物流信息管理平台可实现政府、港口、物流企业三方的电子数据交换,在物流信息交换诸多环节中为各种用户提供综合服务操作平台,使港口信息化建设进一步提高。

The port logistics information management platform will realize the electronic data exchange among the government, port and logistics enterprises, and provide a comprehensive service operation platform for various users in many links of logistics information exchange, so as to further improve the port informatization construction.

通过建设港口综合物流信息服务平台,实现了与港口有关的政府部门履行行政管理的职能,加速了口岸贸易的通关、物流速度,有利于港口城市外向型经济的发展,促进了外贸出口的增加,从而推动了港口城市整体的经济发展。港口物流信息平台将整合港口、船公司、船务代理、检验检疫局、海关海事局及其他用户的信息资源,建立"一站式"对外信息服务窗口,建立面向全球的物流信息服务网络,为货主、船公司、贸易伙伴及其他客户提供优质、全面和准确的信息服务。同时,将进一步提高海关的通关效率、降低交易成本、增加贸易机会,极大改善港口经营环境。

Through the construction of the port integrated logistics information service platform, the government departments related to the port can perform administrative management functions, accelerate the speed of customs clearance and logistics of port trade, facilitate the outward oriented economic development of the port city, promote the increase of foreign trade exports, and thus promote the overall economic prosperity of the port city. The port logistics information platform will integrate the information resources of port, shipping company, shipping agent, inspection and quarantine bureau, customs, maritime bureau and other users, and establish a "one-stop" foreign information service window. Establish a global logistics information service network to provide high-quality, comprehensive and accurate information services for shipowners, shipping companies, trading partners and other customers. At the same time, it will further improve customs clearance efficiency, reduce transaction costs, increase trade opportunities, and greatly promote the improvement of port operating environment.

2.4.3 港口物流管理的支持技术
2.4.3 Support Technology of Port Logistics Management

(1) 电子交换技术
(1) Electronic Exchange Technology
电子数据交换(EDI),指依据统一规定的通用标准格式,运用通信网络传输标准的经济信息,并在贸易伙伴的电子计算机系统之间进行数据交换和自动处理。由于 EDI 能有效减少并最终消除贸易过程中的纸面单证,因而 EDI 也被称作"无纸贸易"。EDI 是进行信息交换和处理的网络化、智能化和自动化系统,并将远程通信、计算机及数据库有机融合于一个系统中,实现数据交换、数据资源共享的一种信息系统。EDI 系统也可作为管理信息系统(MIS)和决策支持系统(DSS)的重要组成部分。

Electronic data interchange (EDI) refers to the standard economical information, which is transmitted through the communication network according to a set of unified standard formats, to carry out data exchange and automatic processing between electronic computer systems of trading partners. EDI is also known as "paperless trade" because it can effectively reduce paper documents in the process of trade until the final elimination. EDI is a networked, intelligent and automatic system for information exchange and processing. It is an information system that integrates remote communication, computer and database to realize data exchange and data resource sharing. EDI system can also be used as an important part of management information system (MIS) and decision support system (DSS).

EDI 系统的三要素为 EDI 软件和硬件、通信网络及数据标准化。构建 EDI 系统需要相应的硬件和软件。EDI 软件将用户数据库系统中的信息翻译成 EDI 的标准形式,以供传输和交换。通信网络是实现数据信息传输和交换的必要条件。同时,EDI 系统需要一个标准的数据格式。

The three elements of EDI system are EDI software and hardware, communication network and data standardization. The realization of EDI system requires corresponding hardware and software. EDI software translates the information in user database system into EDI standard form for transmission and exchange. The communication network is a necessary condition for data information transmission and exchange. At the same time, EDI system needs a standard data format.

(2)地理信息系统
(2) Geographic Information System

地理信息系统(GIS)是 20 世纪 60 年代迅速发展起来的地理学研究新成果,是多学科交叉的产物。地理信息系统以地理空间数据为基础,运用地理模型分析方法,并适时地提供多种空间的和动态的地理信息,为地理研究和地理决策服务。地理信息系统技术作为一种空间信息处理与分析技术,是在信息空间中构建与现实对应的虚拟地理信息空间并在管理决策中应用的核心信息技术,已经成功地应用于高质量制图、资源处理、环境分析、交通管理等方面,具有广泛的应用前景。

Geographic information system (GIS) is a new achievement of geographical research which began to develop rapidly in the 1960s, which is the product of interdisciplinary. The geographic information system is based on geospatial data, uses geographic model analysis methods, and provides a variety of spatial and dynamic geographic information promptly to serve geographic research and geographic decision-making. Geographic information system technology, as a spatial information processing and analysis technology, is the core information technology for constructing virtual geographic information space corresponding to reality in the information space and applying it in management decision-making. It has been successfully applied in high-quality cartography, resource processing, environmental analysis, traffic management, etc., and has a wide application prospect.

伴随世界经济一体化加速发展,传统的港区管理模式愈加不能满足经济快速发展的需要,港口的信息化管理与国际接轨的要求越来越急迫。GIS 技术融合计算机图形和数据库于一体,并作为存储和处理空间信息的高新技术,正是推进港口现代化管理的必要手段。

With the acceleration of world economic integration, the traditional port management mode obviously cannot meet the needs of rapid economic development, and the requirements of port information management and international integration are becoming more and more urgent. GIS technology integrates computer graphics and database, and as a high-tech for storing and processing spatial information, it is a necessary means to promote modern port management.

GIS 技术在港口的应用有如下优势:

The application of GIS in port has the following advantages:

①GIS 的核心功能是空间分析,并是区别于其他信息系统的主要标志,其强大的空间分析能力,在进行港口规划、选址等重大决策时,能够提供最直观的辅助信息。同时在港口联合运输物流管理中,GIS 系统可提供多种合理的运输方式与路线比较方案,并模拟运输过程。

①The core function of GIS is spatial analysis, which is the main mark of GIS different from other information systems. The powerful spatial analysis ability can provide the most direct auxiliary information when making major decisions such as port planning and site selection. At the same time in the logistics management of port combined transportation, GIS system can provide a reasonable comparison scheme of transportation mode and route, and simulate the transportation process.

②GIS 管理注重经济因素和环境因素。以往的管理方式,注重港口项目建设的质量、工期、成本管理。而 GIS 系统更加注重区位机遇与港口发展的作用,以经济地理地图,分析港口的规划与长远发展,同时更加注重港口建设与周边环境的影响,注重港口可持续发展。

②GIS management pays attention to economic factors and environmental factors. The previous management methods focused on the quality, duration and cost management of port project construction. The GIS system pays more attention to the role of location opportunities and port development, analyzes the planning and long-term development of the port with the economic geographical map, pays more attention to the impact of port construction and surrounding environment, and pay more attention to the sustainable development.

(3) 全球定位系统

(3) Global Positioning System

全球定位系统(GPS)是由美国国防部组织研发的第二代卫星导航系统,实现了全球、全天候、连续不间断的实时导航定位。GPS 集当代先进的空间、通信、微电子学、精密时间和计算机技术等技术于一体,其应用已经渗透到社会的各个领域。目前,GPS 已成为国际通行的、用于监控车辆的有效设备。

Global positioning system (GPS) is the second generation of satellite navigation system developed and implemented by the United States Department of defense, which realizes global, all-weather and continuous real-time navigation and positioning. GPS integrates modern advanced space, communication, microelectronics, precise time and computer technology, and its applications have penetrated into all areas of society. At present, GPS has become an internationally accepted and effective device for monitoring vehicles.

GPS 的应用包括以下几方面:

The application of GPS includes the following aspects:

①汽车自定位、跟踪调度及陆地救援。

①Vehicle self-positioning, tracking and dispatching, and land rescue.

车辆导航将成为未来全球卫星定位系统应用的主要领域之一。我国已有数十家公司在开发和销售车载导航系统,中远海、中外运和其他大型国际物流服务企业均建立了载有卫星定位的车队。

Vehicle navigation will become one of the main fields of GPS application in the future. Dozens of companies in China are developing and selling vehicle navigation systems. COSCO, SINOTRANS and other large international logistics service enterprises have established fleets with satellite positioning.

②内河及远洋船队最佳航程和安全航线测定、实时调度、监测和水上救援。

②The best voyage and safe route determination, real-time dispatching, monitoring and water rescue of inland and ocean-going fleets.

在我国,GPS 最先用于为远洋运输的船舶提供导航。我国的三峡工程也已运用了 GPS 来改善船队航运条件、提高航运能力。

In China, GPS is first used in ocean shipping. China's Three Gorges project has also used GPS to improve shipping conditions and capacity.

③空中交通管理、精密进场着陆、航路导航和监视。

③Air traffic management, precision approach and landing, route navigation and monitoring

国际民航组织(ICAO)提出,在 21 世纪将使用未来导航系统(FANS)取代现行导航系统,它是以卫星技术为基础的集航空通信、导航、监视和空中交通管理为一体的导航系统,并利用全球导航卫星系统(GNSS)实现飞机航路、终端和进场导航。

The International Civil Aviation Organization (ICAO) proposes that in the 21st century, the Future Air Navigation System (FANS) will be used to replace the current navigation system. It is a navigation system based on satellite technology that integrates aeronautical communications, navigation, surveillance and air traffic management, and uses the Global Navigation Satellite System (GNSS) to realize aircraft route, terminal and approach navigation.

2.4.4 港航区块链技术应用及展望
2.4.4 Port and Shipping Block Chain Technology Application and Prospects

航运供应链上下游企业涉及港口运营商、水路、公路、铁路等承运单位，与场站、船舶代理、货运代理、报关行及进出口企业多类关系方密切相关，物流链流程长且节点多、中间成本高且信息不透明，运转依靠大量单证，单证存储管理分散、流通过程中修改困难、沟通时效性低。总体而言，关系方繁杂、货物相关单证不唯一，导致不同运输方式业务衔接和信息共享困难，尤其是多式联运一单制难以实施，出错后排错困难，不仅增加了运输成本，也降低了货物的转运效率。

The upstream and downstream enterprises of the shipping supply chain involve port operators, waterways, roads, railways and other carriers, and are closely related to various types of parties such as stations, shipping agencies, freight forwarders, customs brokers, and import and export enterprises. The logistics chain has a long process and many nodes, the intermediate cost is high, and the information is not transparent. The operation relies on a large number of documents, the document storage management is scattered, the modification is complex during the circulation process, and the communication timeliness is low. In general, the complexity of related parties and the non-unique cargo-related documents have led to difficulties in business connection and information sharing between different modes of transportation. In particular, it is difficult to implement the one-order system of multimodal transport and troubleshoot errors, which not only increases transportation costs, but also reduce the efficiency of cargo transhipment.

区块链技术独有的分布式账本、智能合约、实时共识和数据定制加密机制等特点为航运供应链实现产业协同、整体降本增效提供了绝佳的出路。通过区块链技术，整条物流链的信息实现保密、准确、可追溯，数据即时共享为提货单信息的安全和高效流转提供了百分之百、全方位的保障，更为供应链企业实现了整体的降本增效。

The unique features of blockchain technology, such as distributed ledgers, smart contracts, real-time consensus, and data customization encryption mechanisms, provide an excellent way for the shipping supply chain to achieve industrial synergy, reduce overall costs and increase efficiency. Through blockchain technology, the information of the entire logistics chain is kept confidential, accurate, and traceable. The real-time data sharing provides a 100% and all-round guarantee for the safe and efficient flow of bill of lading information, and has achieved overall cost reduction and efficiency enhancement for supply chain enterprises.

需要指出的是，区块链项目的设计和实施对企业的信息化建设和运营能力要求较高，而且对上下游企业甚至行业的无纸化水平和业务整合能力提出较高的要求。2019 年 11 月，上港集团(SIPG)宣布实现全面无纸化。无纸化是港航区块链的重要基础之一，而区块链技术的应用深化，也为无纸化落地和进程加速提供源源不断的助力。早在 2018 年 11 月，上港集团就立项开展全自主知识产权的港航区块链应用示范项目研究，考虑到口岸小提单格式和海运全程提单格式一致性便于全程推广,利用上港集团在上海口岸的号召力可迅速形成规范化应用的优势,上港集团决定以提单为切入口。

It needs to be pointed out that the design and implementation of blockchain projects have higher requirements for the information construction and operation capabilities of enterprises, and higher requirements for the paperless level and business integration capabilities of upstream and downstream companies and even industries. In November 2019, Shanghai International Port Cluster (SIPG) announced that it would become fully paperless. Paperless is one of the important foundations of the shipping blockchain, and the deepening of the application of blockchain technology also provides continuous assistance for the implementation and acceleration of the paperless process. As early as November 2018, SIPG initiated a study on a port and shipping blockchain application demonstration project with fully independent intellectual property rights. Taking into account the consistency of the format of the port small bill of lading (Seaway Bill) and the ocean bill of lading (Bill of Lading) format, it is easy to promote the whole process, and the use of SIPG's appeal at Shanghai port can quickly form the advantage of standardized application. SIPG decided to start with the bill of lading.

历经一年多的努力,基于区块链技术的上港区块链无纸化换单平台实现海运提单的无纸化换单[其间恰逢2019年6月全球航运服务网络(Global Shipping Business Network, GSBN)联盟邀请上港集团加入]。2019年11月,港航联盟链第一个项目“基于区块链技术的口岸电子提单平台”上线试运行,上链的关系方包括:船公司(中远海运、东方海外)及其自有船务代理、货运代理(兴亚报关、畅联国际、三通国际)、货主(特斯拉、上汽通用、3M)。目前,上链企业实现了99%的签发率,已完成近6 000票海运单、近15 000 TEU的货物运转。

After more than a year of hard work, the SIPG blockchain paperless exchange platform based on blockchain technology has realized the paperless exchange of ocean bills of lading (the period coincides with the GSBN alliance's invitation to SIPG to join in June 2019). In November 2019, the first project of the port and shipping alliance chain, “Blockchain technology-based port electronic bill of lading platform”, went online for trial operation. The parties involved in the platform include: shipping companies (COSCO Shipping, OOCL) and its own shipping agents, freight forwarding(Xingya Customs Clearance, Changlian International, Santong International), cargo owner(Tesla, SAIC-GM, 3M). At present, the companies have achieved a 99% issuance rate, and have completed nearly 6,000 sea waybills and nearly 15,000 TEU of cargo operations.

船公司、港务集团、船务代理和货运代理围绕口岸小提单(主要涉及船公司放货和港务集团放货)为特斯拉汽车零部件物流运输提供服务。如特斯拉两条航线同时到港产生单证500票,货运代理企业必须分派跑单人员前往现场窗口提交纸质单证,等待窗口换单人员的审单盖章。通常完成一票审单操作需要花费50~60 s,仅仅船务代理审单环节的500票单证就需要船务代理公司一个窗口服务员不间断工作8 h以上,货运代理公司根据自己单证制作进度需要派遣多名业务员和快递员不断往返船务代理和货运代理公司。部分口岸的港务集团升级为中心化的电子换单模式后可以实现网上换单,节省了时间和人力成本,但仍然需要船务代理逐票审单操作,每票单证还需要盖章留底,且受制于 8 h 人工上班时间限制,效率无法有效提高。区块链模式下,平台真正实现 7×24×365 的全时限一站式服务,大量的业务量将体现更大的效率反差,船务代理不需要逐票审单操作,可以进行批量操作,500 票的换单操作只要三四分钟就可完成。船公司利用区块链应用优化服务、提升客户黏性,也为提升更长链条的物流服务能级奠定了延展基础。

Shipping companies, port cluster, shipping agents and freight forwarders provide services for the logistics and transportation of Tesla auto parts around the port small bill of lading (mainly involving shipping companies and port cluster). For example, if Tesla's two routes arrive at the port simultaneously and produce 500 documents, the freight forwarding company must dispatch the order runners to the on-site window to submit the paper documents, and wait for the window replacement staff to review the documents. Usually it takes 50~60 s to complete a single ticket review operation. For 500 tickets, a shipping agency company's window attendant needs to work for more than 8 hours without interruption. The freight forwarding company needs to send multiple salesmen and couriers to and from the shipping agent and the freight forwarding company continuously according to the progress of its document production. The port cluster at some ports has upgraded to a centralized electronic order exchange mode, which can realize online order exchange, saving time and labor costs. However, it is still necessary for the ship to review the documents on a ticket-by-vote basis. Each ticket and document needs to be stamped, and subject to the 8-hour manual working time limit, and the efficiency cannot be effectively improved. In the blockchain mode, the platform truly realizes 7×24×365 full-time one-stop service, a large amount of business volume will reflect a more excellent efficiency contrast, and shipping agents do not need to review on a ticket-by-vote basis. Batch operations can be performed, and the 500 ticket exchange operation can be completed in only three or four minutes. Shipping companies use blockchain applications to optimize services and enhance customer stickiness, which also lays an extended foundation for improving the logistics service level of a longer chain.

基于上述描述,区块链技术本身并未改变传统行业的固有流程(如支付宝并没有改变支付方式,它改变的是支付的媒介),但一旦发展壮大,其派生出来的多行业叠加效应将会颠覆行业。因此,港航区块链发展将分成两个阶段,第一阶段通过区块链技术与航运物流应用场景的叠加,利用技术热点实现传统业务+互联网应用的融合发展,例如构建一个透明和可靠的公共信息服务平台,各参与方可以实时查看各自节点及相关状态,整个物流过程能够被追溯,航运供应链成本得以降低、效率得以提升。当发生纠纷时,举证和追查也变得更加清晰和容易。第二阶段,随着应用场景深度和广度的拓展,区块链应用证据链充足、信息可信且不可更改,越来越多的跨行业应用将聚合和黏附,跨行业应用场景产生的协同效应将激发更多产业发展空间。例如,通过可信业务网络的建设叠加航运金融保险业,推动传统港航业高质量发展,将供应链中的所有组织电子化链接在一起以实现整个链条的可见性。

Based on the above description, the blockchain technology has not changed the inherent process of traditional industries (for example, Alipay has not changed the payment method, it has changed the payment medium), but once it develops and grows, its derived multi-industry superimposition effect will disrupt the industry. Therefore, the development of the port and shipping blockchain will be divided into two stages. The first stage uses the superposition of blockchain technology and shipping logistics application scenarios to realize the integrated development of traditional business + internet applications by using technical hotspots. For example, to build a transparent and reliable public information service platform, each participant can view their nodes and related status in real-time, the entire logistics process can be traced, shipping supply chain costs can be reduced and efficiency improved. When disputes occur, proof and tracing become clearer and easier. In the second stage, with the expansion of the depth and breadth of application scenarios, the blockchain application evidence chain is sufficient, the information is credible and unchangeable. More and more cross-industry applications will converge and adhere, and the synergistic effects generated by cross-industry application scenarios will stimulate more industry development space. For example, by constructing a trusted business network to superimpose the shipping finance and insurance industry, promote the high-quality development of the traditional port and shipping industry, and electronically link all organizations in the supply chain to achieve the visibility of the entire chain.

因此,区块链可能是一种颠覆行业的技术,航运供应链企业可能通过技术迭代升级辅以跨行业协同实现优胜劣汰,但重要性相较于传统模式会更分散(不同于支付宝中心化的模式)。核心企业或企业联盟在区块链发展中的龙头地位进一步凸显并得以不断发展壮大,中国企业具有良好的发展前景。

Therefore, blockchain may be a technology that disrupts the industry. Shipping supply chain companies may achieve the survival of the fittest through technical iterative upgrades supplemented by cross-industry collaboration, but the importance will be more scattered than the traditional model (different from the centralized Alipay model). The leading position of core enterprises or enterprise alliances in the blockchain development has been further highlighted and continued to grow. Chinese enterprises have good development prospects.

全球主要港航企业在船舶注册登记、单证流程优化、货物追踪、航运保险等领域均开展区块链技术应用,上港集团作为创始会员也加入了全球航运服务网络(GSBN)。马士基为主导的 TradeLens 区块链网络探索与上港集团的合作,上港集团自有的港航区块链物流平台将借助上港集团在上海本埠口岸和长江黄金水道龙头地位的影响力和辐射力,将区块链、无纸化平台先进的技术和业务成果溯游而上,深入长江经济带。

Major global port and shipping companies have carried out blockchain technology applications in the areas of ship registration, document process optimization, cargo tracking, and shipping insurance. SIPG has also joined the Global Shipping Business Network (GSBN) as a founding member. The TradeLens blockchain network led by Maersk explores cooperation with SIPG. SIPG's port and shipping blockchain logistics platform will take advantage of SIPG's leading position in Shanghai's port and the Yangtze River Golden Waterway's leading position in influence and radiation. Extensive application of advanced technologies and business results of blockchain and paperless platforms to promote the joint upgrade and development of ports along the Yangtze River Economic Belt.

未来,针对上海口岸进出口贸易业务,利用区块链技术改造传统航运服务模式和电子单证体系,融合电子订舱、口岸、长江流域、国际航线服务平台,实现多式联运一单制及全程信息共享(操作信息的可追溯、物流信息的唯一性与实时同步性)。降低业务协同成本,提升业务协同效率,构建现代化航运服务业新模式,为进一步改善口岸营商环境、建设交通强国提供基础,并打造中国行业新标准,为供应链金融业务衍生提供基础。

In the future, for the import and export trade business of Shanghai port, blockchain technology will be used to transform the traditional shipping service model and electronic document system, and integrate electronic booking, port, Yangtze River basin, and international airline service platforms. Realize one-order system of multimodal transport and whole-process information sharing (traceability of operation information, uniqueness and real-time synchronization of logistics information). Reduce the cost of business collaboration, improve the efficiency of business collaboration, and build a new model of modern shipping service industry. Improve the port business environment, build a strong transportation country to provide the foundation, and create a new industry standard in China, provide a foundation for the derivation of supply chain financial services.

第3章 港口物流运作流程与管理

Chapter 3 | Port Logistics Operation Process and Management

◆ 3.1 港口物流运作与管理概述

3.1 Overview of Port Logistics Operation and Management

3.1.1 港口物流运作与流程
3.1.1 Port Logistics Operation and Process

港口物流运作是指港口物流活动的运行和操作。它不仅是港口生产活动的客观载体,而且是港口生产的主要表现形式。港口物流运作流程则是指港口物流活动运作的基本流程,例如货物按照何种作业顺序实施装卸、存储以及转运等。虽然在实践中,港口的设计、服务的货类等不尽相同,但港口物流运作的基本流程相似(如图3.1所示),其实质上可被描述为从货物的集运状态到船舶受载状态的切换过程。例如,典型的港口出口物流运作流程可被概括地描述为:转运载具(货车或汽车)卸载→堆场堆存→码头前沿运输→装船作业。基于上述流程,即可实现货物从集运(装载于货车或汽车)状态,切换至港口场(库)的堆存状态,而后通过港内运输设施或设备输送至港口码头前沿,最后通过装卸设施实现船舶受载状态。需要注意的,上述物流流程不仅是单向过程。在实践中,港口物流运作相邻流程均是双向的。例如,货物的堆存流程在进口流程中则可以视为货物载运流程的前序流程。在下文中,我们将上述转运载具(货车或汽车)卸载、堆场堆存、码头前沿运输、装船作业流程称为港口物流作业的基本流程单元。

Port logistics operation refers to the operation of port logistics activities. It is not only the objective carrier of port production activities, but also the main manifestation of port production. Port logistics operation process refers to the basic process of the operation of port logistics activities, such as the order in which cargos are loaded and unloaded, stored, and transferred, etc. Although in practice, the port's design and service categories are not the same, the basic process of port logistics operation is basically similar (as shown in Figure 3.1), which can be essentially described as the switching process from the state of consolidation of cargos to the loaded state of the ship. For example, a typical port export logistics operation process can be broadly described as: unloading of transfer vehicles (trucks or vehicles) → yard storage → quayside transportation of the port → loading. Based on the above process, the cargos can be switched from the state of consolidation (loaded in trucks or vehicles) to the storage state of the port yard (stacking area), and then transported to the quayside of the port through the transportation facilities or equipment in the port, and finally to the loaded state by the loading and unloading facilities. It should be noted that the above-mentioned logistics process is not only a one-way process. In practice, the adjacent processes of port logistics operations are bidirectional. For example, the storage process of cargos can be regarded as the predecessor process of the cargos loading process in the import process. In the following, we will refer to the processes of unloading of the above-mentioned transfer vehicles (trucks or vehicles), yard storage, quayside transportation of the terminal, and loading as the basic process unit of port logistics operation.

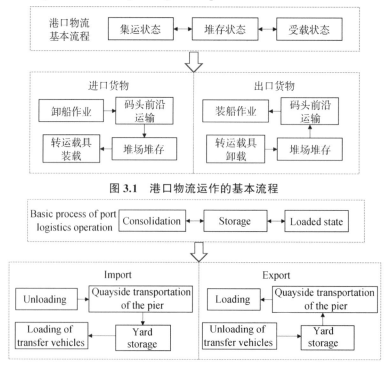

图 3.1　港口物流运作的基本流程

Figure 3.1　Basic process of port logistics operation

　　港口物流运作流程设计与监督控制是港口生产系统设计与日常运营的核心工作。一方面,管理者通过合理的港口物流运作流程设计,实现港口生产系统、港口自然水文条件、港口生产设施以及港口服务对象的优化整合。另一方面,管理者在日常工作中还需要监督和干预港口物流运作,以确保港口生产过程保持在一个理想的状态。这个监督控制行为便是港口物流运作管理。

The design and surveillance of port logistics operation process is the core work of port production system design and daily operation. On the one hand, managers can realize the optimization and integration of port production systems, port natural hydrological conditions, port production facilities, and port service objects through reasonable design of port logistics operation process. On the other hand, managers also need to surveil and intervene in port logistics operation in their daily work to ensure that the port production process remains in an ideal state. This act of surveillance and control is the port logistics operation management.

3.1.2　港口物流运作管理概述与要求
3.1.2　Overview and Requirements of Port Logistics Operation Management

我们将港口物流运作管理定义为对港口物流运作流程的监督与管控。在实践中,港口管理者需要依托一系列生产计划与生产监控控制方法来实现有效的监督与管控。这些计划和方法针对不同类别的港口虽然存在一定的差异,但大致可分为以下几类:

We define port logistics operation management as the surveillance and control of port logistics operation process. In practice, port managers need to rely on a series of production plans and production monitoring methods to achieve effective surveillance and control. Although these plans and methods have certain differences for different types of ports, they can be roughly divided into the following categories:

①针对生产准备过程的计划,简称生产准备计划,例如船舶靠泊计划、船舶装卸计划、堆场使用计划等;

①Plans for the production preparation process, referred to as production preparation plans, such as ship berthing plans, ship loading and unloading plans, stacking area use plan, etc.;

②针对生产过程的注意事项与管理准则,简称基本生产过程规范与守则,例如货物装卸时的设备操作规范、安全守则、日常作业原则等;

②Precautions and management guidelines for the production process, referred to as basic production process specifications and guidelines, such as equipment operation specifications during cargo handling, safety regulations, daily operation principles, etc.;

③为生产过程提供服务的生产服务活动安排,如装卸设备的整备与检查、港口生产过程中相关部门的协调、信息系统的维护和相关数据的获取、存储与使用等;

③Arrangements of production service activities that provide services for the production process, such as the preparation and inspection of loading and unloading equipment, trade-off of relevant departments in the port production process, the maintenance of information systems and the acquisition, storage and use of related data, etc.;

④辅助生产活动规则,如突发事件处理方案、应急处置机制、安全检查规程、物资的准备与补充方案等。

④Rules of auxiliary production activities, such as emergency handling plans, emergency response mechanism, safety inspection procedures, material preparation and supplementary plans, etc.

上述计划、规则以及安排的设计与执行便是港口物流运作日常管理的核心工作,而不同的港口管理者对于这些准则的设计与执行力度的差异,也是导致港口服务能力差异的主要因素。

The design and implementation of the above-mentioned plans, rules and arrangements are the core tasks of the daily management of port logistics operations, and the differences in the design and implementation of these guidelines by different port managers are also the main factors leading to differences in port service capabilities.

综合而言,港口物流运作管理必须遵循以下原则:

In summary, port logistics operation management must comply with the following principles:

(1) 连续性
(1) Continuity

连续性是指在时间与空间层面上,港口物流生产过程的各环节、各工序、各阶段之间的紧密衔接。主要体现在:①各环节、各工序、各阶段之间不中断;②货物作业的连续性,即减少货物的在港时间;③港口具有后备能力,允许有一定的作业中断时间。

Continuity refers to the close connection between the various links, processes, and stages of the port logistics production process at the time and space level. It is mainly reflected in: ①No interruption between the various links, processes, and stages; ②Continuity of cargo operations, that is, reducing the time of the cargo in the port; ③The port has a backup capability that allows for a certain amount of downtime.

(2) 协调性
(2) Trade-off

协调性是指港口物流生产过程的各主要环节之间、作业线上各作业工序之间,保持恰当比例的生产能力(如人力、物力、设备等)。

Trade-off refers to maintaining an appropriate proportion of production capacity (such as manpower, material resources, equipment, etc.) among the main links of the port logistics production process and among the various operating procedures on the operation line.

(3) 均衡性
(3) Balance

均衡性是指在时间与空间层面上,资源和任务配置的均衡。具体表现在:①在时间层面上,相同间隔时间内布置的任务量均衡,即各个阶段、各个作业工序所完成的任务量大体相同;②在空间层面上,各个部门的布局均衡。

Balance refers to the balance of resource and task disposition at the time and space levels. Specifically: ①At the time level, the amount of tasks disposition in the same interval is balanced, that is, the amount of tasks completed in each stage and each work procedure is roughly the same; ②At the space level, the layout of each department is balanced.

（4）经济性
（4）Economy

经济性是指在组织港口物流生产过程中,要兼顾生产效率和经济效益。

Economy means that in the process of organizing port logistics production, both production efficiency and economic benefits must be taken into consideration.

由于各类码头的生产运作特征存在差异,因此各类码头的生产运作系统关注的重点也存在不同。在本章的后续部分,将从港口的布局运营状态等基础理论、港口的生产运作流程以及港口的生产所涉及的相关计划等方面,重点介绍集装箱港口、件杂货港口、干散货港口、石油天然气港口、汽车货港口与冷冻货港口的物流运作与管理知识。

Due to the differences in the production and operation characteristics of various terminals, the focus of the production and operation systems of various terminals is also different. In the subsequent part of this chapter, we will focus on introducing the logistics operation and management knowledge of container port, general cargo port, dry bulk port, oil and gas cargo port, automobile cargo port, and frozen cargo port, in terms of the basic theory of port layout and operation, the production and operation process of port and related plans involved in port production.

◆ 3.2 集装箱港口的物流运作流程与管理
3.2 Logistics Operation Process and Management of Container Ports

3.2.1 集装箱港口概述
3.2.1 Overview of Container Ports

（1）集装箱港口简介
（1）Introduction to Container Ports

港口的物流活动是紧密依托于港口功能、设施设备与生产作业工艺而产生的。因此在介绍集装箱港口的物流活动前,我们首先对集装箱港口的一些基本情况进行介绍。集装箱港口是指包括港池、锚地、进港航道、泊位等水域,以及货运站、堆场、码头前沿、办公、生活区域等陆域范围,能够容纳完整的集装箱装卸作业流程的、具有明确界限的场所。在现代多式联运系统中,集装箱港口是重要的运输与转运节点,也是集装箱类货物在不同运输方式间转运的重要场所。在整个集装箱运输过程中,集装箱港口对加速车辆、船舶和集装箱的周转,提高运输效率和效益,降低整体运输成本都有着十分重要的作用。总之,集装箱港口的功能可以概括为:

Port logistics activities are closely dependent on port functions, facilities and equipment and production processes. Therefore, before introducing the logistics activities of the container port, we first introduce some basic conditions of the container port. A container port refers to a place with strip boundaries including water areas such as harbor basins, anchorages, approach channels, and berths, as well as land areas such as freight stations, yards, quayside of the terminals, office and living areas, etc., which can accommodate a complete container loading and unloading operation process. In modern multimodal transport systems, container ports are important transportation and transhipment nodes, and are also important places for containerized cargo to switch between different transportation modes. In the entire container transportation process, it plays a very important role in accelerating the turnover of vehicles, ships and containers, improving transportation efficiency and benefits, and reducing overall transportation costs. In summary, the functions of a container port can be summarized as:

①货物集散

①Cargo Collection and Distribution

货物集散负责运用各种集疏运工具,来进行集装箱货物出口前的集港业务和进口后的疏港业务,完成港口与货主之间的货物和单证的交接。

Cargo collection and distribution are responsible for the use of various collection and distribution tools to carry out the port collection business before the export of container cargos and the port distribution business after the import, and to complete the handover of cargos and documents between the port and the cargo owner.

②货物堆存

②Cargo Storage

货物堆存是指由堆场负责对进出口的重、空箱进行的堆存保管,以及对中转箱的临时堆存。港内货运站负责拼箱货物的拆、装箱作业。

Cargo storage refers to the storage of heavy and empty containers at the import and export by the yard as well as the temporary storage of transit containers. The freight station in the port is responsible for the unpacking and packing operations of the Less Than Container Load(LCL) cargo.

③装卸搬运

③Loading and Unloading

装卸搬运负责船舶进口靠泊后的集装箱卸载作业,船舶出口离泊前的集装箱装船作业,以及船舶在港内各作业场所之间的水平运输。

Loading and unloading are responsible for the unloading of containers after the import of the ship berths, the loading of the containers before the export of the ship leaves the berth, as well as the horizontal transportation of the ships between the various working places in the port.

④其他服务

④Other Services

其他服务包括船舶靠泊与离泊、集装箱通关、集装箱检验、信息接收处理与传递和其他与集装箱运输和装卸有关的辅助作业。

Other services include ship's berthing and unberthing, container customs clearance, container inspection, information receiving, processing and transmission, and other auxiliary operations related to container transportation and loading and unloading.

经过半个世纪的建设和发展,集装箱港口在全球的分布已经相当广泛,港口的建设逐步显现出如下特征:

After half a century of construction and development, the distribution of container ports in the world has been quite extensive, and the construction of ports has gradually shown the following characteristics:

第一,码头大型化和深水化。随着全球海运贸易量的增加,集装箱运输作为海运的主要运输方式之一发展迅速。21世纪以来,集装箱运输需求快速增长,使得集装箱船舶逐渐向大型化发展。在全球市场的船舶订单中,超巴拿马型船舶所占的比例不断扩大。目前,最大集装箱船舶的载箱量已经超过24 000 TEU。为适应船舶大型化的趋势,集装箱港口开始加快建设专业化深水码头,延长岸线泊位长度,增加码头前沿水深,并扩大整个港口区域,以此来满足需求。

First, large-scale and deep-water terminals. With the increase of global seaborne trade volume, container transportation has developed rapidly as one of the main shipping methods. Since the 21st century, the demand for container transportation has grown rapidly, causing container ships to gradually develop into larger scales. Among ship orders in the global market, the proportion of super-Panamax ships has continued to expand. At present, the carrying capacity of the largest container ship has exceeded 24,000 TEU. In order to adapt to the trend of ship upsizing, container ports began to accelerate the construction of specialized deep-water terminals, extend the length of shoreline berths, increase the water depth at the quayside of the terminals, and expand the entire port area to meet the demand.

第二,搬运机械化和高效化。集装箱货运需求量的不断增加和集装箱船舶逐渐大型化,一方面会使船舶在港作业时间增加,另一方面也会导致船舶的单位停泊和作业成本提高。因此,为了提高船舶航行效率,降低水路运输成本,发挥船舶单位运输成本低的优势,现代集装箱港口不断提高装卸运输设备的性能和适用性,为船舶在港作业配备了专业化、自动化的装卸搬运机械和设备,如自动化双小车岸边集装箱起重机、自动导引车等。自动化的机械设备将具备船舶扫描、自动防摇防扭和设备精准定位等性能,使各作业环节快速衔接,作业故障和失误率有效降低,从而提高港口作业效率。

Second, handling mechanization and high efficiency. Due to the continuous increase in the demand for container freight and the gradual upsizing of container ships, on the one hand, the operation time of ships in the port will increase, and on the other hand, the unit berthing and operating costs of ships will increase. Therefore, in order to improve ship navigation efficiency, reduce waterway transportation costs, and give full play to the advantages of the low unit transportation cost of ships, modern container ports continue to improve the performance and applicability of loading and unloading and transportation equipment, and equip ships with professional and automated loading and unloading machinery and equipment in port operations. Machinery and equipment, such as automated dual trolley quay (ship to shore) container cranes (STS), automated guided vehicles (AGV), etc. Automated mechanical equipment will have the performance such as ship scanning, automatic anti-sway and anti-twist, and precise positioning of the equipment, so that each operation link can be quickly connected, and the operation failure and error rate can be effectively reduced, and improving of efficiency port operation.

第三，管理信息化和智能化。在"互联网+"时代，信息化、智能化技术的应用对港口管理具有重要影响。集装箱货物本身具有批量大、信息量大的特点，集装箱船舶在港作业也需要众多部门之间的协调和调度，如港口内部、外部客户和有关部门之间的联系，港口内部的现场作业和生产指挥中心的联系等。因此，港口必须借助现代科学技术来增加信息传递的便利性和快捷性，实现各部门之间的互联互通，从而提高港口管理的信息化和现代化水平。随着现代科学技术的进步，无线射频技术、大数据、北斗导航定位等智能技术已经在港口管理的过程中得到了应用和推广，以保证信息在港口作业过程中的有效传递，增强港口物流各环节的协调与配合。

Third, informatization and intelligence of management. In the "Internet +" era, the application of informatization and intelligent technology has an important impact on port management. Container cargo itself has the characteristics of large batch and large amount of information, and the operation of container ships in the port also requires trade-off and dispatch between many departments such as the connection between the internal and external customers and relevant departments of the port, the connection between the field operation and the production command center within the port, etc. Therefore, the port must rely on modern science and technology to increase the convenience and speed of information transmission, realize the interconnection between various departments, so as to improve the informatization and modernization of port management. With the advancement of modern science and technology, intelligent technologies such as radio frequency technology, big data, Beidou navigation and positioning have been applied and promoted in the process of port management to ensure the effective transmission of information in the process of port operations and enhance trade-off and cooperation of all aspects of port logistics.

第四，港口发展绿色化。当今社会提倡发展绿色经济和循环经济，港口作为经济发展的重要推动力，同时也是主要耗能单位和污染源头，应当积极发展绿色化港口，推进建设"绿色港口"。绿色港口是指以绿色观念为指导，具备低能耗、低污染、生态保护、资源合理利用等特征的港口。目前，围绕着港口的低碳绿色化，已经有很多成熟的技术（例如，船舶在港节电技术，装卸设施的电气化改造等）被开发出来，并得到了广泛应用，以实现港口生态环境和经济利益之间的平衡发展。相信随着未来人们对运输系统的绿色环保要求的不断提升，集装箱港口将在更多方面围绕环境友好的目标推进技术革新与升级。

Fourth, the development of green ports. Today's society advocates the development of green economy and circular economy. As an important driving force of economic development, ports are also a major energy-consuming unit and pollution source. They should actively develop green port and promote the construction of "green ports". The so-called green port is a port with the characteristics of low energy consumption, low pollution, ecological protection, and rational use of resources, guided by the concept of green. At present, around the low-carbon green port, a lot of mature technologies such as the power-saving technology of ships in the port, the electrification improvement of loading and unloading facilities, etc., and have been developed and widely used to achieve a balanced development between the ecological environment and economic interests of the port. It is believed that with the continuous improvement of people's environmental protection requirements for the transportation system in the future, container ports will promote technological innovation and upgrades in more ways around the goal of environmental friendliness.

（2）集装箱港口的基本布局
（2）Basic Layout of Container Ports

集装箱港口的基础设施与布局是港口物流活动的主要实施区域。常见的集装箱港口作业区域主要由泊位、码头前沿、堆场、货运站和闸口等区域构成，根据不同区域的作业任务，配备有岸边起重机、水平运输机械、堆场起重机等装卸和运输设备。如图 3.2 所示，常规布局方案由海侧区域向陆侧区域依次是：

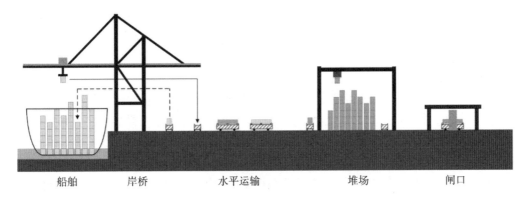

| 船舶 | 岸桥 | 水平运输 | 堆场 | 闸口 |

图 3.2　集装箱港口侧视图

The infrastructure and layout of container port are the main implementation areas of port logistics activities. Common container port operation areas are mainly composed of berths, quayside of the terminals, yards, freight stations and gates. According to the operational tasks in different areas, they are equipped with loading and unloading and transportation equipment such as quay crane, horizontal transportation machinery, and yard cranes. As shown in Figure 3.2, from the seaside area to the landside area, the general layout plan is as follows:

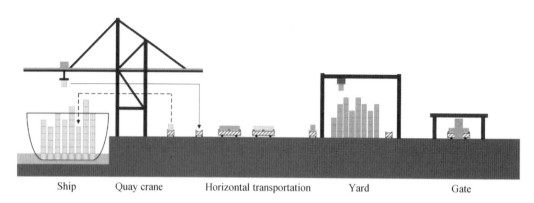

Figure 3.2　Side view of container port

①码头前沿

①Quayside of the Terminals

码头前沿包括泊位和岸桥。泊位是专供集装箱船停靠的位置,长度根据所停靠船舶的主要技术参数及有关安全规定而定。对于集装箱专用码头,一般要求宽度在 300 m 以上。岸边设有集装箱起重机及运行轨道,宽度可根据岸边起重机的跨距和使用的其他装卸机械种类而定,一般为 40 m 左右。

The quayside of the terminal includes berths and quay cranes. The berth is a location exclusively for container ships, and the length is determined according to the main technical parameters of the berthed ship and relevant safety regulations. For special container terminals, the width is generally required to be more than 300 m. There are container cranes and running tracks at the quayside, and the width can be determined according to the span of the quay crane and other types of loading and unloading machinery used, generally about 40 m.

②集装箱堆场

②Container Yard（CY）

集装箱堆场分为前方堆场和后方堆场。前方堆场也称为集装箱编排场,是集装箱的临时堆存地,主要用于将准备装船的集装箱排列待装以及为即将卸船的集装箱准备好堆放位置,从而保证船舶装卸作业可以快速而不间断地进行。后方堆场是指对重箱或空箱进行堆存、保管以及与货主进行交接的场所。堆场面积取决于港口集装箱吞吐量的大小,应根据船舶载运能力及到港的船舶密度、装卸工艺系统、集装箱在堆场上的排列形式等因素综合分析确定。

The container yard（CY）is divided into the front yard and the rear yard. The front yard is also called the container arranging yard, which is a temporary storage place for containers. It is mainly used to arrange the containers to be loaded on the ship and prepare the stacking position for the containers to be unloaded, so as to ensure that the ship's loading and unloading operations can be carried out quickly and continuously. The rear yard refers to the place where heavy or empty containers are stacked, kept, and handed over to the owner. The area of the yard depends on the size of the port's container throughput, and should be determined by comprehensive analysis of factors such as the carrying capacity of the ship, the density of the ships arriving at the port, the loading and unloading process system, and the arrangement of the containers on the yard.

③集装箱货运站(拆、装箱库)

③Container Freight Station (Unpacking and Packing Warehouse)

部分集装箱港口内部设有集装箱货运站(拆、装箱库),一般设置在大门与堆场之间,主要承担出口货物的拼箱作业和进口货物的拆箱作业。在靠近港口大门处,还设有控制塔和维修车间,分别用于指挥、监督集装箱码头的装卸和搬运作业,以及对港口所有机械设备进行维修和保养等工作。

Some container ports are equipped with container freight stations (unpacking and packing warehouse), which are generally set up between the gate and the yard, and are mainly responsible for the packing operation of exported cargos and the unpacking operation of imported cargos. Near the port gate, there are also control towers and maintenance workshops, which are used to direct and surveil the loading, unloading and handling operations of the container terminal, as well as the repair and maintenance of all mechanical equipment in the port.

(3)集装箱港口一般物流活动简介
(3)Introduction to General Logistics Activities of Container Ports

集装箱港口物流活动是指对集装箱的装卸、搬运和堆存作业,是集装箱港口操作部所制订计划的具体实施过程,是在计划指导性文件的指导下,通过有效调动机械和人力,来组织和实施港口的现场作业任务。集装箱港口的物流活动具体包括:

Container port logistics activities refer to the loading and unloading, handling and storage of containers. It is the specific implementation process of the plan formulated by the container port operation department. The purpose of it is to organize and implement the port's field operation tasks through the effective mobilization of machinery and manpower under the guidance of the planning guidance document. The logistics activities of container ports specifically include as follows:

①闸口作业:包括重、空集装箱,集卡进出港。

①Gate operations:including heavy and empty containers, trucks in and out of the port.

②堆场作业:包括交箱、收箱;冷藏箱处理;查验场工作。

②Yard operations:including delivery and collection;reefer container handling;inspection fieldwork.

③货运站作业:包括收货、交货;拼、拆箱、冷藏箱预制冷作业。

③Freight station operations:including receiving and delivery;packing, unpacking, and pre-cooling of refrigerated containers.

④码头前沿作业:包括装船、卸船。

④Quayside of the Port Operations:including loading and unloading.

⑤泊位作业:包括离泊、靠泊。

⑤Berth operations:including departure and berthing.

每一项物流活动的效率都会影响集装箱在港口内流转的速度和船舶在港时间,也会影响港口系统的整体作业效率。影响物流活动效率的因素包括各个物流环节的作业过程,对作业计划的合理安排,作业机械的合理调度,以及作业过程中的协调和控制。因此,集装箱港口需要制订高效且合理的作业和调度计划,来实现港口整体效率和效益的最大化。

The efficiency of each logistics activity will affect the speed of container circulation in the port and the time of the ship in the port, and the overall operating efficiency of the port system. The factors that affect the efficiency of logistics activities include the operation process of each logistics link, and the key lies in the proper arrangement of the operation plan, the reasonable scheduling of the operating machinery, as well as the trade-off and control of the operation process. Therefore, the container port needs to formulate efficient and reasonable operation, and scheduling plans to maximize the overall efficiency and benefit of the port.

3.2.2　集装箱港口物流运作与流程
3.2.2　Logistics Operation and Process of Container Ports

港口的经营模式与业务流程设计决定了港口物流活动的运行规则与效率。为了使船舶在集装箱港口尽快完成装卸货工作,防止装卸船计划发生差错,避免因集装箱在港口滞留时间过长而造成港口生产的混乱和延迟交货,集装箱港口需要对整个业务流程进行合理规划,并同其他部门保持密切联系,做好交接工作。集装箱港口的业务流程主要可分为进口和出口业务(如图 3.3 和图 3.4 所示)。

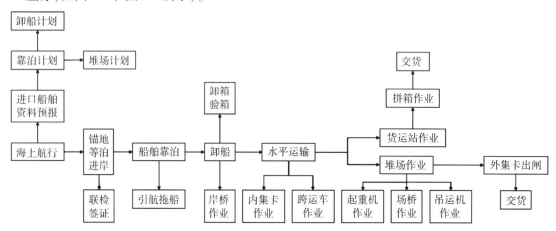

图 3.3　集装箱港口进口业务流程

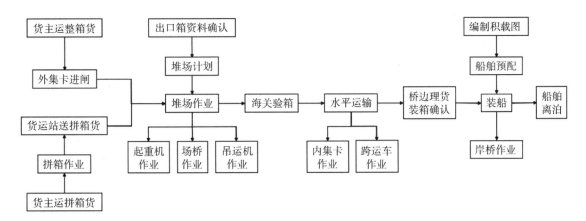

图 3.4 集装箱港口出口业务流程

The port's business model and business process design determine the operating rules and efficiency of port logistics activities. To enable ships to complete the loading and unloading work at the container port as soon as possible, prevent errors in the loading and unloading plan, and avoid the confusion of port production and delayed delivery due to a long detention time of the containers in the port, the container port needs to plan the entire business process reasonably, and keep close contact with other departments to do an excellent job of handover. The business process of container port can be mainly divided into import and export business (as shown in Figure 3.3 and Figure 3.4).

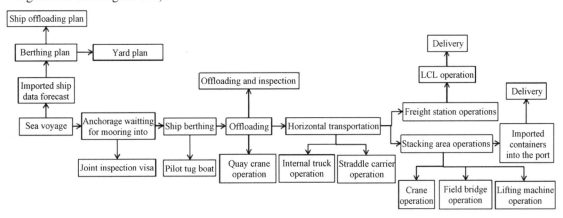

Figure 3.3 Import business process of container ports

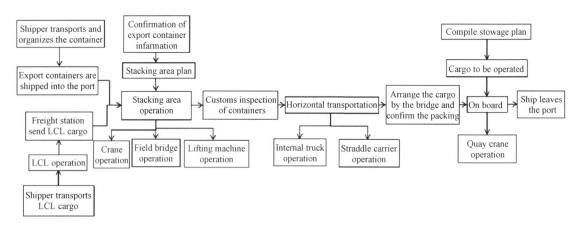

Figure 3.4　Export business process of container ports

进口业务流程:进口船舶在抵达港口前,船公司(或其代理)会将相关单证及船舶信息送交码头业务部门,码头堆场据此安排卸货准备,制订出集装箱靠泊计划、卸船计划、堆场计划和交货计划,并递交至码头计划部门。接着,船舶进入锚地等待进岸,并办理联检和签证手续。检验合格后,引航部门依据靠泊计划安排拖船以协助船舶靠泊。随后,中控部门根据卸船计划和堆场计划调度装卸队进行装卸和水平搬运作业,将集装箱分别运至堆场和港内货运站进行堆存以及拆箱作业。最后,由港外运输机械将进口货物运出港口,向货主交货。

Import business process:Before the imported ship arrives at the port,the shipping lines (or its agent) will send the relevant documents and ship information to the terminal business department,and the terminal yard will arrange unloading preparations accordingly,and formulate a container berthing plan,unloading plan,and yard plan and delivery plan,and submit them to the terminal planning department. Then,the ship enters the anchorage to wait for landing and to go through the joint inspection and visa procedures. After passing the inspection,the pilotage department arranges tug boats to assist the ship in berthing according to the berthing plan. Then,the central control department dispatched the loading and unloading team to carry out loading and unloading and horizontal transportation according to the ship unloading plan and the yard plan, and transported the containers to the yard and the freight station in the port for storage and unpacking operations. Finally,the transport machinery outside the port will transport the imported cargo out of the port for delivery to the owner.

出口业务流程:首先,申报出口集装箱信息,然后进行集港作业,由货主或港外货运站将出口货物装箱后运至港口。根据出口集装箱在闸口登记的信息,码头堆场制订堆场计划,并安排堆场起重机将集装箱堆垛至堆场,同时码头业务部门制订装船计划并编制积载图。随后,海关部门对出口集装箱进行查验并办理通关手续。船舶进港后,中控部门派出运输机械将出口集装箱运至前方堆场或码头前沿等待装船,同时安排理货部门对集装箱进行理货,安排岸边装卸机械对集装箱进行装船,装船完毕后船舶离港。

Export business process:The information of exported containers is declared at first,and then the exported containers are prepared for port collection operations,and the cargo owners or freight stations outside the port will load the exported cargo into the containers and transport them to the port. According to the registered information of the exported container at the gate, the terminal yard formulates a yard plan, and arranges yard cranes to stack the containers to the terminal yard. At the same time, the terminal business department formulates a shipping plan and prepares a stowage plan. Subsequently, the customs department inspected the exported containers and went through customs clearance procedures. After the ship enters the port, the central control department dispatches the transport machinery to transport the exported containers to the front yard or the quayside of the terminal for loading, arranges the tally department to tally the containers, and arranges the shore loading and unloading machinery to load the containers, and the ship leaves the port after the loading is completed.

综合分析上述进出口流程虽然组织复杂,涉及诸多环节和部门,但其本质上可由五个基本业务活动组成,分别为:计划制订、生产调度、作业控制、箱务管理和单证流转,业务活动的各部分内涵如下:

Comprehensive analysis of the above import and export process, although the organization is complex and many links and departments are designed, it can be essentially composed of five basic business activities: plan formulation, production scheduling, operation control, container management and document circulation. The connotations of each part of the business activities are introduced as follows:

(1)计划制订

(1)Plan Formulation

船舶在抵达港口前,船公司或其代理会将下述单证送交码头业务部门:货物舱单、集装箱号码单、积载图、集装箱装箱单、装船货物残损报告和特殊货物表。码头堆场根据这些单证安排卸货准备,制订靠离泊计划、装卸计划、堆场计划和交货计划。

Before the ship arrives at the port, the shipping line or its agent will send the following documents to the pier business department: cargo manifest, container number list, stowage plan, container packing list, ship cargo damage report and special cargo list. The pier yard arranges unloading preparation based on these documents, and formulates berthing/unberthing plans, loading and unloading plans, yard plans and delivery plans.

①靠离泊计划

①Berthing/Unberthing Plans

在船舶预计到港之前,港口工作人员根据船舶预报信息以及计划时间内所有即将到港船舶的信息,为每艘船安排靠泊位置和靠泊时间,制订合理的靠泊计划。在出口货物进港后,根据出口货物信息和船舶卸船信息,工作人员会为船舶规划离港时间,制订离港计划。靠离泊计划可以保持港口航道通畅,使船舶顺利进出港口,尽量减少船舶在港停留时间。

Before the ship is expected to arrive at the port, the port staff will arrange the berthing location and berthing time for each ship based on the ship's forecast information and the information of all the upcoming ships in the planned period, and formulate a reasonable berthing plan. After the export cargoes enters the port, based on the exported cargo information and ship unloading information, the staff will plan the departure time for the ship and make a departure plan. The berthing and unberthing plan can keep the port-channel unobstructed, enable ships to enter and exit the port smoothly, and minimize the time ships stay in the port.

②装卸计划

②Loading and Unloading Plans

为了缩短船舶在港时间,装船与卸船往往需要同时进行。装船和卸船计划对集装箱的装载、卸载顺序,以及在码头前沿的堆存位置进行了合理安排,并配备了充足的装卸机械,目的是保证在最短的时间内使大量的集装箱能顺利地装上或卸下。

To shorten the ship's time in port, loading and unloading often need to be carried out at the same time. The loading and unloading plans make reasonable arrangements for the loading and unloading sequence of containers, and the storage location at the quayside of the pier, and equip with a sufficient number of loading and unloading machinery to ensure that a large number of containers can be loaded or unloaded smoothly in the shortest time.

③堆场计划

③Yard Plan

堆场计划是为进出口集装箱分配装卸搬运机械以及规划合理的堆场堆存位置的计划。它包括卸船场地计划、集港场地计划、场地及场地机械计划。集装箱在港口堆场内能否合理安置,不仅会影响所在船舶的卸船计划和交货计划的执行,还会影响其他船舶在港作业计划的制订和实施。因此,码头堆场应充分考虑卸船的集装箱数量、种类,以及向内地运输和交给收货人的数量,这样才能使集装箱有条不紊地按照相应的计划被卸至堆场,并交给内陆运输的承运人或收货人。

The yard plan is a plan for allocating loading, unloading and handling machinery for import and export containers and formulating a proper yard storage location. It includes ship unloading site plan, collection port site plan, site and site machinery plan. Whether the containers can be reasonably placed in the port yard will not only affect the implementation of unloading plan and delivery plan of the ship, but also affect the formulation and implementation of other ships' operation plans in the port. Therefore, the pier yard shall fully consider the number and types of containers unloaded, and the quantity to be transported to the inland and delivered to the consignee, so that the containers can be unloaded to the yard in an orderly manner according to the corresponding plan, and delivered to the inland transportation carrier or consignee.

④交货计划

④Delivery Plan

交货计划是为了使船上卸下的集装箱不积压在堆场内,并向最终目的地继续运输或直接交给收货人所制订的计划。

The delivery plan is to ensure that the containers unloaded from the ship are not accumulated in the yard, and are continued to be transported to the final destination or delivered directly to the consignee.

船舶到港前,码头业务员接收船公司的资料,并在船舶到港后向船方了解有关箱、货位的实载情况。如果实载情况与原始资料有出入,码头业务员应迅速修改资料信息,并通报给值班主任以及时调整卸船计划和相应的堆场计划。

Before the ship arrives at the port, the pier clerk receives the information from the shipping lines, and learns about the actual loading information of the space of the container and cargo from the ship after the ship arrives at the port. If the actual loading information is different from the original information, the pier clerk should quickly modify the information, and notify the duty supervisor to adjust the unloading plan and the corresponding yard plan in time.

(2)生产调度
(2) Production Scheduling

船舶在港作业的过程中,港口生产调度指挥中心需要根据作业计划,为集装箱的装卸、水平搬运、堆存和集疏港以及船舶的靠离泊等现场作业调配机械及操作人员。生产调度工作要求具有预见性、计划性、集中性和及时性,以保证船舶在港口快速、有序地完成作业。

During the ship's operation in the port, the port production dispatching command center needs to allocate machinery and operators for on-site operations such as container loading and unloading, horizontal handling, storage, collection and distribution, and berthing and unberthing of the ship, according to the operation plan. The production scheduling work requires foresight, planning, concentration and timeliness to ensure that ship's operations can be completed in the port quickly and in an orderly manner.

船舶抵港前,港口生产调度指挥中心要根据船舶预报的船期和泊位空闲情况,对抵港船舶的靠泊时间和靠泊位置进行统一安排,以减少船舶在港时间。靠泊过程中,引航部门需要安排引航员登上船舶,为船舶指引航向,将船舶安全地引进港口并停至泊位。船舶靠泊后,调度指挥中心需要根据预先制订的卸船计划调度岸边装卸机械,将集装箱从船上卸下。这时,岸桥调度应当在满足岸桥之间不可相互跨越并间隔一定安全距离的前提下,进行合理的任务分配和时间分配。而后,调度指挥中心安排最佳数量的水平运输机械,将集装箱搬运至堆场并为其规划最优路径。此时,调度指挥中心一方面要保证最大化运输机械利用率,另一方面要避免运输道路堵塞,降低装卸机械的等待时间。最后,堆场按照堆存计划安排堆场起重机械将集装箱堆垛到合适的箱区和箱位,这不仅需要根据集装箱箱型、装卸工艺和装载货种来合理安排堆存位置,最大化堆场利用率,还要减少翻箱,保证集装箱的堆放安全。在上述作业过程中,调度部门需要确保作业过程的经济性、协调性、均衡性和连续性,在同时考虑生产效率和经济效益的前提下,保证生产各环节、各作业工序之间人员和设备的配备恰当,并且在时间和空间上确保下达和完成的作业任务均衡,使各环节的作业能够协调、连续进行。

Before the ship arrives in the port, the port production dispatching command center shall make suitable arrangements for the berthing time and berthing location for each arriving ship according to the forecasted schedule and berth availability of the ship, to reduce the time of the ship in the port. During the birthing process, the piloting department needs to arrange the pilot to board the ship, guide its course, and introduce the ship to the port safely and park it at the berth.

After the ship is berthed, the port dispatching center needs to dispatch the shore loading and unloading machinery according to the pre-made ship unloading plan to unload the containers. At this time, the quay crane dispatching should carry out reasonable task disposition and time disposition under the premise that the quay cranes cannot cross each other and are separated by a certain safe distance. Then, the port dispatching center arranges the optimal number of horizontal transportation machinery to move the containers to the yard and plans the optimal path for them. At this time, on the one hand, the port dispatching center must ensure the maximum utilization of transportation machinery. On the other hand, it must also avoid blockage of transportation roads and reduce the waiting time of loading and unloading machinery. Finally, the yard arranges the yard crane to stack the containers to the appropriate area and location according to the storage plan. It is necessary to arrange the storage location reasonably according to the container type, loading and unloading process and loading type, and maximize the stacking. It is also necessary to reduce the rate of container turnover to ensure the safety of container stacking. In the above-mentioned operation process, the dispatching department needs to ensure the economy, trade-off, balance and continuity of the operation process. Under the premise of considering production efficiency and economic benefits simultaneously, ensure that the personnel and equipment are equipped properly in each link of production and between each operation process, and ensure the assignment and completion of the tasks are balanced in time and space, so that the operations of each link can be coordinated and carried out continuously.

（3）作业控制
（3）Operation Control

船舶的在港作业情况会对港口的整体作业效率产生重要影响,需要对作业过程进行精准、快速的实时控制。实时控制的实现依赖于码头的软、硬件支持。软件包括现场实时人员与机械的灵活调配,以及高效的数据处理等。硬件包括码头泊位、堆场、闸口摄像装置,岸桥、场桥、叉车、内拖车载处理系统以及完备的通信手段。通过对港口生产作业情况和进度的实时监控,作业中的不平衡现象和突发状况便可被及时发现并处理,从而使港口物流活动顺利完成。

The operation of ships in the port will have a significant impact on the overall operational efficiency of the port, and the operation process needs to be accurately and quickly controlled in real-time. The realization of real-time control depends on the software and hardware support of the pier. The software includes on-site real-time personnel, and flexible deployment of machinery, and efficient data processing. The hardware includes dock berth, yard, gate camera device, quay crane, yard crane, forklift truck, internal trailer handling system, and complete communication means. Through the real-time monitoring of the operation and progress of the port production, the imbalances and emergencies in the operation can be found and dealt with in time, so that the port logistics activities can be completed smoothly.

此外,随着 5G 技术的完善和普及,越来越多的港口开始借助高带宽、低时延的 5G 网络来进行生产作业控制。在集装箱装卸搬运作业中,依托5G网络提供的远程控制通信服务,集装箱装卸桥、集卡等装卸运输机械的自控系统状态信号、视频监控图像信号等信息,以及运行状态参数都可以迅速、实时地被传送到中控室,由生产调度人员在中控台远程判定操作,并下发控制指令。同时,还可以通过监控港区内集装箱的上下船数据、堆存数据、进出港数据等,实现对集装箱在港作业的全流程控制。

In addition, with the improvement and popularization of 5G technology, more and more ports are beginning to use high-bandwidth, low-latency 5G networks to control production operations. In container loading, unloading and handling operations, relying on the remote control communication services provided by the 5G network, the automatic control system status signals of the loading and unloading transportation machinery such as container loading and unloading cranes, trucks, etc., video monitoring image signals and operating status parameters can be transmitted to the central control room quickly and in real-time, and the production dispatcher will remotely determine the operation on the central control station and issue control instructions. At the same time, the total process control of container operations in the port can also be achieved by monitoring the disembarkation data, storage data, and port entry and exit data of containers in the port area.

（4）箱务管理
（4）Container Management

港口箱务管理是指对港口内及港口间集装箱的备用、调运、交接、检验及修理等业务的计划、组织、协调等工作。做好港口集装箱的箱务管理,对降低集装箱的调运成本,加快集装箱周转,提高港口经济效益和市场竞争能力都有着重要的意义。箱务管理主要包括如下五个方面的内容。

Port container management refers to the planning, organization, and trade-off of operations such as backup, dispatch, handover, test, and repair of containers in and between ports. Doing an excellent job in container management of port containers is of great significance for reducing container transportation costs, accelerating container turnover, and improving port economic efficiency and market competitiveness. Container management mainly includes the following five aspects.

①集装箱的调运
①Dispatch of Containers

在集装箱物流活动中,由于集装箱货源的季节波动性和各航线货物流向的不平衡性,各港口所需要的集装箱数量通常与港口堆存的空箱数不对等。此时,需要将各港口的剩余集装箱空箱调运至空箱量不足的港口以供使用。

In container logistics activities, due to the seasonal volatility of container sources and the imbalance of cargo flow on various routes, the number of containers required by each port is usually not equal to the number of empty containers stored in the port. At this time, the remaining empty containers in each port need to be transferred to ports with insufficient empty containers for use.

②集装箱的分配及使用

②Distribution and Use of Containers

班轮公司或其代理人负责制订港口堆场空箱调用计划,装卸工根据其指令装卸指定的集装箱。

Liner companies or their agents are responsible for making the mobilization schedule of empty containers in the port yard. Stevedores will load and unload designated containers according to the instructions.

③集装箱的堆存与保管

③Storage of Containers

集装箱进入货运场站和堆场后,港口应当按照堆存规则对集装箱进行堆垛。这时,港口可按照装卸工艺、箱型状态、进出口业务、装运货种或货载状态合理安排箱区和箱位。这样做的目的是降低翻箱率,缩短桥吊等待时间,提高港口装卸速度和堆场利用率,进而降低港口的生产成本。

After the containers enter the freight station and storage yard, the port shall stack the containers in accordance with the stacking rules. At this time, the port can reasonably arrange the container area and location, according to the loading and unloading process, the status of the container, the import and export business, the type of cargo or the status of the cargo. The purpose of doing this is to reduce the turnover rate, shorten the waiting time of bridge cranes, improve the port loading and unloading speed and the utilization rate of the yard, thereby reducing the port's production costs.

④集装箱的发放和交接

④Issuance and Handover of Containers

应依据进口提单、出口订舱单、场站收据以及这些文件内列明的集装箱交付条款进行集装箱的发放和交接,实行集装箱设备交接单制度。货主及相关单位必须凭集装箱代理人签发的集装箱设备交接单,在港口办理集装箱的提箱、交箱、进场、出场等手续。

The issuance and handover of containers shall be carried out in accordance with the import bill of lading, export booking list, station receipt, and the container delivery terms listed in these documents, and the container equipment delivery order system shall be implemented. The owner of the cargo and related units must have a handover order issued by the agent in order to carry out operations such as picking up and delivering the container, entry and exit at the port.

⑤集装箱的修理及维护保养

⑤Repair and Maintenance of Containers

集装箱在运输、装卸、搬运、堆存过程中由于种种原因造成损坏的,由港口箱管代理人在授权范围内按照报修程序组织修理。当集装箱需要修理时应当根据船公司对集装箱适货的要求,结合 IICL(国际集装箱出租商协会)的验箱标准和推荐的修箱方法进行修理。

In the process of transportation, loading and unloading, handling, and storage, if the container is damaged, the container management agent in the port shall organize the repair in accordance with the repair procedures within the authorized scope. When a container needs to be repaired, it should be repaired in accordance with the shipping line's requirements for the fitness of the container, combined with IICL (Institute of International Container Lessors) inspection standards and recommended repair methods.

（5）单证流转
（5）Document Circulation

集装箱港口业务涉及的单证包括三大类：进口箱业务单证、出口箱业务单证、船舶业务及其他单证。其中，出口运输的主要单证包括：集装箱货物托运单、装箱单、设备交接单、场站收据、提单、集装箱载货清单、预配船图和积载图、理货单等。进口运输的主要单证包括：货物舱单、船舶积载图、理货单、集装箱清单、装箱单、设备交接单、提单和交货记录等。在各作业环节中，各部门之间需要将单证随作业流程的推进进行传递，以确保作业流程有序、准确。由于集装箱运输环节多，涉及大量单证，目前大部分港口均采用 EDI 网络实现信息数据的交换。这为港口、船公司、船务代理、集疏运场站、理货、货主、货运代理和监管职能部门提供了高效、便捷、准确的电子数据交换服务，不仅简化了单证的流转程序，也大幅提升了港口的作业效率。

The documents involved in the container port business include three categories: import container business documents, export container business documents, shipping business and other documents. Among them, the main documents for export transportation include: container cargo consignment list, packing list, equipment delivery list, station receipt, bill of lading, container loading list, pre-configured ship chart and stowage plan, tally receipt, etc. The main documents of import transportation include: cargo manifest, ship stowage plan, tally receipt, container list, packing list, equipment delivery list, bill of lading, delivery record, etc. In each operation link, every department needs to pass the documents along with the progress of the operation process to ensure the order and accuracy of the operation process. As there are many links in container transportation and a large number of documents are involved, most ports currently use EDI networks to exchange information and data. This provides efficient, convenient and accurate electronic data exchange services for ports, shipping companies, shipping agents, collection and distribution yards, tally, cargo owners, freight forwarders, and supervisory departments, which not only simplifies the circulation procedure of documents, but also greatly improves the efficiency of the port's operations.

3.2.3 集装箱港口的物流活动
3.2.3 Logistics Activities of Container Ports

集装箱港口的物流活动主要是根据各类预设好的计划与安排，组织各种装卸机械在装卸、搬运和堆存等环节中迅速、有效地进行集装箱装卸和换装作业，以完成集装箱货物的进口、出口业务。因此,在实践中我们也可以将集装箱港口的物流活动分为进口物流活动和出口物流活动,具体流程如图 3.5 和图 3.6 所示。

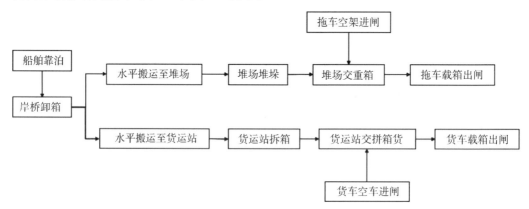

图 3.5 集装箱港口的进口物流活动流程

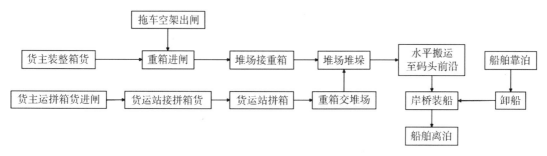

图 3.6 集装箱港口的出口箱物流活动流程

The logistics activities of container ports are mainly to organize various machinery to quickly and effectively carry out container loading and unloading and reloading operations in the links of loading, unloading, handling, and storage according to preset plans, to complete the import and export of container cargos. Therefore, in practice, we can also divide the logistics activities of container ports into import logistics activities and export logistics activities. The specific processes are shown in Figure 3.5 and 3.6.

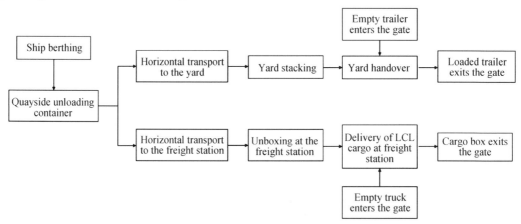

Figure 3.5　The flow of import logistics activities in a container port

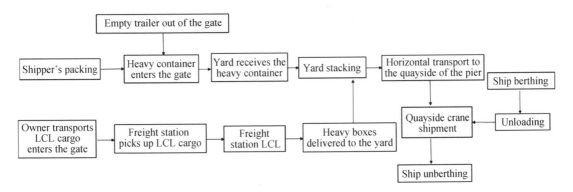

Figure 3.6　The flow of export container logistics activities in a container port

集装箱港口的进口物流活动可简述为:进口船舶按照靠泊计划靠泊后,中控室下达岸桥作业指令并调配港内集卡至码头前沿。码头前沿工作人员按照制订好的卸船计划对进口集装箱进行卸载,并装上内集卡,由内集卡将集装箱运输至堆场或货运站。运至堆场的集装箱由堆场起重机等机械卸下,并按照堆场作业计划,由堆场起重机将其堆垛至指定箱位;而后外集卡进入港口,装载集装箱出闸,交给货主或运至港外货运站;运至货运站的集装箱,由货运站对集装箱进行拆箱作业,并调配货车将货物交给货主,完成进口业务。

The import logistics activities of a container port can be briefly described as: After the imported ships are berthed according to the berthing plan, the central control room issues quay crane operation instructions and deploys inner container trucks in the port to the quayside of the pier. The quayside staff of the pier unload the imported containers according to the formulated ship unloading plan, and load the inner container trucks, and the inner container trucks will transport the containers to the yard or freight station. The containers transported to the yard are unloaded by yard cranes and other machinery, and according to the yard operation plan, they are stacked by the yard crane to the designated container location. And then the external trucks enters into the port, load the containers out of the gate, to the owner or to a freight station outside the port; The containers delivered to the freight station will be unpacked by the freight station, and trucks will be deployed to deliver the cargo to the owners to complete the import business.

集装箱港口的出口物流活动流程包括:货主订舱后,出口货物准备集港。整箱货由货主直接委托集卡运至港口,在闸口登记货物信息后进入堆场,由堆场起重机将集装箱运送至指定箱位并堆垛。拼箱货则由货主运送至货运站进行拼箱作业,装箱完成后运至堆场进行堆存。船舶卸船完成之前,由水平运输机械将出口集装箱搬运至码头前沿进行装船作业,装船完毕后船舶离港。根据集装箱港口的作业地点和作业顺序,可将其物流流程划分为六个步骤,分别为:泊位作业、码头前沿作业、水平搬运、堆场作业、货运站作业和闸口作业。

The export logistics activity process of a container port includes: After the cargo owner has booked the space, the export cargos are ready to be collected in the port. The RCL cargo is transported to the port by the container truck directly entrusted by the owner, and enters the yard after registering the cargo information at the gate. The yard cranes transport the containers to the designated location and stack them. LCL cargo is transported by the owner to the freight station for consolidation operations, and after the packing is completed, it is transported to the yards for stor-

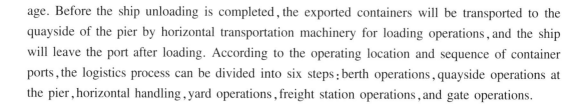

age. Before the ship unloading is completed, the exported containers will be transported to the quayside of the pier by horizontal transportation machinery for loading operations, and the ship will leave the port after loading. According to the operating location and sequence of container ports, the logistics process can be divided into six steps: berth operations, quayside operations at the pier, horizontal handling, yard operations, freight station operations, and gate operations.

（1）泊位作业
（1）Berth Operations

泊位作业主要包括两个环节：第一，船舶到港或离港前的引航、拖船以及泊位计划的制订。在船舶预计到港之前，航运公司会向港口工作人员提供船舶的相关信息以及预计到港时间等信息。工作人员根据某一计划周期内所有到港船舶提供的相关信息，为各船舶安排合理的靠泊位置、靠泊时间以及相关装卸设备并制订泊位计划，使得在满足航运公司要求的条件下，尽量缩短所有船舶的在港时间、提高集装箱港口的作业效率。第二，船舶进出港时的靠、离泊过程。在此过程是由港口的拖船或引航船将集装箱船舶引入泊位或引出港口。引航员要结合当时的环境和条件，根据船舶性能特点以及船舶运动与操纵的相关知识，充分发挥拖船的协助作用来完成引航任务。

Berth operations mainly include two links: First, the pilotage before the ship arrives or departs, the tug boat and the formulation of the berth plan. Before the ship is expected to arrive at the port, the shipping lines will provide relevant information about the ship and the estimated time of arrival to the port staff. According to the relevant information provided by all arriving ships in a certain planning period, the staff arranges the reasonable berthing location, berthing time and related loading and unloading equipment for each ship, and formulates berth plan, so as to meet the requirements of the shipping lines as far as possible shorten the time in port of all ships and improve the operating efficiency of container port. Second, the process of berthing and unberthing. When ships enter and leave the port, the tug boat or pilot boat of the port will lead the container ship into the berth or lead out of the port. The pilot should take into consideration the environment and conditions at the time, according to the ship's performance characteristics and relevant knowledge of ship motion and manoeuvring, and give full play to the assisting role of the tug boat to complete the pilot task.

（2）码头前沿作业
（2）Quayside Operations at the Pier

码头前沿作业主要是指岸边起重机对进出口集装箱进行装船和卸船作业。船舶到达泊位后，港口的工作人员会为每艘船舶指派岸桥、拖车及装卸船工人，并根据装卸船计划为机械和人员安排作业任务，将进口集装箱运至堆场（或将出口集装箱装上船舶）。前沿作业的具体作业流程包括：

The quayside operations at the pier mainly refer to the loading and unloading operations of imported and exported containers by quay cranes. After the ship arrives at the berth, the port staff will assign quay cranes, trailers, and loading and unloading workers for each ship, and arrange tasks for the machinery and personnel according to the loading and unloading plan, and transport the imported containers to the yard (or load the exported container on the ship). The specific operation process of quayside operations includes:

①进口卸船作业

①Import Unloading Operations

集装箱船舶靠港前,将岸桥移动至泊位岸线的大致位置;船舶靠泊之后,船上理货员根据卸船计划中集装箱的卸载顺序,将岸桥指派至集装箱对应的具体作业位置;船上理货员核对箱号,船上工人负责验箱;若是甲板上的货物,船上工人应当在卸箱前打开旋锁和捆绑装置;岸桥将拖车移至船上待卸箱的正上方,放下吊具,将集装箱吊至码头前沿等待的拖车上;外轮理货员核对箱号和封条号码;桥边理货员核对箱号并将信息输入电脑,安排拖车司机将集装箱运至堆场;拖车司机在堆场卸箱后返回岸桥下。循环以上作业顺序,直到所有集装箱卸完为止。

Before the container ship arrives at the port, move the quay crane to the approximate position of the shoreline of the berth; After the ship is berthed, the onboard tally staff will assign the quay crane to the specific operation position corresponding to the container according to the unloading sequence of the containers in the unloading plan; The tally staff on the ship checks the container number, and the workers on the ship are responsible for checking the containers; If it is the cargo on the deck, the workers on the ship should open the twist lock and binding device before unloading; The quay crane lifts the trailer to the ship directly above the unloaded container, puts down the hanger, and hoistes the container to the trailer waiting at the quayside of the pier; The ocean shipping tally staff checks the container number and seal number; The crane-side tally staff checks the container number and enters the information into the computer to arrange for the trailer driver to transport the container to the yard; The trailer driver return to the quay crane after unloading the container at the yard. Repeat the above operation sequence until all containers are unloaded.

②出口装船作业

②Export Loading Operations

船舶到达指定泊位,并进行卸箱作业;拖车根据桥边理货员的指示到堆场提箱,堆场理货员安排堆场起重机将指定集装箱装到拖车上;拖车拖箱到场桥下,外轮理货员及桥下理货员核对箱号和封条号,桥下工人指挥场桥将集装箱吊至船上;船上理货员核对箱号并指示场桥司机该箱的摆放位置,场桥司机将箱装在船上;如果是装载在甲板上的集装箱,桥下工人还应负责安装旋锁,船上工人则应负责锁紧及捆扎集装箱;一个集装箱装上船后,桥下理货员会安排拖车司机去堆场另一个位置取箱。重复上述过程,直到箱位图上每个集装箱都装上船为止。

The ship arrives at the designated berth and unloads the container; The trailer arrives at the yard to pick up the container according to the instructions of the crane-side tally staff, and the yard tally staff arranges the yard crane to load the designated container onto the trailer; The trailer drags the container to the yard crane, the ocean tally and the under-crane tally staff check the container number and seal number, and the workers under the crane direct the yard crane to hoist the container onto the ship; The tally staff on the ship checks the container number and instructs the yard crane driver to place the container, and the yard crane driver loads the container on the ship; If it is the containers loaded on deck, the workers under the crane should also be responsible for installing twist locks, and the workers on the ship should be responsible for locking and binding the containers; After a container is loaded on the ship, the tally under the crane will arrange for the trailer driver to pick up the container from another location in the yard. Repeat the above process until each container on the bay plan is loaded on the ship.

（3）水平搬运
（3）Horizontal Handling

水平搬运主要包括两个过程。第一，岸桥将进口箱卸船后，由水平搬运机械运输至堆场指定箱区的过程；第二，水平搬运机械将出口箱从堆场取走，并运至码头前沿的过程。港口所有集装箱的水平运输都以起重机作为起点和终点，在场桥和岸桥之间进行作业。水平搬运环节是集装箱港口装卸作业的中间环节，其作业能力是否充足是码头前沿作业和堆场作业能力能否得以充分发挥的关键。由于水平搬运机械具有多样性，不同机械的组合可以构成不同的水平搬运系统，每种系统适用的港口类型也不尽相同，因而港口应根据自身情况和作业需要来设置水平搬运系统。常见的几种码头水平搬运系统包括：底盘车系统、跨运车系统、轮胎式龙门起重机系统、轨道式龙门起重机系统。

Horizontal handling mainly includes two processes. The first is the process of unloading the imported containers by the quay crane to the designated container area of the storage yard; The second is the process of removing the exported containers from the yard by the horizontal handling machinery and transporting them to the quayside of the pier. The horizontal transportation of all containers in the port uses cranes as the starting and ending points, and the operations are carried out between the yard cranes and the quay cranes. The horizontal handling is the intermediate link of container port loading and unloading operations. Adequacy of its operating capacity is the key to whether the quayside operations of the pier and the yard can be fully utilized. Due to the diversity of horizontal handling machinery, different combinations of machinery can form different horizontal handling systems, and the types of ports applicable to each system are not the same. Therefore, the port should set up a horizontal handling system according to its own situation and operational needs. Several common pier horizontal handling systems include: trailer chassis system, straddle carrier system, rubber-tired gantry crane system （RTG）, and rail-mounted gantry crane system （RMG）.

（4）堆场作业
（4）Yard Operations

船舶进港前，港口工作人员需要根据航运公司提供的相关信息制订合理的堆场计划。集装箱能否合理地安置在集装箱码头堆场内，不仅会影响卸船计划的执行，而且会显著影响交货计划的执行。因此，码头堆场应在充分考虑卸船的集装箱数量、种类，以及向内地运输和交给收货人的数量的前提下，有条不紊地将集装箱卸下，并立即交给内陆运输的承运人或收货人。堆场作业环节包含两个过程:提箱过程和送箱过程。提箱过程是指堆场装卸机械将堆存在堆场的集装箱卸至水平搬运机械或外集卡上的过程;送箱过程是指堆场装卸机械将水平搬运机械或外集卡送来的集装箱堆存至堆场的过程。

Before the ship enters the port, the port staff need to formulate a reasonable yard plan based on the relevant information provided by the shipping lines. Whether the containers can be reasonably placed in the container pier yard will not only affect the implementation of the unloading plan, but also significantly affect the implementation of the delivery plan. Therefore, the pier yard should unload the containers in an orderly manner, and immediately hand them over to the inland transportation carrier under the premise of fully considering the number and types of containers unloaded, as well as the quantity to be transported to the island and handed over to the carrier. The yard operation involves two processes: The lifting process and the delivery process. The lifting process refers to the process in which the yard loading and unloading machinery unload the containers stacked in the yard to the horizontal handling machinery or outer container truck; The delivery process refers to the process in which the yard loading and unloading machinery stack the containers sent by the horizontal handling machinery or the outer container truck to the yard.

(5)货运站作业
(5) Freight Station Operations

设置在港口内的货运站主要负责与货主交接货物以及拼拆箱作业等业务。货主托运的出口拼箱货均先在码头集装箱货运站集货,在货运站拼箱后转往堆场,准备装船;进口拼箱货则需在卸船后,运至码头集装箱货运站拆箱,然后向收货人送货,或由收货人提货。

The freight station set up in the port is mainly responsible for the delivery of cargos, and splitting and unpacking operations with the consignor. The exported LCL cargo consignment by the consignor is first collected at the pier container freight station, and then transferred to the storage yard for shipment; Imported LCL cargo needs to be unloaded, transported to the pier container freight station for unpacking, and then delivered to the consignee or picked up by the consignee.

(6)闸口作业
(6) Gate Operations

闸口作业主要包括两个过程:出口集装箱的集港操作和进口集装箱的疏港操作。集港操作具体流程包括:集卡将出口集装箱运至码头堆场时,闸口要核对订舱单、码头收据、装箱单等单据,检查集装箱的数量、号码、铅封号码等是否与场站收据记载相一致,查看箱子的外表状况,以及铅封有无异常情况。检查无误后,集卡进场。疏港操作的具体流程包括:集卡空车到码头提取进口集装箱,若所提集装箱手续齐全,闸口根据其在堆场的堆存信息对其进行流向引导,集卡进入堆场提箱。

The gate operations mainly include two processes: The port collection operation of the exported containers and the port distribution operation of the imported containers. The specific procedures of collection operation include: When trucks transport exported containers to the pier yard, the gate must check the booking list, pier receipt, packing list and other documents, check whether the quantity, number, and lead seal number of the container are consistent with the receipt of the station, check the container appearance and whether there is any abnormality in the lead seal. After the inspection is correct, the trucks enter the arena. The specific process of the port distribution operation includes: Empty trucks go to the pier to pick up imported containers, and if the container procedures are complete, the gate will guide the flow of the containers based on their storage information at the storage yard, and the trucks will enter the storage yard to pick up the containers.

在传统集装箱港口中,闸口作业需要人工识别车号和箱号、人工录入的数据、现场箱体检查等。作业效率较低、数据准确性较差,车辆通过闸口的速度也较慢。随着集装箱吞吐量的不断增加和码头大型化的发展,闸口的通过能力对港口整体作业效率的影响越来越大,因此,越来越多的港口开始建设智能闸口。

In traditional container ports, gate operations require manual identification of vehicle numbers and container numbers, manual data entry, and on-site inspection of container body, etc. The operation efficiency is low, the data accuracy is poor, and the speed of vehicles passing through the gate is slow. With the continuous increase of container throughput and the development of large-scale piers, the passing capacity of the gate has an increasing influence on the overall operational efficiency of the port. Therefore, more and more ports have begun to build smart gates.

智能闸口将射频识别、电子数据交换、图像传感器图像采集和实时控制等技术进行有机结合,利用核心控制系统控制各个部分工作,以实现各项业务流程。一般的智能闸口包括闸口预约、电子车牌识别、集装箱箱号识别、集装箱箱体验残、闸口人机交互等多个功能,其具体作业流程如下:

The smart gate organically combines radio frequency identification (RFID), electronic data interchange (EDI), charge coupled device (CCD) image acquisition and real-time control, and uses the core control system to control each part of the work to achieve various business processes. A general smart gate includes multiple functions, such as gate reservation, electronic license plate recognition, container number recognition, damage detection of container body, and gate human-computer interaction. The specific operation process is as follows:

①集卡预约进港。集卡通过系统预约进港送箱(或提箱),系统统计预约信息,方便制订港内作业计划。

①Container trucks enter the port by making an appointment. The trucks makes an appointment in the port for delivery (or pick-up) through the system, and the system counts the reservation information to facilitate the formulation of the operation plan in the port.

②车辆进出闸口时,系统识别电子车牌。进出闸口车辆需要安装电子车牌,并录入车辆的 ID、车牌号、车重等信息,闸口的识别系统全天运行,当电子车牌进入识别区域时,系统会捕获车辆信息,并实时发送给后台。

②When the vehicle enters and exits the gate, the system recognizes the electronic license plate. Vehicles entering and exiting the gate need to install an electronic license plate, and enter the vehicle ID, license plate number, vehicle weight. The recognition system of the gate runs all day, when the electronic license plate enters the recognition area, the system will capture the vehicle information and send it to the backstage in real-time.

③系统识别集装箱信息。集装箱箱号是集装箱唯一的 ID 号,系统通过图像识别技术和 CCD 图像采集技术自动捕获集装箱箱号传递给后台。

③The system identifies the container information. The container number is the unique ID number of the container. The system automatically captures the container number and transmits it to the backstage through image recognition technology and CCD image acquisition technology.

④系统进行集装箱箱体残损检测。集装箱箱体残损检测是集装箱进入港口内不可避免的一项检查工作,目的是避免港口同船方、货方等利益主体因箱体损坏产生纠纷。系统通过逻辑控制系统和图片采集系统将箱面影像呈现在计算机上,由验残员进行检验。

④The system conducts damage detection of the container body. Container damage detection is an unavoidable inspection work when containers enter the port. The purpose is to avoid disputes between the port and the ship and cargo parties due to the damage of the containers. The system displays the container surface image on the computer through the logic control system and the picture acquisition system, and the inspector conducts the inspection.

⑤集卡驾驶员将预约单提交至闸口系统。人机交互系统将预约单的信息自动扫描,存入闸口系统,并将系统反馈的行车指南打印成小票发给驾驶员。驾驶员按照行车指南在港口内行驶,进行提箱或送箱作业。

⑤The truck driver submits the reservation form to the gate system. The human-computer interaction system automatically scans the reservation form information, stores it in the gate system, and prints the driving guide fed back by the system into a small ticket and sent it to the driver. The driver drives in the port according to the driving guide, and carries out the operation of picking up or delivering the container.

◆ 3.3 件杂货港口物流运作流程与管理

3.3 Logistics Operation Process and Management of General Cargo Ports

3.3.1 件杂货港口概述
3.3.1 Overview of General Cargo Ports

与集装箱港口仅用于处理统一化、标准化的运输单元不同,件杂货港口的物流活动与所处理的货物类型、包装、体积等特征密切相关。为了清晰描述件杂货港口的物流活动,我们先介绍件杂货的定义与分类。件杂货是指单件运输、保管的货物。由于件杂货的外形和包装形式多且杂,又被称为杂货。从港口作业角度,件杂货又可被分为袋装类货物、箱装类货物、桶装类货物、捆扎类货物和设备重大件货物,具体如表3.1所示。

表 3.1　不同种类件杂货的概念与分类

种类	概念	分类
袋装	粉末、颗粒状的货物,使用纤维织物(或纸袋)包装形成的物流单元	按自然特性分类,有粮食、糖、化肥、水泥、某些化工原料和矿产品等;按包装材料分类,有麻袋、布袋、塑料编织袋、纸袋、塑料袋及草袋等;按重量分类,1 t 及以上的大型袋装类货物常被称为集装袋(或吨装袋)货物
箱装	一件或一件以上的物品放置于由木材、塑料、纸皮或铁皮等包装材料制成的箱体内,或用上述包装材料将货物包装成箱体状而组成的一个货物单元	箱装类货物按照外包装物材质划分,主要有普通木箱、框架木箱、纸箱、塑料箱和金属箱等
桶装	由木桶、纸桶、铁桶和塑料桶等盛装液体、颗粒、粉状物货物	按桶内盛装货物的物理特性分类,固体的有松香、沥青、烧碱等,液体的有油漆、生漆、颜料、染料、动植物油、矿物油等;按外表包装材质分类,有木桶、纸桶、铁桶和塑料桶包装等
捆扎	将一件或一件以上的货物用捆扎包装材料捆扎在一起,组成一个货物单元的件杂货	捆扎类货物按形状和材料种类综合起来,常见可分成长(条)形钢材类、卷形钢材类、板形金属类、有色金属锭类、成形木材类、轻工产品和农产品类
设备重大件	各种机器、成套设备、车辆和精密仪器等货物	设备重大件货物是件杂货港口常见货物之一,设备重大件货物重量一般在 2~3 t 以上,长度超过 10~12 m。有些超级重件大大超过了普通港口设备的起重能力,一些长大件也超出了单一泊位长度

Unlike container ports that are only used to handle unified and standardized transport units, the logistics activities of general cargo ports are closely related to the type, packaging, and volume of the cargo handled. In order to clearly describe the logistics activities of the general cargo port, we first introduce the definition and classification of general cargo. A pieces of general cargo refer to a single piece of cargo that are transported and kept in storage. Because the shape and packaging of the cargo are many and miscellaneous, they are also called groceries. From the perspective of port operations, general cargo can be divided into bagged cargo, boxed cargo, barreled cargo, bundled cargo and heavy and large piece of equipment, as shown in Table 3.1.

Table 3.1　Concept and classification of general cargo

Type	Concept	Classification
Bagged	Powder and granular cargos are packed in a logistics unit formed by fibre fabric (or paper) bags	Classified by natural characteristics, there are grains, sugar, fertilizers, cement, certain chemical raw materials and mineral products, etc.; Classified by packaging materials, there are sack, cloth bags, plastic woven bags, paper bags, plastic bags and straw bags, etc.; Classified by weight, large bagged cargos of 1 ton and above are often referred to as flexible freight bags (or ton bagged) cargos
Boxed	One or more items are placed in a box made of packaging materials such as lumber, plastic, paper, or iron, or a cargo unit formed by packaging the cargos into a box with the above-mentioned packaging materials	Boxed cargos are classified according to the material of the outer packaging, mainly including ordinary wooden boxes, wooden frame boxes, cartons, plastic boxes and metal boxes
Barreled	Liquid, granular and powder cargos are contained in wooden barrels, paper barrels, iron barrels and plastic barrels	Classified according to the physical characteristics of the cargos in the barrels, solids include rosin, asphalt, caustic soda, etc., and liquids include paint, lacquer, pigment, dye, animal and vegetable oil, mineral oil, etc.; Classified according to the packaging materials, there are wooden barrels, paper barrels, iron barrels and plastic barrels packaging, etc.
Bundled	One or more pieces of cargos are bundled together with strapping packaging materials to form a piece of groceries in a cargo unit	Bundled cargos are integrated according to shape and material types, and are commonly divided into long (strip) steel products, rolled steel products, plate metal products, non-ferrous metal ingots, formed lumber products, light industrial products and agricultural products
Heavy and large piece of equipment	Cargos such as various machines, complete sets of equipment, vehicles and precision instruments	Heavy and large piece of equipment is one of the common cargo in general cargo ports. The weight of heavy and large piece of equipment is generally more than 2 to 3 tons, and the length exceeds 10 to 12 meters. Some super-heavy parts greatly exceed the lifting capacity of ordinary port equipment, and some long and large parts also exceed the length of a single berth

　　件杂货装卸工作存在批量少、货票多、货物双向性的特点,并且多为贵重物品、危险货物或军用货物,需要进行散件装卸运输,所以在装卸时一定要保证其完好无损。因此,件杂货港口物流流程管理的关键在于装卸过程的控制与管理。在进行件杂货装卸作业时,港口应

满足需满足如下要求：(1)工作地点要整洁,对于食品更要注意保持吊货工夹具、机械的工作机构和工作人员的清洁；(2)需要使用合适的、牢固的吊货工夹具；(3)需要正确地将货物安放在吊货工夹具上；(4)平稳地升降货吊,将货物整齐地安放在水平搬运机械上,必要时对货物进行捆扎,以免在运输过程中振落受损。目前,件杂货运输逐渐向成组化、集装箱化的方向发展,然而,有些件杂货难以用集装箱来运输。为满足上述需求,件杂货港口的管理者针对不同种类的件杂货,通常会指定相应的装卸机械与运输管理方法,与集装箱物流活动运作流程存在明显差异。

The loading and unloading of general cargo have the characteristics of fewer batches, more tickets, and two-way cargo. And most of them are valuables, dangerous cargos or military cargos, which need to be loaded and unloaded and transported in bulk, so they must be intact and undamaged when loading and unloading. Therefore, the key to the logistics process management of the general cargo port lies in the control and management of the loading and unloading process. When carrying out general cargo loading and unloading operations, the port should meet the following requirements: (1) The working place should be clean and tidy, and more attention should be paid to keeping the lifting jigs, machinery working mechanism and staff clean for food; (2) Need to use suitable and strong lifting jigs; (3) The cargos need to be placed on the crane jigs correctly; (4) Lift the cargo crane steadily, place the cargo neatly on the horizontal handling machinery, and bundle the cargo if necessary to avoid vibration and damage during transportation. At present, the transportation of general cargo is gradually developing in the direction of grouping and containerization. However, some groceries are difficult to transport in containers. To meet the above needs, the manager of the general cargo port targets different kinds of general cargo, and usually specify the corresponding loading and unloading machinery and transportation management methods, which are obviously different from the operation process of container logistics activities.

3.3.2 件杂货港口物流运作管理
3.3.2 Logistics Operation Management of General Cargo Ports

按照货物在港内流转的过程,件杂货港口物流运作流程和3.1节介绍的基本流程类似,涉及货物装卸、件杂货库场管理以及理货交接等三个部分。相对于集装箱港口而言,件杂货港口不涉及大量资源与作业任务的组织安排,因此其港口物流运作流程较为简单,其主要难点在于货物装卸与件杂货库场管理。

According to the flow of cargo in the port, the logistics operation process of the general cargo port is similar to the basic process introduced in Section 3.1, involving three parts: cargo loading and unloading, general cargo warehouse management and tally delivery. Compared with container ports, general cargo ports do not involve a large number of resources and the organization and arrangement of the operational tasks. Therefore, its port logistics operation process is relatively simple, and its main difficulty lies in cargo loading and unloading and general cargo ware-house management.

（1）件杂货的装卸管理

（1）Loading and Unloading Management of General Cargo

件杂货装卸管理是指在船舶入港前，为了缩短船舶在港时间、提高码头装卸效率，按照港方自身装卸条件以及船方事前提供的信息，对泊位、起重机等码头重要设备进行合理调度的一系列管理活动，通常涉及如下内容。

Loading and unloading management of general cargo refers to a series of management activities in order to shorten the time of ships in the port and improve the efficiency of loading and unloading at the pier before the ship enters the port. A series of management activities for rationally dispatching important pier equipment such as berths and cranes in accordance with the port's own loading and unloading conditions and the information provided by the ship in advance, usually involving the following contents.

①件杂货船舶泊位安排

①Berth Arrangements for General Cargo Ships

件杂货船舶泊位安排指为即将入港的船舶安排靠泊位置。这是制订装卸计划的第一步，需要根据码头在港船舶的装卸进度、入港船舶信息，科学合理地安排船舶停靠泊位，并安排船舶在港作业的各项准备工作。泊位安排具体涉及多艘船舶与多个泊位之间的指派问题，以及泊位服务多个船舶的排序问题。件杂货船舶的泊位安排除了需要考虑船舶技术指标、货主和船方时间与作业需求、港口作业设施的限制外，还需要考虑港口水文自然条件等其他因素。

Berth arrangements for general cargo ships refer to arranging berthing locations for ships about to enter the port. This is the first step in making a loading and unloading plan. It needs to arrange berths for ships scientifically and reasonably, and arrange various preparations for ship operations in the port based on the loading and unloading progress of the ships in the port and the information of the ships entering the port. Berth arrangements specifically involve the assignment of multiple ships and multiple berth activities, as well as the sequencing of berths serving multiple ships. In addition to the berth arrangement of general cargo ships, it is necessary to consider the technical indicators of the ship, the time and operation requirements of the cargo owner and the ship, and the restrictions of port operation facilities. We also need to consider other factors such as port hydrological and natural conditions.

②装卸工艺和流程确定

②Determination of Loading and Unloading Process

装卸工艺和流程确定是指根据抵港船舶信息、作业货物特点、码头装卸设备资源，选择合理的物流活动，以提高货物装卸效率和码头经济效益。

Determination of loading and unloading process refers to the selection of reasonable logistics activities based on the information of the arriving ships, the characteristics of the operating cargo, and the resources of the pier's loading and unloading equipment to improve the efficiency

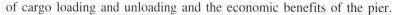

of cargo loading and unloading and the economic benefits of the pier.

③生产要素分配

③Distribution of Productive Factors

根据已确定的物流活动流程、船舶信息、作业货物信息,合理配置装卸设备、企业人力等码头资源,以保证作业的进度要求和质量要求。为保证在作业过程中各环节衔接顺畅,在分配装卸设备时,要注意设备的分配数量应以满足此环节主导机械的作业效率为标准,避免出现主导机械等待或其他设备数量过多等现象。

According to the determined logistics activity process, ship information, and operation cargo information, reasonably allocate pier resources such as loading and unloading equipment and corporate manpower to ensure the progress and quality requirements of the operation. To ensure the smooth connection of all links in the operation process, when distributing loading and unloading equipment, it is necessary to pay attention to the amount of equipment allocated to meet the operating efficiency of the leading machinery in this link as the standard to avoid the phenomenon of waiting of the leading machinery or an excessive number of other equipment.

④协作作业安排

④Arrangements of Collaborative Assignment

根据装卸情况,确定同铁路、驳船及其他协作单位的协同作业关系,并向其提出协作要求,以保证装卸任务顺利进行。

According to the loading and unloading situation, determine the cooperative operation relationship with the railway, barge and other cooperative units, and put forward cooperation requirements to them to ensure the smooth progress of the loading and unloading tasks.

件杂货装卸管理中,要注意码头装卸设备的实际作业效率不仅仅与设备性能参数有关,还会受到货物种类的影响。这主要体现在三个方面:一是受件杂货种类差异影响,例如,装卸作业过程中可能需要更换吊具,避免影响装卸效率;二是受货物自身特性影响,例如钢材等重货,在装卸过程中,设备容易实现满负荷作业,而轻泡货物则难以达到满负荷作业;三是受货物包装形式影响,例如,当货物使用成组网络、托盘进行包装,作业时便应尽量增加装卸设备每次起吊成组网络、托盘的数量。

In the management of general cargo handling, it is important to note that the actual operating efficiency of pier handling equipment is not only related to equipment performance parameters, but also affected by the types of the cargo. This is mainly reflected in three aspects. First, it is affected by differences in the types of groceries. For example, the spreader may need to be replaced during loading and unloading operations, which affects the efficiency of loading and unloading. Second, it is affected by the characteristics of the cargos themselves. For example, heavy cargo such as steel, during the loading and unloading process, the equipment is easy to achieve full load operation, while light foam cargo is difficult to achieve full load operation. Third, it is affected by the packaging of the cargo. For example, when cargos are packaged in-group networks and pallets, the number of groups and pallets that are lifted by the loading and unloading equipment should be increased as much as possible.

（2）库场管理

（2）Warehouse Management

件杂货港口库场是集散货物的主要场所，也是件杂货水路运输中的衔接点。一般情况下，进出口货物在交接前，会在港口库场进行短期储存。由于港口货物运输的非均衡性，进出港口的货物量会出现一定波动。货物的进出港时间以及船舶装卸时间也不可能相同。此时，港口库场的储存功能便为货物运输提供了缓冲空间。货物在保管期间，港口库场也为海关等单位进行货运工作、证件验收、海关验关等必要活动提供了时间和空间。件杂货港口的库场管理主要分为堆存计划与库场评价管理两部分内容。

The general cargo port warehouse is the main place for collecting and distributing bulk cargo, and it is also the connection point in the waterway transportation of general cargo. Under normal circumstances, import and export cargos will be stored in the port warehouse for a short period of time before being handed over. Due to the unevenness of port cargo transportation, the volume of cargo entering and leaving the port will fluctuate to a certain extent. The time of entry and exit of cargo and the time of loading and unloading of ships cannot be the same. At this time, the storage function of the port warehouse provides a buffer space for cargo transportation. During the storage period of the cargos, the port warehouse also provides time and space for the customs and other units to carry out necessary activities such as freight work, document acceptance, and customs inspection. The warehouse management of the general cargo port is mainly divided into two parts: the storage plan and the warehouse evaluation management.

①堆存计划

①Storage Plan

库场的堆存计划明确了一定时期内各种货物的堆存策略，以保证库场使用的计划性、科学性、经济性。科学合理的堆存计划会使货物进出顺畅，装卸作业高效、流畅；反之，则会导致港口物流活动冗杂、倒垛频繁、局部拥堵、库场利用不均等问题，影响码头装卸效率。港口库场的堆存计划管理分为长期规划和短期计划两种。长期规划依据货源、航线以及市场需求等因素进行制订；短期计划是指年度、月度以及昼夜的库场使用计划，需要依据船、货方提供的各种信息，库场使用情况以及码头装卸计划进行制订。在实际操作过程中，最常用也是最重要的是库场昼夜使用计划。堆存计划的编制过程可简述如下。

The storage plan of the warehouse clarifies the storage strategy of various cargos within a certain period of time to ensure the planned, scientific and economical use of the warehouse. A scientific and reasonable storage plan will make the cargo in and out smoothly, and the loading and unloading operations will be efficient and smooth; On the contrary, it will cause problems such as redundant port logistics activities, frequent stacking, local congestion, and uneven utilization of warehouses, which will affect the efficiency of pier loading and unloading. The storage plan management of the port warehouse is divided into long-term planning and short-term planning. Long-term plans are based on factors such as sources of cargos, routes and market demand; Short-term plans refer to annual, monthly, and day and night warehouse usage plans, which need to be formulate based on various information provided by ships and cargo parties, warehouse usage, and pier loading and unloading plans. In the actual operation process, the day and night use plan of the warehouse is the most commonly used and most important. The preparation process of the storage plan can be briefly described as follows.

a. 根据货主提供信息、作业货物信息、库场的现有状况以及昼夜生产计划,进行综合考虑、平衡,编制货物堆存计划。

a. According to the information provided by the cargo owner, the information of the operating cargo, the current status of the warehouse and the day and night production plan, careful consideration and balance are carried out to prepare a cargo storage plan.

b. 为库场使用计划的实施进行准备,包括协调配备相应的机械劳力和库场附属设施的使用。

b. Prepare for the implementation of the warehouse usage plan, including the trade-off of the corresponding mechanical labour and the use of auxiliary facilities in the warehouse.

c. 库场使用计划的下达。

c. Release of warehouse usage plan.

d. 库场使用计划实施过程的监督与指导。

d. Surveillance and guidance of the implementation process of the warehouse usage plan.

e. 库场使用计划实施后的评价与总结。

e. Evaluation and summary after the implementation of the warehouse usage plan.

目前,件杂货码头采用基于货物分类机制的堆存策略。即根据货物属性为不同种类货物分配不同的堆存场所,以满足各类货物的存储特性。具体的货物分类堆存策略包括:对于高周转率的货物,应将其分配在码头作业前沿区域,以保证装船效率;对于大宗货物,由于其被频繁地装卸,应单独堆存来减少设备转场次数;对堆存要求特殊的货物,为便于管理、装卸,应单独堆存;对于性质互抵的货物(如扬尘货物与易被污染货物),不能堆存在一起;对于进口货物,应将其分配在库场的后方,或靠近转运交接点区域,加速货物疏运。

At present, the general cargo pier adopts a storage strategy based on the cargo classification mechanism. That is, according to the attributes of the cargos, different types of cargos are allocated to different storage locations to meet the storage characteristics of various types of cargos. Specific cargo classification and storage strategies include: For high turnover cargo, it should be allocated in the quayside of the pier operation to ensure the efficiency of loading; For bulk cargo, because it is frequently loaded and unloaded, it should be stored separately to reduce the number of equipment transfers; For cargo with special stacking requirements, it should be stored separately for ease of management, loading and unloading; For cargos that are mutually offset in nature (such as dusty cargos and cargos that are easily contaminated), they cannot be stacked together; For import cargos, they should be stored at the rear of the warehouse or close to the transfer junction area to speed up the distribution of cargos.

②库场评价管理

②Warehouse Evaluation Management

件杂货码头的库场是货物的集散地点,由于件杂货种类繁多,存储特性各异,且货物集疏方式、堆存时间也不尽相同。科学合理的堆存计划可以满足不同货物的堆存要求,并提高港口企业的经济效益。因此,港口企业为提高库场管理水平,应制订科学的评价指标,为堆存计划的评价与总结提供依据。件杂货港口库场堆存策略的评价指标的建立可以参考以下几个方面。

The warehouse of the general cargo pier, is the collection and distribution place of the cargo. Due to the wide variety of general cargo, the storage characteristics are different, and the cargo collection and distribution methods and storage time are also different. A scientific and reasonable storage plan can meet the storage requirements of different cargos and improve the economic benefits of port enterprises. Therefore, in order to improve the management level of the warehouse, the port enterprise should formulate scientific evaluation indicators to provide a basis for the evaluation and summary of the storage plan. The following aspects can be referred to for the establishment of the evaluation index of the storage strategy of the general cargo port warehouse.

a. 堆存策略是否具有计划性?

a. Whether the storage strategy is planned?

库场资源是有限的,由于堆存货物种类繁多,且货物的交付基本都在库场进行,因此库场的使用必须遵循计划性,以保证库场堆存的秩序与效率。

The warehouse resources are limited. Due to the wide variety of stockpiled cargos, and the delivery of cargos is basically carried out in the warehouse, the use of the warehouse must follow the plan to ensure the order and efficiency of the warehouse.

b. 库场使用是否科学?

b. Whether the warehouse is used scientifically?

库场使用的科学性是指库场管理工作必须按照科学方法进行组织。首先,库场管理人员必须有严密的分工以及明确的岗位职责。其次,要有健全的库场交接手续、货物保管方法,以保证库场的使用效率和货运质量。此外,还要有一套科学的库场定额与库场使用指标,以保证库场的有效利用并提高港口通过能力。

The scientific nature of the use of warehouse means that the warehouse management must be organized in accordance with scientific methods. First of all, the warehouse management personnel must have a strict division of labour and strip job responsibilities. Second, there must be sound warehouse handover procedures and cargo storage methods to ensure the efficiency of the warehouse and the quality of freight. In addition, there must be a set of scientific warehouse quotas and warehouse usage indicators to ensure the effective use of warehouse and improve port throughput capacity.

c. 库场使用是否经济?

c. Whether the warehouse is used economically?

库场是港口生产不可或缺的重要环节,其使用与管理的情况直接影响港口的经济效益和社会效益。要提高库场的经济性,必须提高库场堆存能力,降低货物堆存时间。提高库场堆存能力是指提高库场的单位面积堆存量。单位面积堆存量是衡量库场通过能力的关键指标,同时也对库场使用效率有直接影响。单位面积的堆存量越大,库场的使用效率越高,库场的通过能力越好;反之,单位面积堆存量越小,堆场的使用效率越低,库场的通过能力也就越差。因此,合理安排货位与空间,提高单位堆存面积,是提高库场管理水平的关键。此外,货物在港堆存时间同样影响着库场通过能力,货物在港堆存时间越短,库场通过能力越强,库场吞吐量也就越大;反之,若货物在港堆存时间过久,则会导致库场可用空间减少,降低库场的堆存能力,导致库场吞吐量减少,从而影响库场的使用效率。因此,加快货物疏运、缩短货物在港时间,是提高港口效益的重要途径。

The warehouse is an indispensable part of port production, and its use and management directly affect the economic and social benefits of the port. To improve the economy of the warehouse, the storage capacity of the warehouse must be improved, and the storage time of the cargo must be reduced. Improving the storage capacity of the warehouse refers to increasing the storage volume per unit area of the warehouse. The storage volume per unit area is a key indicator to measure the throughput capacity of the warehouse, and it also has a direct impact on the efficiency of the warehouse. The larger the storage volume per unit area, the higher the efficiency of the warehouse, and the better the throughput capacity of the warehouse. Conversely, the smaller the storage volume per unit area, the lower the usage efficiency of the warehouse, and the worse the throughput capacity of the warehouse. Therefore, rationally arranging cargo locations and space and increasing the storage area per unit are the keys to improving the management level of the warehouse. In addition, the storage time of the cargo in the port also affects the throughput capacity of the warehouse. The shorter the storage time of the cargo in the port, the stronger the throughput capacity of the warehouse, and the greater the throughput of the warehouse; Conversely, if the cargos is stored in the port for a long time, the available space of the warehouse will be reduced, the storage capacity of the warehouse will be reduced, resulting in the reduction of the throughput of the warehouse, thus affecting the efficiency of the warehouse. Therefore, speeding up the cargo distribution and shortening the time of the cargo in port are important ways to improve port efficiency.

d. 货物是否妥善保管?

d. Whether the cargo is properly kept?

作为货物集疏场所,确保货物在收发保管过程中的质量,是库场的基本职责和要求。件杂货种类、储存特性差异较大,因而在保管过程中稍有不慎,就会出现货损货差。因此,正确地收发、保管货物,是提高货运质量的保证,也是保证库场效益的基本要求。

As a place for collecting and distributing the cargo, it is the basic responsibility and requirement of the warehouse to ensure the quality of the cargo in the process of receiving, dispatching and storing. The types and storage characteristics of the general cargo vary greatly, so if you are careless in the storage process, there will be poor cargo damage. Therefore, the correct delivery and storage of the cargo is a guarantee for improving the quality of freight, and it is also a basic requirement for ensuring the efficiency of the warehouse.

e. 港口库场的使用是否具有可持续性?

e. Whether the use of port warehouses is sustainable?

货物堆存应在库场额定负荷内使用。库场堆存场所内均有单位面积荷重定额,它是指库场堆存场所的单位面积最大承重能力。在库场使用过程中,货物的单位面积堆存重量不能超过所在场地的最大承重能力,否则将会降低库场的使用寿命,增加库场维护费用。堆存货物时,库场工作人员要依据单位面积最大承重能力来决定货物的堆码方式和堆码高度。

The storage of cargos shall be used within the rated load of the warehouse. There is a load quota per unit area in the warehouse, which refers to the maximum load-bearing capacity per unit area of the warehouse. During the use of the warehouse, the weight per unit area of the cargos should not exceed the maximum load-bearing capacity of the warehouse. Otherwise the service life of the warehouse will be reduced, and the maintenance cost of the warehouse will increase. When stacking up cargos, the warehouse staff should determine the stacking method and stacking height of the cargos based on the maximum load-bearing capacity per unit area.

f. 堆存策略的制订是否考虑作业任务整体?

f. Whether the storage strategy takes into account the overall task?

货物堆存应尽可能保证周转货物存放至前方堆场,待装货物在后方堆场。前方堆场靠近码头作业前沿,供出港货物装船前集中堆放以及进港货物临时堆放,以缩短货物运输距离,提高作业效率。因此,在制订堆存策略时,不仅应考虑库场情况与货物堆存要求,而且要从码头作业任务整体出发,以提高整个作业系统的效率。

As far as possible, the storage of cargos shall ensure that the turnover cargos are stored in the front yard, and the cargos to be loaded are in the rear yard. The front yard is close to the quayside of the pier, for centralized storage of outbound cargo before loading and temporary storage of incoming cargo to shorten the distance of cargo transportation and improve operation efficiency. Therefore, when formulating a storage strategy, we should not only consider the warehouse conditions and cargo storage requirements, but also start from the overall task of the pier to improve the efficiency of the entire operating system.

g. 港口库场的使用是否具有安全性?

g. Whether the use of port warehouses is safe?

港口库场使用的安全性主要体现在危险货物的堆存管理。危险货物堆存管理是指对于具有爆炸、易燃、有毒、腐蚀、放射性等性质的货物,委托人应按照相应的货物运输规定进行妥善包装,并粘贴危险品标志和标签,以保证货物堆存安全的一项工作。进行委托时,港口经营人应将货物的正式名称、危害性质以及应当采取的预防措施以书面形式通知港口经营人。港口经营人按照《水路危险货物运输规则》的有关规定在库场内进行作业或堆存。如委托人未按要求通知或通知有误,港口经营人可以在任何时间、任何地点根据情况需要停止作业、销毁货物或者使之不能为害,且不承担赔偿责任。委托人对港口经营人因作业此类货物所受到的损失,应当承担赔偿责任。港口经营人知道危险货物的性质并且已同意作业的,仍然可以在该项货物对港口设施、人员或者其他货物构成实际危险时,停止作业、销毁货物或者使之不能为害。

The safety of the port warehouse is mainly reflected in the storage management of dangerous cargos. Dangerous cargo storage management means a safe job that for cargos with explosive, flammable, toxic, corrosive, radioactive, etc., the consignor shall properly package them in accordance with the corresponding cargo transportation regulations, and stick dangerous cargos signs and labels to ensure the storage of cargos. When entrusting, the port operator shall be notified in writing of the official name of the cargo, the nature of the hazard and the preventive measures that shall be taken. The port operator shall carry out operations or stockpiles in the warehouse in accordance with the relevant provisions of the "Rules for the Transport of Dangerous Cargos by Waterway". If the consignor fails to notify as required or the notification is incorrect, the port operator can stop the operation, destroy the cargo or make it incapable of harm at any time and at any place according to the situation, without being liable for compensation. The consignor shall be liable for compensation for the losses suffered by the port operator due to the operation of such cargos. If the port operator knows the nature of the dangerous cargos and has agreed to the operation, he can still stop the operation, destroy the cargos or make it incapable of harm when the cargos pose a real danger to port facilities, personnel or other cargos.

（3）理货交接
（3）Tally Handover

理货是指在装卸搬运过程中，根据货运票据和货运规章制度，对货物进行点数、计量、分票、分标志、分清货物残损、办理货物交接签证和指导货物装卸、堆码等多项工作的总称。理货是一项复杂的工作，其业务内容主要包括在货物运输过程中的各环节之间，按照票据对货物数量与质量进行核对。理货业务是第三方公证性质，参与方主要有货方、船方、港口。这些人员在货物交接过程中，为弄清货物数量和质量协同工作。理货工作涉及各方利益。数字的准确无误，货物状态明确都有利于货物的顺利交接与装卸工作的进行，并可加快货物运输速度。按照交接双方的身份，件杂货码头理货货运交接种类可分为：港口与船方的交接、港口与货方的交接、港口与理货机构的交接、港口内部间的交接等。

Tally is a general term referred to counting, measuring, dividing, marking, sorting out damaged cargo, applying for cargo handover visas, and guiding cargo loading and unloading, stacking up and other tasks in the process of loading, unloading and handing according to freight bills and freight rules and regulations. Tally is a complicated task, and its business content mainly includes checking the quantity and quality of cargos according to the bills between each link in the process of cargos transportation. Tallying business is notarized by a third party, and participants are mainly cargo, ship, and port. These personnel work together to ascertain the quantity and quality of the cargo during the cargo handover process. The tally work involves the interests of all parties. The figures are accurate and the status of the cargos is clear, which is conducive to the smooth handover and loading, unloading and handing of the cargos, and speeds up the transportation of cargos. According to the identities of the handover parties, the types of general cargo pier tally handover can be divided into: the handover between the port and the ship, the handover between the port and the cargo, the handover between the port and the tally agency, the handover within the port, and so on.

①港口与船方的交接

①Handover Between the Port and the Ship

港口与船方的交接是指港口与船方按照约定方式在装卸过程中对货物进行交付与接受,并在交付接受完成后,共同就货物数量与货物状态等内容在有关货运单证上签字确认的过程。港口与船方交接主要涉及的货运单证包括货运交接清单和货运记录。货运交接清单主要记录货物实际交接数量与货运记录的编号;货运记录主要记录在装卸过程中发现的货物残碎或灭失等情况。对于港口直装、直提的货物,由于货物基本不在港口掌管范围内,因此此类情况原则上应由货方与船方进行交接。

The handover between the port and the ship refers to the process in which the port and the ship deliver and accept the cargos in the process of loading and unloading in an agreed method, and they jointly sign the relevant shipping documents for confirmation on the quantity and status of the cargos after the completion of the delivery and acceptance. The shipping documents mainly involved in the handover between the port and the ship include the cargo handover list and the freight record. The freight handover list mainly records the actual number of cargos handed over and the number of the freight record; the freight record mainly records the broken or lost cargos found during the loading and unloading process. For cargo directly loaded or picked up directly at the port, since the cargo is basically outside the scope of the port's control, the cargo and the ship should take over such cases in principle.

②港口与货方的交接

②Handover Between the Port and the Cargo

港口与货方的交接是指港口与货方按照约定的方式在货物进出库场时,对货物数量以及状态进行核实,并在交付接受完毕后,共同就交接货物的数量与状态等内容在有关货运单证上进行签字确认的过程。出口货物入库时,港口以及作业合同中的有关内容对入库货物的名称、包装、规格、标志等进行验收,货物验收完毕后,港口应向货主签发收据。进口货物出库时,每票货物出库完毕后,货主也应签认收据。若在货物验收过程中,出现了货物残损情况,双方应共同编制货运记录。

The handover between the port and the cargo refers to the process in which the port and the cargo verify the quantity and status of the cargo when the cargo enters and exits the warehouse in an agreed manner, and they jointly sign the relevant shipping documents for confirmation on the quantity status of the cargos after the completion of the delivery and acceptance. When export cargos are put into the warehouse, the port and the relevant content in the operation contract shall check and accept the name, packaging, specifications, and signs of the incoming cargos, and the port shall issue a receipt to the cargo owner after the cargos have been checked and accepted. When the import cargos are out of the warehouse, the cargo owner should also sign the receipt after each cargo shipment is out of the warehouse. If damage to the cargos occurs during the inspection and acceptance of the cargos, the two parties shall jointly compile freight records.

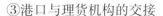

③港口与理货机构的交接

③Handover Between the Port and the Tally Agency

国际运输以件交接的货物、集装箱货物和集装箱,船方应当通过理货机构与港口经营人交接,这是专门针对国际运输货物而做出的具有特定使用范围的强制性规定。在没有做出强制性规定的情况下,船方可以自行理货也可以选择由理货机构与港口经营人进行交接。对于每作业班次的交接数量,双方应共同签认技术单。对于货物出现残损或者灭失等情况,双方还应共同签认现场记录。在全船理货交接完毕后,理货机构按照计数单和舱单,汇总编制货物溢短单;按照现场记录,汇总编制货物残损单。对于出口货物,理货机构根据计数单以及装货单,制作货物分舱单和记载图。对非强制性的委托理货业务,委托方可以是船方,也可以是收、发货人,理货机构则可以看成是委托方的受雇人(或者代理人)。此时,港口与理货机构之间的交接,可以用港口与货方及港口与船方间的交接方式和内容进行调整。

For cargos, containerized cargos and containers that are delivered by pieces in international transportation, the ship should be delivered to the port operator through a tally agency. This is a mandatory provision with a specific scope of use explicitly made for the international transportation of cargo. In the absence of compulsory regulations, the ship may tally the cargo on its own or choose to have the tally agency and the port operator carry out the handover. For the number of handovers for each work shift, both parties shall jointly sign the technical sheet. In the event of damage or loss of cargo, both parties shall also jointly sign on-site records. After the delivery of the whole ship tally is completed, the tally agency will compile the cargo overfill and short list according to the counting list and warehouse receipt; and compile the cargo damage list according to the on-site records. For export cargo, the tally agency prepares the cargo sub-manifest and record chart based on the counting list and the loading order. For non-compulsory entrusted tally business, the entrusting party can be the ship, the consignee or the consignor, and the tally agency can be regarded as the servant (or agent) of the entrusting party. At this time, the handover between the port and the tally agency can be adjusted by the way and content of the handover between the port and the cargo and the port and the ship.

④港口内部间的交接

④Handover Within the Port

港口内部间的交接指的是货物在港作业及堆存期间,港口货运部门内部依据有关货运程序进行的货物与货运单证的交接。

The handover within the port refers to the handover of cargos and shipping documents carried out by the port freight department following the relevant freight procedures during the operation and storage of the cargos in the port.

3.3.3　件杂货港口的物流活动
3.3.3　Logistics Activities of General Cargo Ports

（1）件杂货装卸操作的总体概述
（1）Overview of General Cargo Loading and Unloading Operations

件杂货港口的物流活动的关键在于装卸活动。因此,我们在本节着重介绍件杂货的装卸环节的相关理论。件杂货港口装卸活动流程与港口的装卸工艺布局密切相关。在我国最常见的布局有两种:一是船舶装卸设备与水平搬运机械组成装卸布局,该装卸布局局限性较大。能否正常进行作业,很大程度上取决于船舶是否配备装卸设备。但该布局对于港口条件、码头泊位要求低,港口建设投资少。二是由岸上装卸设备与水平搬运机械组成装卸布局。这种布局不受限于作业船舶设备情况,且码头岸机的工作范围较大,便于码头前沿堆场上的货物装卸。若作业船舶本身也配备装卸设备,则岸机可以配合船吊对船舶进行装卸,因此工作效率较高。件杂货港内装卸模式大致可分如下六类:

The key to the logistics activities of the general cargo port is the loading and unloading activities. Therefore, in this section, we focus on the relevant theories of the loading and unloading links of general cargo. The process of loading and unloading of general cargo in the port is closely related to the layout of the port's loading and unloading process. There are two most common layouts in China: One is the loading and unloading layout composed of ship loading and unloading equipment and horizontal handling machinery, and this loading and unloading layout has more significant limitations. Whether the operation can be carried out normally depends mainly on whether the ship is equipped with loading and unloading equipment. However, this layout has low requirements for port conditions and berths, and port construction investment is low. The second loading and unloading layout is composed of shore loading and unloading equipment and horizontal handling machinery. This layout is not limited to the operating ship equipment, and the operating range of the pier shore machine is large, which is convenient for cargo loading and unloading on the quayside of the pier. If the working ship is equipped with loading and unloading equipment, the shore machine can cooperate with the ship crane to load and unload the ship, so the work efficiency is higher. The loading and unloading modes of general cargo in the port can be roughly divided into the following six categories:

模式1被称为"船—船运作模式"。该模式可进一步分为船—船外挡过驳作业和船—船里挡过驳作业。①船—船外挡过驳作业,即装货船靠在卸货船的外挡,卸货船利用自身配备的装卸设备将货物直接从外挡卸至装货船。这种作业流程不需占用港口泊位,但受外挡水域条件与作业船舶设备配置的限制。②船—船里挡过驳作业,即装货船与卸货船停靠在相邻的泊位,使用岸吊或者船吊从卸货船上卸下货物,通过牵引车将货物运送至装货船停靠的泊位,再由岸吊或者船吊进行装船作业(如图3.7所示)。船—船作业模式下,货物不进入码头堆场而只在码头前沿流转,可以有效缓解码头堆场压力,节约码头人力资源,具有较高的装卸效率。

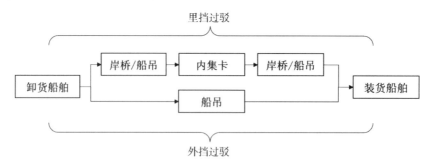

图 3.7 船—船运作模式

(图片来源:杨茅甄.件杂货港口管理实务[M]. 2 版. 上海:上海人民出版社,2015.)

Mode 1 is called the "ship – ship operation mode". This mode can be further divided into ship – outboard barge transfer operations and ship – inboard barge transfer operations.①Ship – outboard barge transfer operations,that is,the loading ship is leaning on the outer barge of the unloading ship,and the unloading ship uses its own loading and unloading equipment to unload the cargos directly from the outer barge to the loading ship. This kind of operation process does not need to occupy a port berth,but is restricted by the conditions of the outer water area and the equipment configuration of the operation vessel.②Ship – inboard barge transfer operations,that is,the loading ship and the unloading ship are docked at adjacent berths,the quay crane or ship crane is used to unload the cargo from the unloading ship,and the cargo is transported to the berth where the loading ship is docked by the tractor,and then the ship loading operations are carried out by quay cranes or ship cranes (as shown in Figure 3.7). In the ship – ship operation mode,the cargo does not enter the yard but only circulates at the quayside of the pier,which can effectively relieve the pressure on the dock,save the pier human resources,and has a higher loading and unloading efficiency.

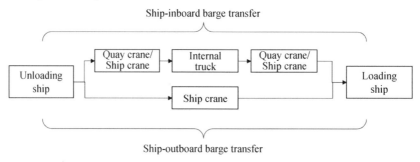

Figure 3.7 Ship – ship operation mode

模式 2 被称为"船—场运作模式"。该模式下,货物由船吊或岸吊卸下,再通过牵引车将货物运送至堆场,由场桥进行堆垛作业(如图 3.8 所示)。该模式也可按逆方向运用于件杂货装船作业。

图 3.8 船—场运作流程

Mode 2 is called the "ship – yard operation mode". In this mode, the cargo is unloaded by a ship crane or quay crane, and then transported to the yard by a tractor, and the yard crane is used for stacking operations (as shown in Figure 3.8). This mode can also be used in the reverse direction for general cargo loading operations.

Figure 3.8 Ship – yard operation mode

模式 3 被称为"船—车运作模式"。该模式下,货物通过作业设备从船上卸下后,不进入码头堆场,而是直接装上提货卡车或火车(如图 3.9 所示)。该作业流程也可按逆方向运用于件杂货装船作业。这种作业流程的操作环节少,能够节约码头堆场空间,提高码头作业效率,加快货物运输速度。由于岸吊作业效率高于卡车或火车的作业效率,可能导致岸吊等待卡车,从而出现作业中断的现象。而若配备足够多的卡车配合岸吊作业,则有可能导致道路拥堵。为解决此问题,件杂货码头通常将"船—卡车"和"船—场"两种作业流程同时进行。在提货车辆到达时,通过"船—卡车"作业流程,直接将货物装车;在提货车辆未到达时,码头将卸下的货物运送至堆场保管,车辆直接去码头堆场提货装车。

图 3.9 船—车运作模式

Mode 3 is called the "ship – vehicle operation mode". In this mode, after the cargo is unloaded from the ship through the operating equipment, it does not enter the dockyard, but is directly loaded onto the pick-up truck or train (as shown in Figure 3.9). The operational process can also be applied in the reverse direction for general cargo loading operations. This kind of operation process has few operation links, which can save the space of the yard, improve the efficiency of the pier operation, and speed up the transportation of cargo. Since the operation efficiency of the quay crane is higher than that of a truck or train, it may cause the quay crane to wait for the truck, and the operation may be interrupted. If enough trucks are equipped to work with quay cranes, it may cause road congestion. In order to solve this problem, general cargo piers usually carry out the two operating processes of "ship – truck" and "ship – yard" at the same time. When the pick-up vehicle arrives, the cargo is directly loaded into the vehicle through the "ship – truck" operation process; When the pick-up vehicle does not arrive, the pier will transport the unloaded cargos to the yard for storage, and the vehicle will pick up and load the truck directly at the yard.

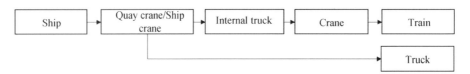

Figure 3.9　Ship－vehicle operation mode

模式 4 被称为"场—车运作模式"。这种模式是指货物从码头堆场通过火车或卡车运出码头(如图 3.10 所示)。若选择卡车出栈,则货物在码头堆场拆垛后,直接装上提货卡车运出码头。若选择火车出栈,则货物在码头堆场拆垛后,需要通过牵引车将货物运送至铁路线,再通过作业设备装上火车运出码头,该运作流程同样可逆。

图 3.10　场—车运作模式

Mode 4 is called the "yard－vehicle operation mode". This mode means that cargos are transported from the pier yard by train or truck out of the pier (as shown in Figure 3.10). If the truck is selected to be out of the stack, the cargos will be directly loaded onto the pick-up truck and transported out of the pier after the cargos are unstacked at the pier yard. If the train is selected to be out of the stack, the cargos need to be transported to the railway line by a tractor after the cargos are unstacked at the pier yard, and then loaded on the train by the operating equipment to be transported out of the pier, this operation process is also reversible.

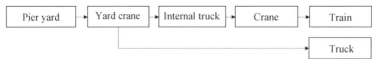

Figure 3.10　Yard-vehicle operation mode

模式 5 称作"场—场运作模式",指由于某种需求,需要将码头内某处堆场的货物转移至另一堆场,或转移至港外疏运堆场(见图 3.11)。具体作业流程为:货物在某堆场由场桥进行拆垛,然后通过牵引车将货物运送至另一处堆场,最后由场桥进行堆垛。该作业模式的实施,有利于提高码头库场的管理水平,保证了码头库场的堆存能力。

图 3.11　场—场运作模式

Mode 5 is called "yard－yard operation mode", which refers to the need to transfer cargo from a particular yard in the pier to another yard or transfer to a deportation stacking area outside the port due to a particular demand (as shown in Figure 3.11). The specific operation process is: the cargos are unstacked by the yard crane at a particular yard, and then the cargos are transported to another yard by a tractor, and finally stacked by the yard crane. The implementation of this operation mode is conducive to improving the management level of the pier warehouse and ensuring the storage capacity of the pier warehouse.

Figure 3.11　Yard-yard operation mode

模式6称为"车—车运作模式",是指货物从火车卸下,装上卡车出栈,或以卡车形式进栈,再被装上火车出栈(如图 3.12 所示)。这种运作流程要求码头配备火车轨道等基础设施。

图3.12　车—车运作模式

Mode 6 is called "vehicle-vehicle operation mode", which means that the cargos are unloaded from the train, loaded on the truck and out of the stack, or put into the stack in the form of a truck, and then loaded on the train and removed from the stack (as shown in Figure 3.12). This operation process requires the pier to be equipped with infrastructure such as train tracks.

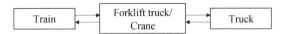

Figure 3.12　Vehicle-vehicle operation mode

不论采用上述何种装卸作业模式,件杂货港口的作业活动均涉及如下几个具体的物流作业,具体包括舱底作业、起落舱作业、水平搬运作业、车内作业以及库场作业等。

Regardless of the loading and unloading operation mode as mentioned above, the operations of the general cargo port involve the following specific logistics operations, including bilge operations, landing cabin operations, horizontal handling operations, in-vehicle operations, and warehouse operations.

①舱底作业

①Bilge Operations

装船和卸船时,件杂货舱底作业工序包括在舱内摘挂钩、拆码货组、拆码垛及平舱、清舱等作业。因为件杂货在水路运输过程中,多以单件堆装,故在卸船作业时,需工作人员进入舱内,利用托盘、网络对件杂货分组,然后才能调运出舱;在装船作业时,也相应需要安排工作人员进舱拆组。故舱底作业消耗大量人力、时间成本,但由于件杂货单件运输的性质,改进此作业较为困难,因此这一物流作业活动是件杂货码头作业线中最容易造成效率"瓶颈"的工序。

The bilge operation process of general cargo includes unloading hooks in the cabin, unstacking cargo group, unstacking, trimming and clearing the cabin during loading and unloading. Because general cargos are primarily stacked in single piece during waterway transportation, so during unloading operations, workers need to enter the cabin and use pallets and networks to group the general cargos into groups before they can be transported out of the cabin; It is also necessary to arrange workers to enter the cabin and disassemble the group accordingly during the loading operation. Therefore, the bilge operation consumes a lot of workforce and time cost. However,

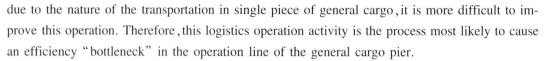
due to the nature of the transportation in single piece of general cargo, it is more difficult to improve this operation. Therefore, this logistics operation activity is the process most likely to cause an efficiency "bottleneck" in the operation line of the general cargo pier.

②起落舱作业

②Landing Cabin Operations

起落舱作业工序包括装船和卸船时船舱到岸、岸到船舱、船舱到车辆、车辆到船舱以及船舱到船舱的作业。该作业工序是船舶装卸作业流程中的主导环节。作业过程中,主要使用船吊机械与岸吊机械,工人在此环节主要承担船边拆挂钩和喊钩等辅助任务。

The landing cabin operation process include cabin-to-shore, shore-to-cabin, cabin-to-vehicle, vehicle-to-cabin, and cabin-to-cabin operations during loading and unloading. This operation procedure is the top link in the ship loading and unloading operation process. During the operation, ship crane machinery and quay crane machinery are mainly used, and workers mainly undertake auxiliary tasks such as the ship side dismantling of hooks and calling hooks in this link.

③水平搬运作业

③Horizontal handling Operations

水平搬运作业工序主要是货物在码头库场车辆间的搬运作业。码头前沿与码头后方堆场通过此工序连接。作业任务主要由水平搬运机械承担,如牵引车、挂车等。在进行船舶装卸作业时,应注意协调水平搬运作业效率与起落舱作业效率,避免出现岸吊等车或作业中断等现象。

The horizontal handling operation process is mainly the handling of cargos between vehicles in the pier warehouse. The quayside of the pier and rear yard are connected through this process. The task of this operation is mainly undertaken by horizontal transportation machinery, such as tractors and trailers, et al. When carrying out ship loading and unloading operations, attention should be paid to coordinating the efficiency of horizontal transportation with the efficiency of landing cabin operation to avoid the phenomenon of quay crane waiting for vehicles or interruption of operations.

④车内作业

④In-vehicle Operations

车内作业工序包括装卸车辆时的上下搬动、拆码货组及车内的拆码垛作业。车内作业一般需要考虑库场装卸作业机械。

The in-vehicle operation process includes the up and down movement when loading and unloading the vehicle, the unstacking cargo group and the unstacking operation in the vehicle. In-vehicle operations generally need to consider the loading and unloading machinery of the warehouse.

⑤库场作业

⑤Warehouse Operations

库场作业工序是指库场内的拆码垛、拆码货组等作业。该作业工序包括库场内货物的拆码垛、拆码货组、供喂料、理货分唛等工作。其中,拆码垛是指将成垛货物拆开和码好;供喂料是指将物料按照顺序运送至作业机械的过程。理货分唛是指件杂货在库场作业时,需要按唛头进行区分,这是装卸过程中必须存在的环节,但也是一项烦琐、耗时的作业。

Warehouse operation process refers to the operations such as unstacking and unstacking cargo groups in the warehouse. The operation process includes unstacking, unstacking cargo groups, the feeding, and the tally marking in the warehouse. Among them, unstacking refers to unpacking and stacking up the piled cargos. Feeding refers to the process of transporting materials to the operating machinery in order. Tally marking refers to the need to distinguish the general cargos according to their marks when operating in the warehouse. This link must exist in the loading and unloading process, and it is also a tedious and time-consuming operation.

件杂货码头装卸作业系统是一个典型离散动态事件系统。因件杂货物种类繁多,外形尺寸不一,装卸机械新旧状况、作业负荷不同,且作业过程中涉及汽车、火车、航运等多种运输方式,码头作业系统具有较高的复杂性。因此,在涉及件杂货码头装卸工艺时,要求装卸设备具有一定的通用性,且适应进口与出口的双向货流作业。同时,为了提高码头经济效益,在装卸过程中,还应要求各作业环节的生产率应服从主导机械的作业能力,即各环节配备的机械数量,应以满足主导机械的作业效率为标准。

The loading and unloading operation of the general cargo pier system is a typical discrete dynamic event system. Due to the wide variety of general cargo, different dimensions, new and old conditions of the loading and unloading machinery, different operating loads, and various transportation modes such as automobiles, trains, and shipping and so on in the operation process, the pier operating system has a high complexity. Therefore, when it comes to the loading and unloading process of general cargo piers, the loading and unloading equipment must have a certain degree of versatility and adapt to the two-way cargo flow operation of import and export. At the same time, in order to improve the economic efficiency of the pier, during the loading and unloading process, the productivity of each operation link should be required to obey the operating ability of the leading machinery, that is, the number of machines equipped in each link should meet the operating efficiency of the leading machinery as the standard.

（2）袋装类货物装卸活动实务
(2) Practice of Loading and Unloading Bagged Cargos

件杂货装卸工作一般采取成组运输的方式,以提高工作效率。但对于不同种类的货物,其成组方式各有侧重、不尽相同。因此,这里首先对袋装类货物装卸作业中的成组方式做简单介绍,其典型成组方式主要有网络、托盘、集装袋三种。

The loading and unloading of general cargo generally adopt group transportation to improve work efficiency. However, for different cargos, the grouping methods have different emphasis and are not the same. Therefore, here is a brief introduction to the grouping methods in the loading and unloading operation of bagged cargos. The typical grouping methods mainly include networks, pallets, and container bags.

网络成组,即利用网络,按照规定堆垛方法,通过人工将额定数量的袋装类货物(单件重量在30~50 kg)放入成组;托盘成组,即利用托盘,按照规定堆垛方法,将额定数量的袋装类货物(单件重量不超过30 kg)放入成组;集装袋成组,即利用强力纤维制作,类似于网络但比网络更为韧性的集装袋,将小包装袋装类货物放入成组,一般在港口或库场完成。

The network is grouped, that is, using the network, according to the prescribed stacking method, to manually put the rated quantity of bagged cargos (the weight of each piece is 30~50 kg) into the group. The pallet is grouped, that is, using pallets, according to the prescribed stacking method, to put the rated quantity of bagged cargos (the weight of single piece is not exceeding 30 kg) into the group. The flexible freight bags is grouped, that is, it is made of strong fibre, which is similar to the network but is more flexible than the network, put the small package bag cargos into groups, which are usually completed at the port or warehouse.

袋装类货物常用装卸工具主要包括:绳索、链条钩、网络、托盘等。装卸中应根据货物的属性来配置不同的网络。同时必须遵循安全规定,定时、定点检查工属具,立即更换损坏超过安全规定的工具。

Commonly used tools and attachments for bagged cargo mainly include: ropes, chain hooks, networks, pallets, etc. During loading and unloading, different networks should be configured according to the attributes of the cargo. At the same time, the safety regulations must be followed, the tools and attachments must be checked regularly and at fixed points, and the tools that are damaged beyond the safety regulations must be replaced immediately.

码头前沿垂直作业时,以船舶装卸设备(起重双吊、起重单吊等)和码头岸机(门式起重机、高架起重机、轮胎式龙门吊等)为主;水平运输作业时,一般使用牵引车拖带挂车。在配置牵引车时,必须遵循水平运输能力必须大于等于垂直运输能力的原则:当水平运输距离小于250 m时,一般以一台牵引车、两台平板车的组合为主;当水平运输距离大于等于250 m时,一般以两台(或两台以上)牵引车,三台或三台以上平板车的组合为主;库场作业时,通常使用轮胎式龙门吊堆桩。仓库内作业,也可以使用叉车。

When working vertically at the quayside of the pier, ship loading and unloading equipment (double cranes, single cranes, etc.) and pier quay cranes (gantry cranes, overhead cranes, rubber tired gantry cranes, etc.) are mainly used; For horizontal transportation, a towage is generally used to tow a trailer. When configuring a tractor, the principle that the horizontal transportation capacity must be greater than or equal to the vertical transportation capacity must be followed; When the horizontal transportation distance is less than 250 m, generally a combination of one tractor and two flatbed vehicles is the main choice; When the horizontal transportation distance is greater than or equal to 250 m, generally a combination of two (or more than two) tractors and three or more flatbed vehicles are the main choice; For warehouse operations, rubber tired gantry cranes are usually used to stack the piles. For operations in the warehouse, forklifts truck can also be used.

袋装货物装卸人力安排的基本原则:为了使配备机械主机得到充分发挥,工人的作业能力应大于等于机械的作业效率,且应配备专人指挥。袋装类货物装卸流程较为复杂,装卸效率低、成本高,故应优先采取船—船、船—车直取作业,尽量减少操作环节,并运用成组方式进行搬运、堆拆垛。袋装货物装卸操作要求结合船舶货舱等条件,综合考虑货物妥善、安全、合理的装卸与货物运输保管要求等条件,保证货物完好交付,按时到达。下面我们重点介绍袋装货物舱、库、车内的各装卸操作流程。

The basic principle of manpower arrangement for bagged cargos loading and unloading: in order to make the machine equipped with the main engine fully utilized, the working ability of the workers should be greater than or equal to the operation efficiency of the machine, and special personnel should be assigned to command. The loading and unloading process of bagged cargo is more complicated, with low loading and unloading efficiency and high cost. Therefore, direct ship – ship and ship – vehicle pickup operations should be given priority to minimize operation links, and use group methods for handling, stacking and unstacking. The handling of bagged cargos requires the combination of ship's cargo cabin and other conditions, comprehensive consideration of conditions such as proper, safe, and reasonable loading and unloading of cargos, and cargo transportation and storage requirements, so as to ensure that the cargos are delivered in good condition and arrives on time. Below we focus on the loading and unloading operation procedures of the bagged cargos in the cabin, warehouse, and vehicle.

①袋装货物舱内操作

①Cabin Operation of Bagged Cargos

装船作业直接影响到船舶航行的安全和货物运输的质量,因此需要总揽全局、综合考虑,而重中之重考虑的还是如何实现正确、合理的配载,装船工作中采用的操作方法是否正确、货舱关系、货货关系能否得到正确处理。装船作业时,舱内用人力散堆,一般采用顺船打墩子,然后由四周向舱口逐层堆码的作业方法。若舱内空间较大,即舱壁与舱口的距离较远时,可选择适合的机具配合工人进行搬运,来减少工人劳动量,提高安全性;若舱内采取分段装载,分段长度一般不小于舱口长度的1/2,处于间隔分段位置的袋装货物应顺船头方向堆码,且货物密封口方向应当朝里。

Ship loading operations directly affect the safety of ship navigation and the quality of cargo transportation. Therefore, it is necessary to have an overview and comprehensive consideration. The most important consideration is how to achieve the correct and reasonable stowage, whether the operating methods adopted in the loading work are correct, and whether the cargo-hold relationship and the cargo-cargo relationship can be handled correctly. When loading the ship, the cabins are scattered and piled by manpower. Generally, piles are built along the ship, and then stacked layer by layer from all sides to the hatch. If the space in the cabin is large, that is, when the distance between the bulkhead and the hatch is long, suitable machinery can be selected to cooperate with the workers to carry it, so as to reduce the workload of workers and improve safety. If the cabin is loaded in sections, the section length is generally not less than 1/2 of the length of the hatch. The bagged cargos in the spaced section position should be stacked in the direction of the bow, and the sealing part direction should be inward.

卸船作业时,首先应开舱通风,且通风时间自开启舱盖后,不应少于2 h。如若舱内通风设备不完备,无法实现顺畅通风,应配备风机等机具通风,且严令禁止工人盲目下舱。时刻观察反映工人情况,如有异状,应立即召集所有工人撤离。卸船时,分票卸货,由舱口向四周发散式逐层处理,且应该时刻关注货物残损情况。对于在卸货过程中发现的残损货物,应当及时与船方沟通,取得签认,并做好记录,再搬运出舱。

When unloading the ship, the cabin should be opened for ventilation first, and the ventilation time should not be less than 2 h after opening the hatch. If the ventilation equipment in the cabin is not complete and smooth ventilation cannot be achieved, fans and other equipment should be equipped for ventilation, and workers are strictly prohibited from getting out of the cabin blindly. Observe and report the workers' conditions at all times. If there is any abnormality, all workers should be called to evacuate immediately. When unloading the ship, the cargo is unloaded in batches, and the cargo is handled layer by layer in a divergent manner from the hatch to the surroundings, and the damage of the cargo should always be paid attention to. For damaged cargos found during unloading, they should communicate with the ship in a timely manner, obtain an approval, and make a record before moving them out of the cabin.

②袋装类货物库场操作

②Warehouse Operation of Bagged Cargos

首先要清理现场,这项流程位于所有库场堆垛作业之前,以达到平整路面,稳固搬运所需道路的作用。若货物易受潮,还需铺垫木板等。而后,进行库场堆垛。应尽可能采用机械成组堆垛的方式,提高效率且保障作业人员安全。若需要工人登高进行堆垛作业,应选择好站立位置,且时刻为工人留好空余位置,防止坠落等问题发生。接着进行拆垛。拆垛工人应先检查货垛是否牢固,有无倾倒危险。拆垛作业必须自上而下依次进行,不得反向操作,以免货垛倒塌伤人,且应指定专人负责发出信号指挥机械司机。

The first step is to clean up the site. This process is located before all warehouse stacking operations to level the road surface and stabilize the required road for transportation. If the cargo is susceptible to moisture, planks should be laid. After that, the warehouse stacking is carried out. The mechanical group stacking method should be used as much as possible to improve efficiency and ensure the safety of operators. If workers are required to climb high for stacking operations, they should choose a standing position, and keep a free position for workers at all times to prevent problems such as falling. Then proceed to unstack. The workers should first check whether the stacks are firm and there is no danger of dumping. The unstack operation must be carried out sequentially from top to bottom, and the reverse operation is not allowed, so as to avoid the collapse of the stack and hurting people, and a special person should be designated to send a signal to command the mechanical driver.

③袋装类货物车内操作

③In-vehicle Operation of Bagged Cargos

袋装类货物进出件杂货港口主要依靠水路、公路和铁路运输。故除船舶装卸外,港口还有大量汽车和铁路车辆的装卸作业。与船舶装卸相比,车辆装卸工作空间小,单位装卸量小,作业频率高,装卸效率低。因其特殊性,必须充分重视车辆装卸作业的管理。袋装类货物车内操作时,首先要做好车厢清洁,以保证货物包装不会受到污染;装车时,要注意货物密封口向车里,严禁倒关。当一块网络使用完毕后,应该及时回收,可以通过工人带回,也可以挂在叉车或者吊机的钩头上顺便带回。若车内货物系拆组堆码,作业时袋装货物应沿车宽方向横向堆码,并逐层堆码、摆放整齐;装车后,应针对车厢盖好防雨篷布,系好固定绳并仔细检查。如果货物包装在卸货过程中损坏,应区分作业残损和原有残损,并做好货运记录,同时及时收集、堆放泄漏货物,更换损坏的货物包装。

The entry and exit of bagged cargos in and out of general cargo ports mainly relies on waterway, road and rail transportation. Therefore, in addition to the loading and unloading of ships, there are also a large number of loading and unloading operations of automobiles and railway vehicles in the port. Compared with the loading and unloading of ships, the work space of the loading and unloading of vehicles is small, the unit loading and unloading volume is small, the operation frequency is high, and the loading and unloading efficiency is low. Due to its particularity, full attention must be paid to the management of the loading and unloading operations of ships. When handling bagged cargos in the vehicle, the compartment must be cleaned first to ensure that the packaging of the cargos will not be contaminated; When loading the vehicle, pay attention to the sealing of the cargos into the vehicle, and it is strictly forbidden to go back. When a piece of network is used up, it should be recycled in time. It can be brought back by workers, or hung on the hook of a forklift truck or crane. If the cargo in the vehicle is disassembled and stacked, the bagged cargo should be stacked horizontally along the width of the vehicle during operation, and stacked layer by layer and placed neatly; After loading the vehicle, cover the compartment with a rainproof tarp, fasten the fixing rope and check carefully. If the packaging of the cargos is damaged during the unloading process, distinguish the operation damage and the original damage, and make a record of the freight. At the same time, collect and stack the leaked cargos in time, and replace the packaging of damaged cargos.

(3) 箱装类货物装卸活动实务
(3) Practice of Loading and Unloading of Boxed Cargos

箱装类货物的成组方式与袋装类货物相比较为简单。但面对不同客户需要,其在各个场景下是否选择成组,需要综合考虑。其成组方式一般为"单纯成组",即利用特定设备,将单件货物集合成一组,然后由装卸设备进行作业。根据运输过程中是否依然成组,可进一步分为两种情况:若成组运输,其优点是工人劳动强度较低,运输效率较高,缺点是投入的工具成本较高;若单件运输,其优点是投入的工具成本较低,缺点是工人劳动强度较高。

The grouping of boxed cargos is simpler than that of bagged cargos. However, in the face of different customer needs, whether they choose to form a group in each scenario needs to be considered comprehensively. The grouping method is generally "simple grouping", that is, using specific equipment to gather single pieces of cargos into a group, and then the operations are carried out by loading and unloading equipment. According to whether the transportation is still in groups, it can be further divided into two situations: If the transportation is in a group, the advantages are low labor intensity of workers, and higher transportation efficiency, the disadvantage is the higher cost of input tools; If the transportation is in a single, the advantage is the lower cost of input tools, but the disadvantage is that the labor intensity of workers is relatively high.

箱装类货物的常用工具主要有:托盘、撑杆和吊索等。托盘,又称货板或托架,属于箱装货物成组作业的主承载工具。撑杆,又称吊架,属于箱装货物成组作业的间接工具,是货盘的配套工具,可以起到改变吊具的吊挂模式,避免吊索直接与货物外包装接触,导致货物挤压受损。与货盘配套的吊索也属于主承载工具,是指在起重机械和货盘之间起柔性连接作用的工具,常用的吊索包括钢丝绳吊索与纤维绳吊索。钢丝绳吊索属于传统的常用吊索,价格低廉,比较耐用,但表面较硬、容易产生毛刺,有可能对货物表面造成刮擦。纤维绳吊索属于近年来出现的新型吊索,其强度高、柔软、重量轻,不会对货物造成刮擦,但其价格相对较高。箱装类货物的装卸操作主要分为舱内操作、库场操作和车内操作三部分。

Commonly used tools for boxed cargos mainly include: pallets, struts and slings. The pallet, also known as the tray or bracket, is the main load-bearing tool for group operation of boxed cargos. The strut, also known as the hanger, is an indirect tool for the group operation of boxed cargos. It is a supporting tool for the pallet, which can change the hanging mode of the spreader and avoid the direct contact between the sling and the outer packaging of the cargos, which may cause the cargos to be squeezed and damaged. The sling matched with the pallet also belongs to the main load-bearing tool, which refers to the tool that acts as a flexible connection between the hoisting machinery and the pallet. Commonly used slings include wire rope sling and fiber rope sling. Wire rope slings are traditional and commonly used slings. They are inexpensive and durable, but the surface is hard and prone to burrs, which may cause scratches on the surface of the cargos. Fiber rope slings are new types of slings that have appeared in recent years. They are high in strength, soft, and light in weight. They will not scratch the cargos, but their tariff are relatively high. The loading and unloading operations of boxed cargos are mainly divided into three parts: cargo cabin operation, warehouse operation and in-vehicle operation.

①箱装类货物舱内装卸操作

①Cabin Operation of Boxed Cargos

箱装类货物舱内装卸操作,是指货物在船舱内(包括舱口围及舱四周)的装卸作业。箱装类货物舱内作业时要注意以下事项:装卸作业开始前,应先对货舱进行通风换气,排除有害气体,确认安全并达到适工条件后,作业人员才能下舱作业;随后相关人员应先对货物的状态、规格、单重、积载进行核实,若有货损,应及时通知相关部门进行处理;上述工作完成后,作业人员开始评估舱口长度、船机设备等情况,安排装卸方案。选用吊具时,应优先选用专用吊具,对货运质量有要求的货物应选用纤维绳吊索。在舱内作业过程中,箱类货物除体积过大或者单件重量过大不宜成组外,凡批量过大,规格相同的货物,应采用托盘进行成组装卸。舱内卸载时,应先卸舱口围,后卸舱四周。在船舱四周卸货作业时,一般使用装卸机械,协助作业人员将货物搬移至舱口沿,再进行成组。进行装载作业时,应该按照装载图要求进行作业,先装舱四周,后装舱口围,并按照要求堆放整齐、稳固。

Cabin operation of boxed cargos refers to the loading and unloading operations of boxed cargos in the cabin (including the hatch and around the cabin). When working in the cargo cabin of boxed cargo, pay attention to the following: Before loading and unloading operations, the cargo cabin should be ventilated to remove harmful gases, and after the safety is confirmed and the working conditions are met, the operator can disembark. Afterwards, the relevant personnel should first verify the status, specifications, unit weight, and stowage of the cargo. If there is damage to the cargo, they should notify the relevant departments for handling; After the completion of the above work, the operators begin to assess the length of the hatch, the ship's machinery and equipment, etc., and arrange the loading and unloading plan. When selecting spreaders, special spreaders should be preferred, and fiber rope slings should be used for cargos that require freight quality. In the process of cabin operations, except for boxed cargos that are too bulky or too heavy for a single piece to be grouped, cargos with too large batches and the same specifications should be assembled and unloaded on pallets. When unloading in the cabin, the cargos around hatch coaming should be unloaded, and then cargos around the cabin. When unloading cargo around the cabin, the loading and unloading machinery is generally used to assist the operators in moving the cargo to the edge of the hatch, and then forming a group. When carrying out the loading operation, the operation should be carried out in accordance with the requirements of the loading plan. The cargos around the cabin should be loading first, and then the cargos around hatch coaming should be loading, and the stack should be neat and stable according to the requirements.

②箱装类货物库场操作

②Warehouse Operation of Boxed Cargos

箱装类货物库场操作,是指货物在仓库或露天堆场内的装卸作业。库场作业过程中,应按照符合有关规定的堆垛标准进行铺垫和堆垛,拆、堆货垛应一票一清,一码一清,且货物堆放应按照库场有关工作人员的要求和货物特性、包装、摆放的要求进行。货堆之间,货堆与墙之间,应视货物种类与库场条件不同,留出合适的通道。堆垛作业时,堆垛高度应符合安全标准,且货物应重不压轻、大不压小,货物堆垛稳固牢靠。拆垛作业时,应符合安全要求,从上到下分层分批进行作业。

Warehouse operation of boxed cargos refers to the loading and unloading operations of cargos in warehouses or open yards. During the operation of the warehouse, paving and stacking should be carried out in accordance with the stacking standards that meet the relevant regulations. Destacking and stacking should be cleared for each ticket and cleared for each yard, and the storage of cargos should be carried out in accordance with the requirements of the relevant staff of the warehouse and the characteristics of the cargos, packaging and placement. Appropriate passages should be set aside between cargo piles and between cargo piles and walls, depending on the types of cargos and the conditions of the warehouse. During the stacking operation, the stacking height should meet the safety standards, and the cargo should be heavy not pressing light, large not pressing small, and the cargos should be stacked firmly and securely. During the unstacking operation, the safety requirements should be met, and the operation should be carried out in batches from top to bottom.

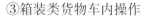

③箱装类货物车内操作

③In-vehicle Operation of Boxed Cargos

箱装类货物车内操作,是指货物在铁路车辆(棚车、敞车)和汽车(平板车)内的装卸作业。作业开始前,工作人员应检查车辆状况,并根据作业货物种类和要求对车厢进行铺垫和清扫。开始装卸作业前,应检查装卸设备作业范围内有无障碍物,保证装卸过程的顺利进行。铁路敞车作业时,货物积载应符合铁路部门的规定,装载货物均衡,不集重,不偏重,不超重,装载货物顺序应先里后外。货物装卸汽车作业时,货物积载应符合交通规定,装卸货物时应轻搬轻放,按层次从车辆行驶方向的前端,依次向后装载。

In-vehicle operation of boxed cargos refers to the loading and unloading operations of boxed cargos in railway vehicles (box vehicles, gondola vehicles) and vehicles (flat vehicles). Before the start of the operation, the staff should check the condition of the vehicle, prepare and clean the compartment according to the type of cargos and requirements of the operation. Before starting the loading and unloading operations, check that there are no obstacles in the working range of the loading and unloading equipment to ensure the smooth progress of the loading and unloading process. When operating a railway gondola vehicles, the stowage of cargos shall comply with the regulations of the railway department. The load shall be balanced, not heavy, partial, and overweight. The order of loading cargos shall be inside first and then outside. When loading and unloading cargos by vehicles, the stowage of cargos shall comply with the traffic regulations. When loading and unloading cargos, they shall be carried lightly and lowered gently and shall be loaded from the front end of the vehicle's driving direction according to the level, in turn backward loading.

(4)桶装类货物装卸活动实务

(4) Practice of Loading and Unloading of Barreled Cargos

桶装类货物成组方式主要有"上吊"和"下托"两种。上吊成组,即利用吊架(矩形),通过吊机等专用吊具将桶装货物均匀悬挂在吊架上成组,其多运用于直立运输的桶装货物的吊运操作;下托成组,即利用托盘,通过吊机等专用吊具将桶装货物整齐布置在托盘上成组。成组前需要人工在托盘上堆码,成组后可以保持成组于全物流过程,有利于提高后程效率。

There are mainly two ways of grouping barreled cargos:"hanging" and "dropping". Hanging into groups, that is, using a hanger (rectangular) to evenly suspend the barreled cargos on the hanger through special spreaders such as cranes to form a group, which is mostly used for the lifting operation of the barreled cargos for vertical transportation; Dropping into groups, that is, using a pallet to neatly arranged the barreled cargos on the pallet through special spreaders such as cranes to form a group. Manual stacking on pallets is required before grouping. After grouping, the group of cargos can be kept in the whole logistics process, which is beneficial to improve the efficiency of the next process.

桶装类货物装卸过程一般由"船—场""船—船""船—车""场—车""场—场"等五种物流运作流程组成,这些流程都可以双向运作。桶装类货物不同的装卸工艺流程,应相应配备不同的装卸设备、装卸工具和进行人力安排。

The loading and unloading process of barreled cargos is generally composed of five kinds of logistics operation processes:"ship-yard","ship-ship","ship-vehicle","yard-vehicle" and "yard-yard". These processes can all operate in both directions. Different loading and unloading process of barreled cargos should be equipped with different loading and unloading equipment,loading and unloading tools and manpower arrangements accordingly.

桶装类货物常用工属具主要有:卧式桶钩、三爪桶钩、立式桶钩等。卧式桶钩适用于装卸在船舱或车厢(卡车或铁路敞车车厢)内横卧装载的桶装货物。在操作上,卧式桶钩在挂钩时,为避免翻钩,应先注意理顺链条;三爪桶钩和立式桶钩均用于装卸在船舱或车厢(卡车或铁路敞车车厢)内直立装载的桶装货物。在使用三爪桶钩和立式桶钩时,为避免挂钩脱落,必须选定好较为合适的挂钩位置,并在挂钩后上好保险,保持挂钩的稳定。上述三种桶钩,一般均只适用于以铁桶包装的桶装货物。

Commonly used tools for barreled cargos mainly include horizontal barrel hooks,three-claw barrel hooks,and vertical barrel hooks. The horizontal barrel hook is suitable for loading and unloading barreled cargos loaded horizontally in the cabin or carriage (truck or railway gondola). In operation,when the horizontal barrel hook is hooked,in order to avoid turning the hook,you should first straighten out the chain;Both three-claw barrel hooks and vertical barrel hooks are used for loading and unloading barreled cargos that are loaded upright in the cabin or carriage (truck or railway gondola). When using three-claw barrel hooks and vertical barrel hooks,in order to prevent the hooks from falling off,it is necessary to select a more suitable hook position, and secure the hook,to maintain the stability of the hook. The above three barrel hooks are generally only suitable for barreled cargos packed in iron barrels.

垂直运输作业时,码头前沿可选用门式起重机、船用起重机、轮胎式起重机等。库场或装卸卡车、铁路敞车,一般使用轮胎式起重机等;水平运输作业时,码头前沿与库场之间的水平运输,可以选用汽车、牵引车、叉车等。对于叉车来说,可以装配堆叠叉,使其既可以进行桶装货物的水平运输,也可以进行堆垛作业。

For vertical transportation operations, gantry cranes, marine cranes, and rubber-tired cranes can be used at the quayside of the pier. Warehouse yards or loading and unloading trucks, railway gondola vehicles, generally use tire cranes, etc.;During horizontal handling operations, for horizontal transportation between the quayside of the pier and the warehouse yard,you can use vehicles,tractors,forklifts,etc. For forklifts,stacking forks can be assembled so that they can be used for horizontal transportation of barreled cargos and stacking operations.

在配工方面,"上吊"和"下托"两种装卸方式是有所差别的:用"上吊"方式进行成组装卸作业时,舱内或车内仅需配备两个工人,进行挂、拆钩作业,对工人体力要求不大,但需要工人挂钩经验丰富。因为在上吊货物过程中,挂钩的选位非常重要,直接影响作业的效率和安全程度;如用下托方式进行成组装卸作业,则舱内会根据垂直运输机械效率而决定配工人数,一般都会配备较多组工人。桶装类货物的装卸操作具体内容如下:

In terms of workmanship,there is a difference between the two loading and unloading methods：When using the hanging method for assembly and unloading operations, only two workers in the cabin or in the vehicle need to be equipped for hooking and unhooking operations, which does not require much physical strength for the workers, but require the worker with rich hooking experience. Because in the process of hanging cargos, the selection of the position of the hook is very important, which directly affects the efficiency and safety of the operation. If the assembly and unloading operations are carried out by the dropping method, the number of workers in the cabin will be determined according to the efficiency of the vertical transport machinery, and generally there will be more groups of workers. The specific contents of the loading and unloading operations of barreled cargos are as follows：

①桶装类货物舱内操作

①Cabin Operation of Barreled Cargos

由于桶装货物经常装有化工制品，故应严格执行开舱通风(具体操作可参考袋装类货物舱内作业时通风流程)。务必确认工作环境检测达标后，方能开展下舱作业。卸船作业，应遵循由舱口向四周按顺序逐层进行。针对卧式放置的桶装货物，应配备有足够数量的楔形木塞，卸货时垫在货物下方，防止桶装货物四处滚动，造成不必要的货损和安全事故；针对直立放置的桶装货物，舱内卸货一般采用翻倒滚动的方式，故必须准备旧轮胎等作为缓冲，且禁止从一定高度直接将桶装货物翻滚下落。装船作业，舱内装载一般应由船舷边向舱口逐层立放，桶口向上，堆叠应排列整齐，成行成线。由于桶装货物横卧时易发生滚动，造成事故，故装卸桶装货物时，尤其是横卧装载的桶装货物，应特别注意保持船体平衡，船舶横倾不应大于3°。

Since barreled cargo is often filled with chemical products, open-cabin ventilation should be strictly implemented (The specific operations can refer to the ventilation process during operation in the bagged cargo cabin). Be sure to confirm that the working environment is up to the standard before proceeding to go down the cabin. Ship unloading operations should be carried out layer by layer in order from the hatch to the surrounding area. For barreled cargos placed horizontally, a sufficient number of wedge-shaped corks should be provided, and placed under the cargos when unloading to prevent the barreled cargos from rolling around, causing unnecessary cargo damage and safety accidents；For upright barreled cargos, the unloading in the cabin generally adopts the method of overturning and rolling, so it is necessary to prepare old tires as a buffer, and it is forbidden to roll the barreled cargos directly from a certain height. For ship loading operations, the loading in the cabin should generally be placed layer by layer from the side of the ship's gunwale to the hatch. The barrel mouth should be upward, and the stack should be neatly arranged in rows and lines. As barreled cargos are prone to rolling when lying horizontally, and causing accidents, special attention should be paid to maintaining the balance of the hull when loading and unloading barreled cargos, especially those loaded horizontally. The ship's heel should not be greater than 3°.

②桶装类货物库场操作

②Warehouse Operation of Barreled Cargos

所有库场作业之前首先要清理现场，达到平整路面，稳固搬运所需道路的作用。如有不平,应采用木板铺平。而后执行堆垛作业,货物堆叠不应超过规定的堆位线,一般不应超过4 m。立式堆垛应桶口向上,下大上小,逐层收缩卡缝;卧式堆垛时,打底一层应用木塞塞紧,使桶货绝对无法滚动,然后逐层收缩堆垛。

Before all warehouse operations, the site must be cleaned up to level the road surface and stabilize the road required for transportation. If there is any unevenness, it should be flattened with wooden boards. After the stacking operation is performed, the stacking of the cargos should not exceed the specified stacking line, generally not more than 4 m. For vertical stacking, the mouth of the barrel should be upward, the bottom is large and the top is small, and the seams should be shrunk layer by layer; For horizontal stacking, the bottom layer should be plugged tightly with a cork to prevent the barrels from rolling, and then the stack should be shrunk layer by layer.

③桶装类货物车内操作

③In-vehicle Operation of Barreled Cargos

桶装类货物的车内操作,应遵循不超重,重量分布均衡,不浪费容纳体积的原则。车内装载作业应从汽车前部依次向后逐层进行。桶装类货物立式装载时,液体桶装货物应桶口向上,高出车厢车帮部分,不应超过桶高的二分之一;卧式装载时,高出车厢围板部分不应超过桶身直径的三分之一。

The in-vehicle operation of barreled cargos should follow the principles of not overweight, balanced weight distribution, and no waste of containment volume. Loading operations in the vehicle should be carried out layer by layer from the front of the vehicle to the back. When barreled cargos are loaded vertically, the mouth of the barrel for loading liquid cargos should be upward, higher than the upper part of the carriage, and should not exceed one-half of the height of the barrel; When loading horizontally, the part higher than the hoarding of the carriage should not exceed one-third of the diameter of the barrel.

(5)捆扎类货物装卸活动实务

(5) Practices of Loading and Unloading of Bundled Cargos

捆扎类货物,因其本身就有捆扎束缚,故在装卸过程中一般不采用成组作业。捆扎类货物可按捆扎方式进行划分,包括包捆、裸捆等。包捆就是先在包装件表面上用包装材料封闭地包装起来,然后用捆扎材料捆扎起来。包捆可以起到保护货物免受污染的作用。裸捆顾名思义就是在原包装件上,直接用捆扎材料捆扎起来。捆扎类货物的装卸工属具有很多种,大体上主要工具可分为吊钩、吊索、吊架(杆)等通用工具,以及各种形式的夹、钳、钩等专用工具。捆扎类货物的装卸操作主要分为舱内操作、库场操作和车内操作三个部分。

Bundled cargos are not generally used in group operations during loading and unloading due to their own binding constraints. Bundled cargos can be classified according to the way of strapping, including packing bundle, bare bundle, etc. The so-called packing bundle means that the package is first sealed and wrapped with packaging materials on the surface of the package, and then tied up with the strapping material. The packing bundle can protect the cargos from pollution. As the name implies, the bare bundle is directly tied up with strapping materials on the original packaging. There are many types of loading and unloading tools for bundled cargos. In general, the main tools can be divided into general tools such as hooks, slings, hangers (rods), and various forms of special tools such as clamps, pliers, and hooks. The loading and unloading operations of bundled cargos are mainly divided into three parts: cabin operation, warehouse operation, and in-vehicle operation.

①捆扎类货物舱内操作

①Cabin Operation of Bundled Cargos

开舱通风,务必确认工作环境检测达标后,方能开展下舱作业;工作人员应在作业前对货物进行确认核实,内容包括有货物单重、规格、积载等情况,从而选择合适的工属具(优先选用吊具);舱内卸货原则仍是自舱口向舱内四周逐层作业。舱内装载货物时,则采取相反顺序,先装舱四周,后装舱口围,并按要求铺垫、隔票及堆放整齐、稳固。以长(条)形钢材舱内装卸作业为例:

Open the cabin and ventilate, and be sure to confirm that the working environment is up to the standard before proceeding to go down the cabin. The staff should confirm and verify the cargos before the operation, including the weight of the cargos, specifications, stowage, etc., so as to choose the appropriate tools (spreaders are preferred). The principle of unloading in the cabin is still to operate layer by layer from the hatch to the cabin's surroundings. When the cargo is loaded in the cabin, the reverse order is adopted, the cabin's surroundings are loading first, and the hatch coaming is loading second, and be padded, separated, and stacked neatly and stably as required. Take the loading and unloading operations in the long (strip) steel cabin as an example:

打码时,若货物长度大于舱口对角线长度,可用"三七"或"二八"码穿套式打码倾斜起吊出舱。起吊时,应注意清空周围无关人员,相关作业人员应保持安全距离;对于如钢管、工字钢和钢轨等货物应尽量选用专用吊具,而对货运质量有特殊要求的货物应选用纤维绳吊索;装卸钢管、圆钢时,未吊及落码后的货物可能会发生滚动,伤害到工作人员,要垫塞好楔块(三角木)。

When coding, if the cargo length is greater than the diagonal length of the hatch, you can use the "37" or "28" code to pass through the code and lift out of the cabin obliquely. When lifting, pay attention to empty the irrelevant personnel around, and the related operators should keep a safe distance; For cargos such as steel pipes, I-beams and rails, special spreaders should be used as much as possible, and fibre rope slings should be used for cargos with special requirements for freight quality. When loading and unloading steel pipes and round steel, the cargos that are not hoisted or dropped may roll and hurt the staff, and wedges (triangular wood) should be padded.

②捆扎类货物库场操作

②Warehouse Operation of Bundled Cargos

捆扎类货物库场操作要求如下:库场作业中,按照标准进行拆、堆垛,有利于货物的保管、后续清点和日常检查工作,同时,可以有效利用库场,避免空间浪费,即确定需要进行作业的货垛数目正确,货垛安置整齐,堆垛牢固。货垛摆放位置需综合考虑仓库实际情况和货物特性,货货之间、货墙之间应视为差异货种,留有空间恰当的通道。捆扎类货物的堆垛作业应注意垛与垛底边之间的距离应大于等于1 m,垛底边至作业机械轨道距离不少于1.5 m,货垛高度应考虑堆垛机械、堆场承载能力来确定。拆垛作业应呈阶梯形落高,并从上到下分层分批进行。以长(条)形钢材舱内装卸作业为例:

The requirements for warehouse operation of bundled cargos warehouse are as follows: In warehouse operations, unstacking and stacking are carried out by standards, which is conducive to the storage of cargos, subsequent inventory and daily inspections. At the same time, the warehouse can be effectively used to avoid waste of space. It is determined that the number of stacks to be operated is correct, the stacks are arranged neatly, and the stacks are firm. The placement of the stacks needs to be considered comprehensively according to the actual situation of the warehouse and the characteristics of the cargos. Between cargos and between cargos and walls should be regarded as different types of cargos, leaving an appropriate passage with space. The stacking operation of bundled cargos should pay attention to the distance between the stack, and the bottom edge of the stack should be greater than or equal to 1 m, the distance between the bottom edge of the stack and the track of the operating machine should not be less than 1.5 m, and the stack height should consider the stacking machinery and the load of the stacking yard ability to determine. The unstacking operation should be stepped down and carried out in batches from top to bottom. Take the loading and unloading operations in the long (strip) steel cabin as an example:

堆垛作业前,应先清理场地,且对场地进行平整,在不平处垫好木板,对于木方的铺垫,"十字形"垛形要求只对底层进行铺垫;而"一字形"垛形则需一层一垫。堆垛高度视库场荷载而定,通常为散支长(条)形钢材的堆垛高度不宜超过3 m,十字路口两侧,铁路轨边的堆垛高度不宜超过2 m。圆形货物(如钢管)要注意管口等的堵塞工作,还要在最外端使用绳索进行束缚。拆垛作业时,要由上而下逐层进行。

Before stacking operations, the site should be cleaned up first, and then leveled, and the uneven areas should be padded with wooden boards. For the wooden paving, the "cross" stack shape requires only the bottom layer to be padded, while the "in-line" stack shape requires paving one layer and one pad. The stacking height depends on the load of the warehouse. Usually, the stacking height of loose-supported long (strip) steel should not exceed 3 m, and the stacking height on both sides of the intersection and the railroad track should not exceed 2 m. For round cargos (such as steel pipes), attention should be paid to the clogging of the nozzles, and ropes must be used at the outermost end for restraint. When unstacking, it must be carried out layer by layer from top to bottom.

③捆扎类货物车内操作

③In-vehicle Operation of Bundled Cargos

装卸前,应先查看车辆状态,例如其车门、车窗是否完好,并与车辆人员核实情况,同时要根据货车车型和货物种类综合考虑，对车厢清洁打扫，还可进行一些垫层的铺垫，保护货物和货车；装车作业时，货物积载与盖、垫应符合铁路部门的要求，装载应先里后外，装严码紧，应均衡，不集重，不偏重，不超重，不应碰撞、砸压车帮和货码下降速度过快。

Before loading and unloading, check the vehicle's status, such as whether its doors and windows are intact, and verify the situation with the vehicle personnel. At the same time, it is necessary to comprehensively consider the types of trucks and the types of cargos, and clean the carriages, and also make some cushions to protect the cargos and trucks. During the loading operation, the cargo stowage, cover, and pad should meet the requirements of the railway department. The loading should be inside and out, tightly packed, balanced, and should not be concentrated, partial, overweight, and collided or crushed. The lowering speed of the vehicle body and cargo code should not be too fast.

使用叉车叉载货物进出卡车时，按需要配用移动平台，叉车叉运下坡时，应倒车行驶。起重机装车作业时，其吊运范围内应无其他障碍或作业。装卸作业完成后，应将工具、设备与货物堆放在铁轨一侧，且与铁轨保持1.5 m以上的安全距离。以长（条）形钢材舱内装卸作业为例：平板车装载时，应在平板车两边设置插桩，插桩应牢固有效；捆装或单支钢管装车时，其超出车厢或护栏的高度不应大于单捆或单支直径的1/3；装、卸铁路车辆作业，应打开车门板，并指定专人负责指挥；吊运钢材进出车厢时，车厢内不应有人；作业人员使用长杆钩在车厢外稳码；钢材放稳后，作业人员才可进车厢摘钩。

When using a forklift to load cargos in and out of the truck, a mobile platform is equipped as needed. When the forklift is moving downhill, it should be reversed. During the loading operation of the crane, there should be no other obstacles or operations within the lifting range. After loading and unloading operations are completed, tools, equipment and cargo should be stacked on one side of the rail, and a safe distance of more than 1.5 m should be kept from the rail. Take the loading and unloading operations in the long (strip) steel cabin as an example: When the flat vehicles is loaded, inserting piles should be installed on both sides of the flatbed, and the inserting piles should be firm and practical. When the bundled or single steel pipe is loaded into the vehicle, the height beyond the carriage or guardrail shall not be greater than 1/3 of the diameter of the single bundle or single steel pipe. When loading and unloading railway vehicles, the door panels should be opened, and a designated person should be assigned to be responsible for the command. When hoisting steel in and out of the carriage, there should be no person in the carriage. The operator uses a long rod hook to stabilize the code outside the carriage. After the steel is stabilized, the operator can enter the carriage and take off the hook.

（6）设备重大件货物装卸活动实务
(6) Practice of Loading and Unloading of the Heavy and Large Piece of Equipment

设备重大件货物装卸活动一般由"船—场""船—船""船—车""场—车""场—堆"五种物流作业流程组成。注意这些流程都可以双向运作。因为设备重大件货物本身自重非常大，装卸作业不易受到天气情况的影响，故在无大风等极端恶劣条件下，一般都由件杂货码头为设备重大件货物装卸而成立的专业队伍采取直取、直放的方式,通常采用纤维编织而成的吊带或钢丝绳作为吊索,此外更多的是一些辅佐工具,例如吊梁、护垫等。

The loading and unloading activities of the heavy and large piece of equipment generally consist of five types of logistics operation processes: "ship - yard", "ship - ship", "ship - vehicle", "yard - vehicle", and "yard - yard". It should be noted that these processes can operate in both directions. Because of the heavy and large piece of equipment itself, the loading and unloading operations are not easily affected by weather conditions. Therefore, in the absence of extreme conditions such as strong winds, a professional team established by the general cargo pier for loading and unloading the heavy and large piece of equipment is generally carried out. It is usually loaded and unloaded by direct taking and direct placing, and the sling wire rope or steel is woven by fibre is used as the sling. In addition, some additional tools, such as hanging beams, cushions, etc., will be used.

①设备重大件货物的舱内操作

①Cabin Operation of the Heavy and Large Piece of Equipment

舱内作业前,相关工作人员应首先核实查清设备重大件货物情况,例如其重量、重心、起吊标志。若没有标清起吊标志,应由工作人员根据货物特征计算确定起吊位置;装船作业时,注意保持船体平衡,横倾不应大于3°,装卸顺序和其他类货物无较大差别,装载时由周围舱壁向舱口、舱内至甲板顺序布置,卸货作业时则相反。同时注意必须对设备重大件货物进行加固。若加固工作不到位,易造成较大财产损失。当有重大件与件杂货混合积载时,宜先卸完周围件杂货后,再卸重大件。设备重大件货物于舱内的位移工作一般采用合适负荷的叉车来解决。若货物重量太大或受限于现场条件,可使用导向滑车,由船舶起货机把货物先拖移到目的位置。

Before carrying out operations in the cabin, the relevant staff should first verify and clarify the situation of the heavy and large piece of equipment, such as its weight, center of gravity, and lifting signs. If there is no standard-definition lifting mark, the staff shall calculate the lifting position based on the characteristics of the cargo. When loading the ship, pay attention to maintaining the balance of the hull, and the heel should not be greater than 3°. The order of loading and unloading is not much different from other types of cargos. It is arranged in order from the surrounding bulkhead to the hatch, from the cabin to the deck during loading, and the opposite is true during unloading operations. At the same time, pay attention to the need to strengthen the heavy and large piece of equipment. If the reinforcement work is not in place, it is easy to cause significant fiscal losses. When there is a mixed stowage of heavy items and general cargo, it is advisable to unload the surrounding general cargos before unloading the heavy cargo. The displacement of heavy and large piece of equipment in the cabin is generally solved by a forklift truck with a suitable load. If the weight of the cargo is too large or limited by the site conditions, a guide block can be used, and the cargo will be towed to the destination by the ship's crane firstly.

②设备重大件货物的库场操作

②Warehouse Operation of the Heavy and Large Equipment

库场操作时,应综合考虑到设备重大件的重心位置和现场情况,使其能够实现平稳、整齐堆放,要特别注意起吊标志的箭头朝上。若是露天库场,应在工作结束后用帆布盖好货物。对于重心较高、受风面积较大、稳定性不好的货物,堆放作业完成后还应另加其他支撑。

When operating in the warehouse, the position of the center of gravity of the heavy and large equipment and the on-site conditions should be comprehensively considered, so that it can be stacked in a stable and orderly manner. In particular, it is necessary to pay attention to the arrow of the lifting sign facing upward. If it is an open warehouse, the cargos should be covered with canvas after the work. For cargos with a high center of gravity, a large wind area, and poor stability, other supports should be added after the stacking operation is completed.

③设备重大件货物的车内操作

③In-vehicle Operation of the Heavy and Large Equipment

进行设备重大件货物的车内操作,应将货物重心对准运载车辆中心,放正、垫稳、不偏重、不集重。如装载完毕,应做好加固工作;如卸载完毕,则要收拾好帆布、紧固带等。装卸铁路车辆,应听取铁路部门的意见。

For in-vehicle operation of the heavy and large equipment, the center of gravity of the cargo should be aligned with the center of the carrying vehicle, and positioned, stable, not concentrated, not partial. If the loading is completed, reinforcement work should be done. If the unloading is completed, the canvas, fastening straps, etc. must be packed. When loading and unloading railway vehicles, the opinions of the railway department shall be heeded.

◆ 3.4 干散货港口物流运作流程与管理

3.4 Logistics Operation Process and Management of Dry Bulk Ports

3.4.1 干散货港口概述
3.4.1 Overview of Dry Bulk Ports

干散货是指不加包装的呈松散颗粒(或者粉末状态),以散装的形式处理和运输的货物,如煤炭、铁矿石和粮食谷物等。干散货港口是指专门装卸大宗干散货的专用港口,通常由外锚地区域、港内水域、码头前沿区域、货物堆存区域以及办公生活区域共五大区域构成。这类港口一般都配置针对干散货装卸搬运的大型专用装卸设备,其效率高,成本低。

Dry bulk refers to unpackaged cargos in loose granules (or powder state) and handled and transported in bulk, such as coal, iron ore, and grains. A dry bulk cargo port refers to a dedicated port that specializes in loading and unloading dry bulk cargo. It usually consists of five areas: outer anchorage area, port water area, pier quayside area, cargo storage area, and office and living area. Such ports are generally equipped with large-scale particular loading and unloading equipment for dry bulk handling, with high efficiency and low cost.

干散货港口进行装船或卸船,既可采用固定式装卸船机也可采用移动式装卸船机,并通常采用带式输送机(皮带机)输送货物。因此,干散货港口除了可采用集装箱港口和件杂货港口普遍采用的顺岸式码头外[如图3.13(a)所示],也可采用栈桥式码头[如图3.13(b)所示]。栈桥式码头是指由陆岸向水域中伸出的码头。它的优点是可以充分利用岸线前沿的水深,并且栈桥的两侧和端部均可系靠船舶。只要占用少量岸线,就能获得较多的泊位。干散货港口设置固定式装卸船机时可采用顺岸式码头,设置移动式装卸船机时需采用栈桥式码头。干散货港口通常只需要设置露天堆场,而不需要仓库,比如煤炭、矿石等散货港口[如图3.14(a)和图3.14(b)所示]。散粮由于具有食用性、清洁性等特点,港口[如图3.14(c)所示]通常设置筒仓用于堆放以及储存货物。

When loading or unloading a ship in a dry bulk port, either a fixed ship loader or a mobile ship loader can be used, and a belt conveyor (belt conveyor) is usually used to transport the cargo. Therefore, dry bulk cargo ports can not only use the shore-based wharf commonly used in container ports and general cargo ports [as shown in Figure 3.13(a)], but also can use trestle-type wharf of docks [as shown in Figure 3.13(b)]. The trestle-type wharf refers to the pier that extends from the land bank to the water. Its advantage is that it can make full use of the water depth at the front of the shoreline, and both sides and ends of the landing stage can be moored to ships. As long as a small amount of shoreline is occupied, more berths can be obtained. When a dry bulk cargo port is equipped with a fixed ship loader, a shore-based wharf can be used, and when a mobile ship loader is installed, a trestle-type wharf is required. Dry bulk cargo ports usually only need to set up open yards instead of warehouses, such as coal, ore and other bulk cargo ports [as shown in Figure 3.14(a) and Figure 3.14(b)]. Due to the characteristics of edibility and cleanliness of agribulk, ports [as shown in Figure 3.14(c)] usually set up silos for stacking and storing cargos.

(a)顺岸式码头　　　　　　　　　　　　(b)栈桥式码头

(a)Shore-based wharf　　　　　　　　　(b)Trestle-type wharf

图 3.13　码头布置形式

Figure 3.13　Wharf layout form

（a）煤炭码头

（a）Coal wharf

（b）矿石码头

（b）Ore wharf

（c）散粮码头

（c）Agribulk wharf

图 3.14　干散货码头

Figure 3.14　Drybulk wharf

3.4.2　干散货港口业务流程与计划管理
3.4.2　Business Process and Plan Management of Dry Bulk Ports

（1）干散货港口进出口业务流程
（1）Import and Export Business Process of Dry Bulk Ports

干散货港口进出口业务流程指的是贸易流转过程中,干散货在港口经过装卸、搬运以及堆存等作业环节到最后运离港口的整个作业流程。常见的干散货港口业务流程可以分为进口业务流程和出口业务流程两大类。根据具体作业操作,干散货进出口业务流程又可分为装卸船前流程,装卸船作业流程以及装卸船后船舶离泊流程三个环节。

The import and export business process of dry bulk cargos refers to the entire operation process of dry bulk cargos leaving the port after loading,unloading,handling and stocking at the port in the process of trade circulation. Common dry bulk port business processes can be divided into two categories:Import business processes and export business processes. According to specific operations,the dry bulk import and export business process can be divided into three links:

The process before loading and unloading, the loading and unloading process, and the ship's unberthing process.

①干散货港口进口业务流程

①Import Business Process of Dry Bulk Ports

a. 卸船前流程

a. Process Before Unloading

如图 3.15 所示,船、货运代理将船舶、货物信息向港方申报后由货运部受理业务、办理手续,并把相关信息通知到各个业务部门。船舶及货物信息要一般要提前一周左右通知到码头业务部门;收到通知后,港方调度计划员编制船舶计划(旬计划、五日计划、昼夜进出港计划等)及作业计划(昼夜作业计划等),同时进行船舶的预、确保管理并沟通理货员选择最优路径制订码头料场堆位计划;最后由码头作业员根据计划员编制的昼夜作业计划执行作业计划安排,同时进行船舶的靠、移、离等船舶动态的管理工作。船舶靠泊前相关部门要检查确认作业线中所有机械设备是否能正常运作,并将相关信息反馈给码头调度计划员。

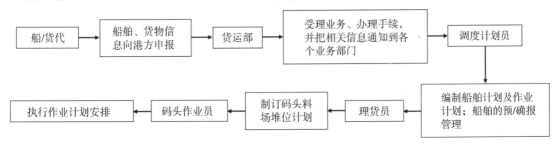

图 3.15 干散货港口进口业务卸船前流程图

As shown in Figure 3.15, after the shipping agency and freight forwarders declare the ship and cargo information to the port, the freight department will accept the business, go through the formalities, and notify the relevant information to each business department. Ship and cargo information should generally be notified to the pier business department about one week in advance. After receiving the notice, the port dispatch planner prepares ship plans (ten-day plan, five-day plan, day and night arrival and departure plan, etc.) and operation plans (day and night operation plan, etc.), and meanwhile carries out the nautical forecast and confirmation management and communicates with the tally staff to choose the best route to formulate the storage location plan of the pier material yard. Finally, the pier operator executes the operation plan according to the day and night operation plan prepared by the planner, and at the same time carries out the management of ship dynamics such as the berthing, moving, and departure of ships. Before the ship berths, the relevant departments should check whether all the mechanical equipment in the operation line can operate normally, and feedback relevant information to the pier dispatch planner.

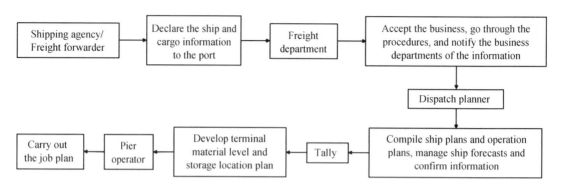

Figure 3.15 Flow chart of dry bulk cargo port import business before unloading

b. 卸船作业流程

b. Ship Unloading Process

如图 3.16 所示,首先由码头作业员安排船舶靠泊,根据调度计划员编制的昼夜作业计划安排作业线,并进行卸船机械的安排,同时记录船舶靠泊时间,并在作业完成后对作业票进行审核、确认;接下来由机械队根据调度安排的作业线安排具体的卸船作业机械及司机,作业之前要注意检查卸船流程中所需的所有机械设备是否能正常运转并将设备信息反馈给调度计划员,作业完成后记录作业完成时间并填写机械作业票;然后由装卸队根据调度安排的作业线进行装卸工的安排,作业完成后记录作业完成时间并填写装卸作业票;理货员根据安排进行理货作业,在确认所有舱位已清空时通知卸船司机停止卸船作业,同时记录卸船完成时间,作业完成后填写作业票及理货票;最后由库管员将作业完成后的理货信息形成台账(库存信息及出入库记录)。在整个卸船作业中,调度计划员要做好全程跟踪监督工作,参与卸船作业的各个部门要及时反馈作业情况并做好各项记录。

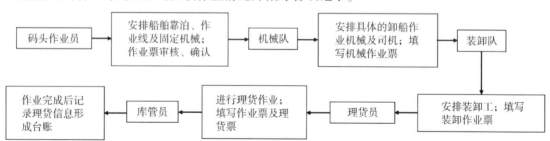

图 3.16 干散货港口进口业务卸船作业流程图

As shown in Figure 3.16, the pier operator arranges the ship's berthing firstly, and then arranges the operation line according to the day and night operation plan prepared by the dispatch planner, and arranges the unloading machinery. At the same time, the berthing time of the ship should be recorded, and the work ticket should be reviewed and confirmed after the operation is completed. Next, the machinery team arranges specific ship unloading machinery and drivers according to the operation line arranged by the dispatcher. Before the operation, pay attention to check whether all the mechanical equipment required in the unloading process can operate normally, and feedback the equipment information to the dispatch planner. After the job is completed, record the completion time of the job and fill in the machinery work ticket. Then the loading and unloading team arranges the loading and unloading workers according to the dispatching operation line. After the job is completed, the completion time of the job is recorded, and the loading and unloading work ticket is filled in. The tally clerk carries out the tally operation according to the arrangement. When confirming that all the spaces have been cleared, the unloader should be notified to stop the unloading operation, and at the same time, the unloading completion time should be recorded. After the operation is completed, the work ticket and the tally ticket should be filled in. Finally, the warehouse clerk forms the ledger (inventory information and warehousing records) with the tally information after the job is completed. In the entire ship unloading operation process, the dispatch planner must surveil the whole process, and all departments involved in the ship unloading operation must promptly feedback the operation situation and make various records.

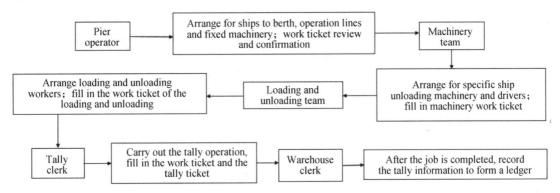

Figure 3.16　Flow chart of dry bulk cargo port import business when unloading

c. 卸船后离泊流程

c. Unberthing Process After Unloading

如图 3.17 所示,卸船作业完成后,调度计划员确认船方已完成交接手续并付清相关费用后,即可通知系解缆工人解缆准备离泊并记录离泊时间,船只离泊后由清洁工人清洁库场及码头卫生,进口卸船流程完成。

图 3.17　干散货港口进口业务船舶离泊流程图

As shown in Figure 3.17, after the unloading operation is completed, the dispatch planner confirms that the ship has completed the handover procedure and paid the relevant fees, and then informs the mooring worker to prepare to leave the berth and record the time of leaving the berth. The ship leaves the berth afterwards, cleaners will clean the warehouse and pier, and the import unloading process will be completed.

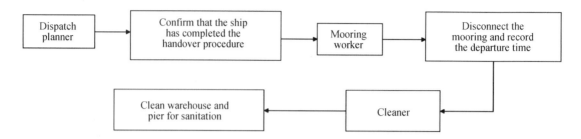

Figure 3.17 Flow chart of unberthing of bulk cargo port import business

②干散货港口出口业务流程

②Export Business Process of Dry Bulk Ports

a. 装船前流程

a. Process Before Loading

如图 3.18 所示,船、货运代理向港方发出发货申请后,由货运部按港务商务发货管理制度进行货物放行及货权确认,并把相关信息通知各个业务部门;港方收到通知后由调度计划员编制船舶计划(旬计划、五日计划、昼夜进出港计划等)及作业计划(昼夜作业计划等),同时进行船舶的预、确保管理并沟通理货员选择最优路径制订码头料场堆位计划;最后由码头作业员根据计划员编制的昼夜作业计划执行作业计划安排,同时进行船舶的靠、移、离等船舶动态的管理工作。船舶靠泊前,相关部门还要检查确认作业线中所有机械设备是否能正常运作并将相关信息反馈给码头调度计划员。

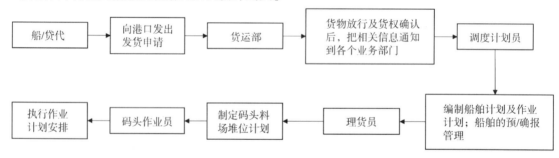

图 3.18 干散货港口出口业务装船前流程图

As shown in Figure 3.18, after the ship agency and freight forwarder submit the delivery application to the port, the freight department will release the cargo and confirm the rights of the cargo by the port business delivery management system, and notify the relevant business departments of the relevant information; After the port receive the notification, the dispatch planner prepares the shipping plan (ten-day plan, five-day plan, day and night arrival and departure plan, etc.) and operation plan (day and night operation plan, etc.), and at the same time carries out the ship's forecast and confirmation management and communicates with the tally clerk to choose the best route to formulate the storage location plan of the pier material yard; Finally, the pier operator executes the operation plan according to the day and night operation plan prepared by the planner, and at the same time carries out the management of ship dynamics such as the berthing, moving, and departure of ships. Before the ship berths, the relevant departments should check whether all the mechanical equipment in the operation line can operate normally and feed the relevant information back to the pier dispatch planner.

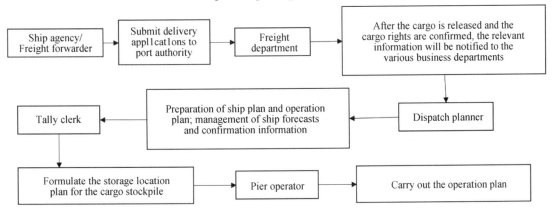

Figure 3.18 Flow chart of dry bulk cargo port export business before loading

b. 装船作业流程

b. Ship Loading Process

如图 3.19 所示,首先由码头作业员安排船舶靠泊,根据调度计划员编制的昼夜作业计划安排作业线,并进行装船机械的安排,记录船舶靠泊时间,并在作业完成后对作业票进行审核、确认;接下来由理货员确定装船取料方案,且装船作业期间理货员应不间断巡查作业流程,如有异常情况及时反馈给码头调度计划员,作业完成后记录作业完成时间并填写理货作业票;然后由机械队根据调度安排的作业线,安排具体的装船作业机械及司机,作业之前要注意检查装船流程中所需的所有机械设备是否能正常运转并将设备信息反馈给调度计划员,作业完成后记录作业完成时间并填写机械作业票;随后由装卸队根据调度安排的作业线进行装卸工的安排,作业完成后记录作业完成时间并填写装卸作业票;最后由库管员将作业完成后的理货信息形成台账(库存信息及出入库记录)。在整个装船作业流程中,理货员及调度计划员要做好跟踪监督工作,参与装船作业的各个部门要及时反馈作业情况并做好各项记录。

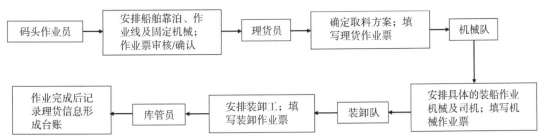

图 3.19 干散货港口出口业务装船作业流程图

As shown in Figure 3.19, the pier operator arranges the berthing of the ship firstly, and then arranges the operation line according to the day and night operation plan prepared by the dispatch planner, and arranges the loading machinery, records the berthing time of the ship and performs the work ticket after the completion of the operation is reviewed and confirmed. Then the tally clerk should determine the loading and reclaiming plan and continuously inspect the operation process during the loading operation, and timely feedback to the pier dispatch planner if there is any abnormality, and record the completion time after the operation is completed then fill in the tally work ticket; The machinery team arranges specific ship loading machinery and drivers according to the operation line arranged by the dispatcher. Before the operation, check whether all the machinery and equipment required in the shipping process are functioning normally and feedback the equipment information to the dispatch planner, after the job is completed, record the completion time of the job and fill in the mechanical work ticket. Then the loading and unloading team arranges the loading and unloading workers according to the dispatching operation line, after the completion of the job, record the completion time of the job and fill in the work ticket of the loading and unloading. The warehouse clerk forms a ledger (inventory information and warehouse entry and exit records) with the tally information after the job is completed. In the entire shipping process, the tally staff and dispatch planners should do an excellent job of tracking and surveillance, and all departments involved in the shipping operations should report back the operation in a timely manner and make various records.

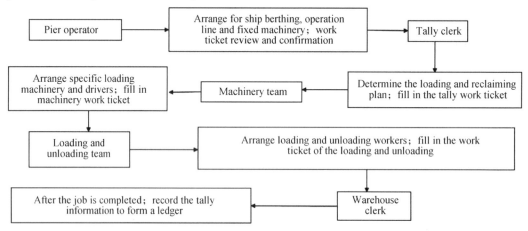

Figure 3.19 Ship loading operation flow chart of dry bulk cargo port export business

c. 装船后离泊流程

c. Unberthing Process After Loading

如图 3.20 所示,装船作业完成后,调度计划员确认船方已完成交接手续并付清相关费用后,即可通知系解缆工人解缆准备离泊并记录离泊时间,船只离泊后由清洁工人清洁库场及码头卫生,出口装船作业完成。

图 3.20 干散货港口出口业务船舶离泊流程图

As shown in Figure 3.20, after the loading operation is completed, the dispatch planner confirms that the ship has completed the handover procedures and paid the relevant fees, and then informs the mooring workers to prepare to leave the berth and record the time of leaving the berth. The ship leaves the berth afterwards, cleaners will clean the warehouse and pier for sanitation, and the export and shipping operations will be completed.

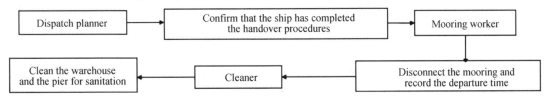

Figure 3.20　Flow chart of unberthing of dry bulk cargo port export business

（2）干散货港口业务流程的计划与管理
（2）Planning and Management of Dry Bulk Port Business Process

干散货港口业务流程的计划与管理指的是干散货港口进出口业务流程中各项具体操作环节的调度与安排,主要包括船舶靠离泊计划与管理,装卸船作业计划与管理和堆场计划与管理。

The planning and management of dry bulk port business process refer to the dispatching and arrangement of various specific operation links in the dry bulk port import and export business process, mainly including ship berthing and unberthing planning and management, loading and unloading operation planning and management, and yard planning and management.

①船舶靠离泊计划与管理

①Planning and Management of Ship Berthing and Unberthing

在船舶到达港口之前,码头调度计划员应根据船期编制船舶计划(旬计划、五日计划、昼夜进出港计划等)。船舶进出港作业流程通常包括船舶抵港后按进港次序在进港时段内进港,进行靠泊作业。当船舶完成装卸作业后,在出港时段按次序出港。

Before the ship arrives at the port, the pier dispatch planner should prepare ship plans (ten-day plan, five-day plan, day and night arrival and departure plan, etc.) according to the shipping schedule. The operation process of ships entering and leaving the port usually includes the arrival of the port in the order of entry period to perform berthing operations. After the ship has completed the loading and unloading operations, it will leave the port in sequential order during the departure time.

制订船舶靠泊计划时,码头调度计划员要配合理货员根据港口的现有存货量,平衡供求关系,尽量减少港口库存,确保船只有地方停放的同时合理安排对应堆场。泊位的安排还应该考虑船舶的尺寸、泊位的水深、系泊设备等因素,并将整体船只在泊时间作为泊位调度标准。调度工作中的基本约束包括:

When formulating a ship berthing plan, the pier dispatch planner shall cooperate the tally clerk to balance the supply and demand relationship based on the existing inventory in the port, and reduce the port inventory as far as possible to ensure that the ship has a place to park and reasonably arrange the corresponding yard. The berth arrangement should also consider factors such as the size of the ship, the depth of the berth, and the mooring equipment. The overall ship berth time should be used as the berth scheduling standard. The basic constraints in the dispatching work include:

a. 船型。大型船只必须停放到较深泊位,船只吃水量较大,与泊位相匹配,小型船只停靠在水位较浅位置。

a. Ship type. Large ships must be parked at a deeper berth, and the draft of the ship is larger, which matches the berth, and small ships must be parked at a shallower water level.

b. 船货匹配。签订合同时指定船只装载何种货种,船只就只能装载相应货种,否则不予分配泊位。

b. The cargo is matched. When the contract is signed, the ship to load what kind of cargo, the ship can only load the corresponding cargo. Otherwise, no berth will be allocated.

c. 一次性服务。泊位具有时效性,尽量减少船只换泊位装船、卸船等工作。

c. One-time service. Berths are time-sensitive, minimizing the need for vessels to change berths for loading and unloading.

d. 对应关系。泊位与相关堆存位须对应,转运繁忙时优先装载对应关系的船舶。

d. Correspondence. The berth must correspond to the relevant storage space, and priority will be given to loading the corresponding ship when the transhipment is busy.

e. 泊位不能共享。在某一时间段内,必须保证一船一泊位。

e. Berths cannot be shared. One berth per ship must be guaranteed within a certain period of time.

船舶离泊之前港方应提前与船方做好交接,确认装卸船等各项工作完成后方可通知解系缆工人解缆离泊。

Before the ship leaves the berth, the port should complete the handover with the ship in advance, and only after confirming the completion of the loading and unloading of the ship, can the mooring worker be notified to unmoor.

②装卸作业计划与管理

②Planning and Management of Loading and Unloading Operation

在船舶靠泊进行装卸货作业之前,码头调度计划员应提前沟通参与装卸作业的各个部门,认真组织机械队、装卸队、理货员及其他作业人员开好船前会,详细布置船舶靠泊位置、靠泊注意事项、货物的名称、货物的重量以及货物堆放位置等具体情况,并提出作业要求及安全注意事项;在卸船作业中,调度计划员坚守作业岗位,加强作业巡查,严格按照船舶装卸货顺序组织作业,确保作业生产的安全、质量,如遇特殊情况,严格按公司下发的文件和要求认真执行。

Before the ship berths for loading and unloading operations, the pier dispatch planner should communicate with all departments involved in the loading and unloading operations in advance, carefully organize the machinery team, the loading and unloading team, and the tally and other operators to hold a pre-ship meeting, and arrange the berthing location of the ship in detail, mooring precautions, cargo name, cargo weight and cargo stacking location and other specific conditions, and put forward operation requirements and safety precautions. During unloading operations, the dispatch planner should stick to the job position, strengthen operation inspections, and organize operations in strict accordance with the ship's loading and unloading sequence, to ensure the safety and quality of operation and production, in case of special circumstances, strictly implement the documents and requirements issued by the lines.

机械队应根据装卸货设备的特性,包括码头额定的装卸货速度、使用装卸设备的数量等制订装卸设备计划,并检查作业线中的所有机械设备能否正常运行。装卸船作业过程中,机械队要严格按照码头调度计划员的安排进行作业。

The machinery team should formulate a loading and unloading equipment plan based on the characteristics of the loading and unloading equipment, including the rated loading and unloading speed of the pier, the number of loading and unloading equipment used, etc., and check whether all the mechanical equipment in the operation line can operate normally. During the operation of loading and unloading ships, the machinery team shall work strictly in accordance with the arrangements of the pier dispatch planner.

装卸队应根据货种、货量提前做好人员计划。装卸船作业过程中,组织好巡检人员加强现场的巡视,重点部位要重点检查,发现问题及时组织人力进行修复,尽最大努力缩短流程停机时间,确保生产高效、优质地完成。

The loading and unloading team should make a personnel plan in advance according to the cargo type and volume. During the loading and unloading operations, the inspection personnel should be organized to strengthen the on-site inspection, and the key parts should be inspected. If problems are found, they will be organized to repair them in time, and try their best to shorten the process downtime, to ensure that the production is completed efficiently and with high quality.

理货员应严格按照码头调度计划员安排的装卸货位置,在作业前将场地情况报告给码头调度计划员并做好卸货准备。作业时理货员要及时将装卸货位置通知机械队,并指挥机械队到达指定位置。作业中随时掌握堆场的堆码情况,最大限度地保证堆场利用率,并及时向码头调度计划员反馈堆场信息,保障作业不间断进行。

The tally should strictly follow the loading and unloading positions arranged by the pier dispatch planner, and report the site conditions to the pier dispatch planner to prepare for unloading before the operation. During the operation, the tally should timely notify the machinery team of the loading and unloading position, and direct the machinery team to the designated position. Keep track of the stacking situation of the yard at any time during the operation, ensure the utilization rate of the yard to the greatest extent, and feedback the yard information to the pier dispatch planner in time to ensure uninterrupted operation.

③堆场计划与管理

③Planning and Management of Yards

大多数散装货场的货位布置形式均采用分区分类布置,即对储存货物在"三一致"(即性能一致、养护措施一致、消防方法一致)的前提下,对堆场划分为若干保管区域;根据货物大类和性能等划分为若干类别,以便分类集中堆存。堆场分区分类的方法具体分为下面两种。

Most of the bulk cargo yards are arranged by zoning and classification, that is, the yard is divided into several storage areas under the premise of "three consistency" (that is, the same performance, the same maintenance measures, and the same fire protection method). Divided into several categories according to the categories and performance of the cargos, so that they can be classified and stored in a centralized manner. There are two specific methods for the classification of yard zones.

a. 按照货物种类和性质进行分区分类。这是大多数堆场采用的分类分区方法,就是按货主单位经营货物来分类,把性能互不影响、互不抵触的货物,在同一堆场内划定在同一货区里集中储存。

a. Zoning and classification according to the type and nature of the cargo. This is the classification and zoning method adopted by most yards, which is to classify the cargo operated by the owner's unit, and delimit the cargos that do not affect each other or conflict with each other in the same yard for centralized storage in the same cargo area.

b. 按照货物发往地区进行分区分类。这种方法主要适用于储存期限不长,而进出数量较大的中转性质的堆场。具体做法是,货物按照交通工具划分为公路、铁路、水路,再按到达站、港的线路划分。这种分区分类方法虽然不分货物种类,但是对于危险品、性能互相抵触的货物,也应该分别存放。

b. Zoning and classification according to the area where the cargo is sent to. This method is mainly suitable for transit yards with a short storage period and a large number of transhipment. The specific method is that the cargo is divided into roads, railways, and waterways according to the means of transportation, and then divided according to the routes of arrival stations and ports. Although this zoning and classification method does not distinguish the types of cargos, the dangerous cargo and cargo with conflicting properties should also be stored separately.

在进行散货装卸之前,码头调度计划员与理货员需要制订合理的堆场计划,具体实施过程中需要落实以下原则:根据昼夜生产计划合理安排堆场,保证港口作业的顺利进行,从而加快货物周转、提高港口吞口量;根据货种、流向及货物性质对储存的不同要求,合理选用堆场,充分发挥堆场的功能,提高堆场的利用率;确定有流向的货物堆放在前方堆场,无流向的堆放在后方堆场,合理安排堆取次序,避免交叉作业和交通冲突,保证作业的连续性;货物在堆场存放期间,理货员要做好降尘措施并且在货物运出堆场之后,清洁人员应及时做好堆场卫生清洁工作。

Before carrying out loading and unloading of bulk cargo, the pier dispatch planner and tally need to formulate a reasonable yard plan. The following principles need to be implemented in the specific implementation process: Arrange the yard reasonably according to the day and night production plan to ensure the smooth progress of port operations, thereby speeding up cargo turnover and improving port throughput; According to the different storage requirements of cargo type, flow direction and nature of cargo, rationally select the yard, give full play to the functions of the yard, and increase the utilization rate of the yard; Determine the flow of the cargo to be stacked in the front stack in the yard, the stacking yard with no flow direction should be arranged in the rear yard, and the stacking order should be reasonably arranged to avoid cross operations and traffic conflicts to ensure the continuity of the operation; During the storage of the cargo in the yard, the tally should take dust reduction measures after carry out the cargo. After the the cargo is shipped out of the yard, the cleaner should do a good job of sanitation and cleaning of the yard in time.

3.4.3 干散货港口物流作业一般流程
3.4.3 General Logistics Operation Flow of Dry Bulk Ports

干散货港口按照运输货物的种类可以分为煤炭港口、铁矿石港口、散粮港口等,虽然不同港口装卸搬运的货物不同,但它们在物流作业过程中存在着一定共性。干散货港口的物流作业通常都是由装卸船作业、装卸车作业、堆场作业以及相关的辅助作业组成。本节主要针对干散货港口物流作业的一般流程进行介绍。针对重点货物,如煤、铁矿石、散粮码头的特别作业要求将在下节进行介绍。

Dry bulk ports can be divided into coal ports, iron ore ports, bulk grain ports, etc. according to the types of cargo transported. Although different ports handle different cargos, they have certain commonalities in the logistics operation process. The logistics operations of dry bulk ports usually consist of ship loading and unloading operations, loading and unloading machine operations, yard operations and related auxiliary operations. This section mainly introduces the general flow of dry bulk port logistics operations. The special operation requirements for key cargo such as coal, iron ore, and agribulk wharf will be introduced in the next section.

(1) 干散货港口装船流程
(1) Loading Process of Dry Bulk Ports

干散货港口装船流程主要包含场—船、车—船、船—船三种情况。三种情况通常都会使用到的设备是装船机,装船机按照整机的结构特点及作业方式可分为固定式、移动式和摆动式三大类。固定式装船机机身不能移动且结构简单,适用于中小型船舶作业。移动式装船机较为灵活,可以沿平行于码头布置的轨道行走,目前在干散货码头中应用得较为广泛。摆动式装船机分为直线摆动式装船机和弧线摆动式装船机两种,摆动式装船机虽然也具有结构简单的特点,但由于其占地面积大,轨道建设也较为困难,所以目前更多地在国内河港码头上使用。在对干散货装船机有了初步认识后,接下来将对三种装船流程分别展开作简要介绍。

The loading process of dry bulk ports mainly includes three situations: yard – ship, vehicle – ship, and ship – ship. The equipment usually used in the three situations is the ship loader. The ship loader can be divided into three categories: fixed, mobile and swing according to the structural characteristics and operation methods of the whole machine. The fuselage of the fixed ship loader cannot be moved and has a simple structure, which is suitable for small and medium-sized ships. The mobile ship loader is more flexible and can walk along a track arranged parallel to the pier. It is currently widely used in dry bulk cargo piers. Swing ship loader is divided into linear swing ship loader and arc swing ship loader. Although swing ship loader also has the characteristics of simple structure, because of its large footprint, track construction is also more difficult. So it is currently used more on domestic pier of river ports. After having a preliminary understanding of the dry bulk ship loader, the three loading processes will be briefly introduced next.

"场—船"的物流作业流程(如图 3.21 所示)主要是借助取料机(或堆取料机)将干散货从堆场运送至装船机带式输送机系统。针对这一作业过程通常采用斗轮式堆取料机,该机械工艺布置简单、性能全面,同时具备堆料取料两种能力,可以提高作业效率。但作业时要注意针对不同货物种类所选取的机械性能应有所区别。例如,铁矿石码头就要选择比煤炭码头更耐用的机械型号。货物到达装船皮带式输送机系统后,通过水平运输再将货物运送到装船机,然后完成装船作业。散粮、煤炭等一般干散货的装卸通常都使用带式输送机来完成大容量、长距离、高效率的运输。

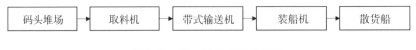

图 3.21　场—船物流作业流程

The logistics operation process of "yard - ship" (as shown in Figure 3.21) mainly uses reclaimers (or stackers and reclaimers) to transport dry bulk from the yard to the ship loader belt convey or system. For this operation process, a bucket wheel stacker and reclaimer is usually used. The mechanical process layout is simple, the performance is comprehensive, and it has both stacking and reclaiming capabilities, which can improve operating efficiency. However, the mechanical properties that should be selected for different types of cargos are different during operation. For example, iron ore piers have to choose mechanical models that are more durable than coal piers. After the cargos arrive at the ship's belt conveyor system, they will be transported to the ship loader through horizontal transportation, and then the loading operations are finished. The loading and unloading of general dry bulk, such as bulk grain and coal, usually use belt conveyors to complete large-capacity, long-distance, and high-efficiency transportation.

Figure 3.21　Yard - ship logistics operation process

车—船的物流作业流程(如图 3.22 所示)主要是装载干散货的火车/车,通过卸车机系统(将在装卸车部分进行介绍)将货物卸下,接着通过皮带机系统进行水平运输将货物运送至装船机完成装船作业。和之前介绍的工艺相比,此种工艺在对货物的运输过程中不经过堆场,直接在火车/车和船驳之间建立联系,所以可以省去货物进入堆场、从堆场取料等操作环节,因此货物在码头的作业速度会更快,但同时对火车/车和船时间上配合的准确性有着更高的要求,而要满足这样的要求在实践操作中十分困难,因此限制了此种流程在日常作业中的使用。

图 3.22　车—船物流作业流程

The vehicle – ship logistics operation process (as shown in Figure 3.22) is mainly to load dry bulk trains/trucks, unload the cargos through the unloader system (which will be introduced in the loading and unloading section), and then proceed through the belt conveyor system. The cargos are moved to the ship loader to complete the loading operation by horizontal transportation. Compared with the process introduced before, this process does not pass through the yard during the transportation of the cargos, and directly establishes a connection between the train/truck and the barge, so it can save the cargos from entering the yard and taking them from the yard. Therefore, the operation speed of the cargo at the pier will be faster, but at the same time, there are higher requirements for the accuracy of the time trade-off between the train/truck and the ship. It is tough in practice to meet such requirements. Therefore, the use of this process in daily operations is restricted.

Figure 3.22　Vehicle–ship logistics operation process

"船—船"的物流作业流程(如图 3.23 所示)主要是货物从船上卸下后,不进入堆场,而直接被装入其他船舶。具体又可分成两种情况:一是"船—船"外挡过驳作业,即卸货船用船吊将货物卸到停靠在其外挡的装货船中。二是"船—船"里挡过驳作业,即卸货船上的货物被卸船机械卸下后,通过带式输送机、转接塔被运到装船机上,再由装船机装入装货船。

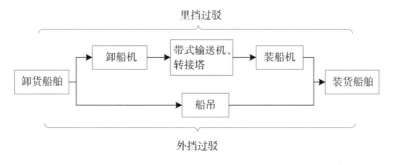

图 3.23　船—船物流作业流程

(图片来源:杨茅甄. 件杂货港口管理实务[M]. 2 版.上海:上海人民出版社,2015.)

The ship – ship logistics process (as shown in Figure 3.23) is mainly about after unloading from the ship, the cargos are directly loaded into other ships instead of entering the yard. Specifically, it can be divided into two cases: The first is a ship-outboard barge transfer operation, in which a ship's crane unload cargo on the unloading ship to a loading ship anchored in its outside gear. The second case is ship-inboard barge transfer operation, that is, after the cargos on the unloading ship are unloaded by the unloading machinery, they are transported to the ship loader through the belt conveyor and transfer tower, and then, loaded by the loader into the cargo ship.

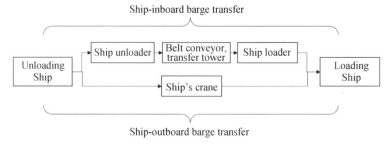

Figure 3.23　Ship – ship logistics operation process

（2）干散货港口卸船流程
（2）Unloading Process of Dry Bulk Ports

干散货港口的卸船作业流程主要包括船—场、船—船和船—车三种情况。三种情况通常都会使用的设备是卸船机,常用的干散货卸船机有链斗式卸船机、斗轮式卸船机、螺旋式卸船机和气力式卸船机。链斗式卸船机作业效率高,操作过程简单,卸船能力在 200～4 500 t/h,适用于堆积密度小、粒度不大的物料,如石灰石、煤炭、磷酸盐、矿砂和原糖等;斗轮式卸船机挖掘能力很强,因此适用于大部分货种,但出于经济因素的考虑,更多地用于较难挖取的重散粒物料,如矿石、煤炭、砂石、泥土等;螺旋式卸船机和气力式卸船机有一些共同特点:一是规模小且可以在密闭条件下完成作业,二是能做到无物料洒落,三是不受气候条件的限制。其中,螺旋式卸船机可以用来装卸搬运水泥、谷物、煤、各类化肥及化学原料等;气力式卸船机卸船物料则多用于粉料或粒度较小的物料,如散装水泥、粮食、生石灰、煤炭等,当其用于散粮卸船时也被称作吸粮机。实际操作中,应当按照现实情况灵活选择相应的卸船机械,鉴于船—船(驳)的情况上面已经介绍过,接下来主要对船—场、船—车的作业流程进行介绍。

The unloading process of dry bulk cargo ports mainly includes ship – yard, ship – ship and ship – vehicle. The equipment usually used in the three cases is a ship unloader. The commonly used dry bulk cargo ship unloader is chain bucket ship unloader, bucket wheel ship unloader, screw ship unloader, and pneumatic ship unloader. The chain bucket ship unloader has high operation efficiency and a simple operation process. Its unloading capacity is 200 ~ 4,500 t/h. It is suitable for materials with small accumulation density and small particle sizes, such as limestone, coal, phosphate, ore and raw sugar. The bucket wheel ship unloader has strong mining capacity, so it is suitable for most kinds of cargos. However, for the consideration of economic factors, it is more used for unloading heavy bulk materials which are complex to be dug, such as ore, coal, sand and soil, etc. The screw ship unloader and pneumatic ship unloader have the following common characteristics: The first point is that the scale of both is very small; The second point is that both can complete the operation under closed conditions, and can do no material falling; The third point is that neither is subject to climatic conditions. Among them, the screw ship unloader can be used to load and unload cement, grain, coal, all kinds of chemical fertilizers and chemical raw materials, etc. The pneumatic ship unloader is mainly used for powder or small particle size materials, such as bulk cement, grain, quicklime, coal, etc. When it is used for bulk grain unloading ship, it is also called grain suction machine. In actual operation, the ship unloading machinery should be flexibly selected according to the actual situation. Given the situation of ship – ship (barge) has been introduced above, the following mainly on ship – yard, ship – vehicle operation process is introduced.

　　"船—场"的作业过程与"场—船"的作业过程相反(如图 3.24 所示)。其主要作业流程是装载着干散货的船在到达港口之后,通过卸船机将货物卸下,运送至带式输送机,再通过带式输送机和堆场带式输送机的连接,将货物运送至堆场进行堆料。在通常的情况下,从船到堆场的卸船工艺仅通过一条带式输送机很难实现作业,多条带式输送机相互转接并处于封闭状态才能更好地完成这个部分的作业。

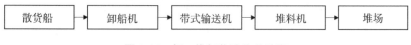

图 3.24　船—堆场物流作业流程

　　The operation process of "ship – yard" is opposite to that of "yard – ship" (as shown in Figure 3.24). The primary process is that when a ship carrying dry bulk cargo arrives at the port, unload the cargos through the ship unloader and transport them to the belt conveyor. Then through the connection of the belt conveyor and yard belt conveyor, the cargos are transported to the yard for stacking. It is difficult to unload the shipment from the ship to the yard with only one belt machine. In order to better complete this part of the operation, multiple belt conveyors are in a closed state and transferred to each other.

Figure 3.24　Ship – yard logistics operation process

　　船—车的物流作业流程(如图 3.25 所示)为:装载着干散货的船在到达港口之后,通过卸船机将货物卸下,运送至带式输送机,再通过装车机系统将干散货运至火车/车。同样地,由于卸船量与火车运量相差较大,且火车和船舶的到港时间难以匹配,这种运作流程也较少实施。

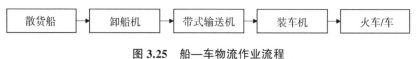

图 3.25　船—车物流作业流程

　　The logistics operation process of ship – vehicle (as shown in Figure 3.25) is as follows: After arriving at the port, ships carrying dry bulk cargo are unloaded by ship unloader, then transported to belt conveyor, and dry bulk cargo is delivered to the train/truck by loader machine system. Similarly, due to the significant difference between ship unloading and train volume, and the mismatch between train and ship arrival times, this operation process is rarely implemented.

Figure 3.25 Ship – vehicle logistics operation process

（3）干散货港口装卸车流程

（3）Loading and Unloading Machine Process of Dry Bulk Ports

干散货的装卸车工艺主要由车—场的卸车流程和场—车的装车工艺两部分构成。这里主要对卸车系统展开介绍。在卸车作业过程中,通常要使用卸车机。常用的卸车机包括门式链斗卸车机、螺旋卸车机和翻车机。门式链斗卸车机不用打开车门即可进行作业,可以简化作业流程、节约作业成本,适于松散、粒度较小的物料如粮食、煤等;螺旋卸车机结构较为简单,主要利用物料向下自流的特点完成作业,卸车能力通常在400~600 t/h,由于作业时不用对物料的提升做功,因此卸车效率高而能耗较低,同样适用于松散、粒度小的粮食煤等,但螺旋卸车机的缺点是卸车过程中流量很不均匀,开始阶段较后续阶段快很多;翻车机的形式主要有转子式和侧倾式两种,作业效率很高,一台翻车机的日平均综合生产能力可达15 000 t左右(昼夜),适用于运输量大的港口的煤炭、焦炭、矿砂等物料装卸。在实际操作中应当根据货种的现实情况选择相适应的机械。下面对卸车流程和装车流程分别展开简要介绍。

Loading and the unloading process of dry bulk cargos are mainly composed of the vehicle – yard unloading process and yard – vehicle loading process. Here mainly introduces the unloading system. Unloading machine is usually used during unloading operation. Commonly used unloading machine includes gantry chain bucket unloading machine, screw unloading machine and dump machine. The gantry chain bucket unloading machine can operate without opening the door, which can simplify the operation process and save the operation cost. It is suitable for loose and small granular materials such as grain and coal. The structure of screw unloading machine is relatively simple, mainly using the characteristics of downward material gravity to complete the operation. The unloading capacity of the screw unloading machine is usually 400 ~ 600 t/h. Because the operation does not need to work on the material promotion, the unloading efficiency is high, and the energy consumption is low. Screw unloading machine is also suitable for loose, small grain coal, etc. However, the disadvantage of the screw unloading machine is that the flow is very uneven in the unloading process, and the initial stage is much faster than the subsequent stage. There are two main types of dump machine: Rotor type and tilt type. The operation efficiency of dump machine is very high, and its daily average comprehensive production capacity can reach about 15,000 t (day and night). Dump machine is suitable for loading and unloading coal, coke, ore and other materials in ports with large transportation volumes. In actual operation, the appropriate machinery should be selected according to the actual situation of the cargos. The following is a brief introduction of unloading process and loading process.

车—场的卸车作业流程(如图3.26所示)主要是装载着干散货的火车/车在到达港口之后,通过卸车系统将货物卸下,通过固定皮带式输送机输送系统将货物运送至堆场进行堆存。运输干散货的车辆主要分为敞车和翻车两种形式,其中较为通用的车辆类型是敞车,它的利用率较高,可以装运散粮、散矿以及各种包装散货。自卸车相比较而言专用性较高,其造价也较高,但载重量利用率低,因此不如敞车使用广泛。

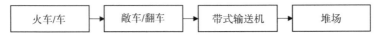

图 3.26　火车/车—堆场卸车作业流程

The vehicle - yard unloading process (as shown in Figure 3.26) is mainly that after arriving at the port,the train/truck loaded with dry bulk cargo is unloaded through the unloading system, and then transported to the yard through the fixed belt conveyor system. Dry bulk cargo transport vehicles are mainly divided into two types:open wagon and dump truck,among which the more common vehicle type is a open wagon. The open wagon utilization rate is higher. It can carry bulk grain, bulk ore and all kinds of packaged bulk cargos. Compared with open vehicles,dump trucks have higher specificity and higher cost,but a low load utilization rate. Therefore,dump trucks are not as widely used as open wagon.

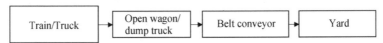

Figure 3.26　Train/Truck - yard operation process

场—车装车作业过程(如图 3.27 所示)主要是通过取料机将存放在堆场的干散货取出,通过装车机进而完成相应的装车作业。装车机可以选取如桥式起重机抓斗、装卸桥抓斗的装车机械,也可以选择装车机械化系统。

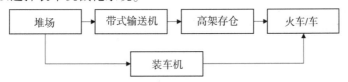

图 3.27　堆场—火车/车装车作业流程

(图片来源:刘翠莲. 港口装卸工艺[M]. 大连:大连海事大学出版社,2013.)

Yard - vehicle loading operation process (as shown in Figure 3.27) is mainly that the dry bulk cargos stored in the yard are taken out by the material making machine. And the corresponding loading operation is completed by the loading machine. Loading machine can be selected,such as bridge crane grab, loading and unloading bridge grab. A mechanized loading system is also an option.

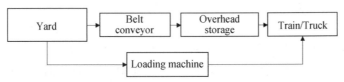

Figure 3.27　Yard - vehicle loading operation process

（4）干散货港口堆场作业流程

（4）Yard Operation Process of Dry Bulk Ports

干散货港口的堆场作业包括货物在堆场及堆场到车、船之间进行的水平运输（如图3.28 所示）。通过上述作业可以实现对货物的堆料、取料以及转堆，以便完成货物的集散工作，发挥其在货物水路运输和陆路运输之间的价值。在货物到达港口之后，可以在堆场对货物进行清理检查、计量验收、拆包重组等一系列的处理工作，确保货物的质量以及使用价值。同时，由于不同的货物具有不同的性质和用途，对于运输时间的要求也有所区别，因此堆场还可以为干散货的运输提供一个衔接过渡的平台，对到港的货物装卸分配作业起到一定调节缓冲的作用。

图3.28　干散货港口堆场作业流程

Yard operation of dry bulk ports includes horizontal transportation of cargos in the yard and from yard to vehicle and ship（as shown in Figure 3.28）. In order to complete the collection and distribution of cargos, play its value between water transportation and land transportation of cargos, through the above operations, we can realize the stacking, taking and stacking of cargos. In order to ensure the quality and use-value of the cargos, the cargos can be cleaned, inspected, measured and accepted, unpacked and reorganized in the yard after they arrive at the port. At the same time, different cargos have different properties and use, and the requirements for transportation time are also different. Therefore, the yard can also provide a transition platform for dry bulk cargo transportation, and play a role of adjustment and buffer for the cargo loading, unloading and distribution operations at the port.

Figure 3.28　Yard operation process of dry bulk ports

（5）相关辅助作业

（5）Related Auxiliary Operation

①干散货的计量作业

①Measuring Operation of Dry Bulk Cargo

无论是装船、卸船还是装卸车作业流程，在作业过程中都会涉及干散货的计量问题。干散货的计量可以采用像地磅称重、水尺计量、振动给料高速净重、自动散装谷物秤称重等方式。具体而言，地磅称重法是在煤炭码头堆场的卡车与火车出口，配备地磅称重的设备，利用地磅称重空载和满载公路车辆，并根据环境和当地要求选择合适的类型和尺寸。在大多数情况下，设备运行的温度条件为−10 ℃到+50 ℃，地磅称重的范围可以从20 t（5千克级）到80 t（20千克级）。选用地磅称重在使用的过程中要注意去掉车皮的重量。水尺计量又称"水尺检量"，是指将船舶作为一个大型衡器，通过读取加载货物前后的吃水量，将两个数字的差作为装载货物的重量。此种方法操作过程简单,但其缺点是在装卸过程中,很难保证除货物移动外不发生其他重量的变动,所以不太可能准确计算所涉及的压载物的确切数量。振动给料高速净重这类机器通常用于煤炭、焦炭、加工燃料和类似商品的称重,可实现 25 kg/min 的五次称重或 50 kg/min 的四次称重且预计精确度会优于 1.0%。自动散装谷物秤称重可以对从升降机、传送带、储料斗或筒仓进料的谷物和自由流动的物料进行称重,记录从 30 kg 到 5 t 的重量,且以高达每小时 1 000 t 的速度交付。在定期检查、维修和维护下预计精确度可达到谷物贸易中的一般要求±0.1%。

Whether it is the process of ship loading and unloading operation or loading and unloading machines, the measurement of dry bulk will be involved in the operation process. Dry bulk can be weighed by the methods such as weighing platform, water gauge, vibrating feed high-speed net weight, automatic bulk grain weighing, etc. Specifically, the weighing platform method is to equip the platform weighing equipment, at the truck and train exit of the coal pier yard, equipped with, use the platform to weigh empty and full load vehicles, and select the appropriate type and size according to the environment and local requirements. In most cases, the operating temperature of the equipment is from −10 ℃ to +50 ℃, and the weighing of the platform scale can range from 20 t (5 kg class) to 80 t (20 kg class). When using the weighing platform method, pay attention to removing the weight of the vehicle. Water gauge, also known as "water gauge measurement", refers to the use of a ship on a large scale, reading the draught before and after loading the cargo, and taking the difference between the two numbers as the weight of the loaded cargo. The operation process of this method is simple, but its disadvantage is that it is challenging to ensure that no other weight changes occur except for the movement of the cargo during the loading and unloading process, so it is impossible to accurately calculate the exact amount of ballast involved. Vibrating feed high-speed net weight measurement is commonly used for weighing coal, coke, processed fuels and similar commodities. It can achieve five weighing of 25 kg/min or four weighing of 50 kg/min, and the accuracy is expected to be better than 1.0%. Automatic bulk grain weighing can weigh grains and free-flowing materials fed from elevators, conveyor belts, storage hoppers or silos, recording weights ranging from 30 kg to 5 t, and up to 1,000 tons per hour speed deliver. Under regular inspection, repair and maintenance, the accuracy is expected to reach ±0.1%, which is the general requirement in the grain trade.

②干散货的防尘作业

②Dust-proof Operation of Dry Bulk Cargo

干散货在运输过程中十分容易发生粉尘污染,严重时会威胁到当地的环境质量状况和当地居住人民的身体健康。因此,干散货的防尘工作十分重要。为了能够有效地缓解一般干散货扬尘的问题,可以采取喷雾洒水和防尘的方法。喷雾洒水能够有效抑制粉尘的扩散,干散货港口货物通常贮存量大、运转速度快,喷雾洒水的方法符合方便、经济的原则。遮挡物防尘是在干散货的运输车辆上加盖雨布等遮挡物,减少风力对货物的影响,缓解货物在运输过程中洒落引起的地面扬尘问题。另外,可以将码头考虑建在远离住宅区的偏远位置(如大型的海上煤炭和矿石码头)并且在满足作业条件的前提下尽可能选用更环保的机械。例

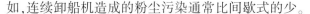

如,连续卸船机造成的粉尘污染通常比间歇式的少。

Dry bulk cargo is prone to dust pollution during transportation, which can threaten the local environmental quality and the health of local residents in severe cases. Therefore, dust prevention of dry bulk cargo is essential. In order to more effectively alleviate the dust problem of dry bulk cargo, spray water and dust-proof methods can be adopted. Spray water can effectively inhibit the spread of dust. Dry bulk cargo usually has a large storage capacity and fast operation. The spray water method conforms to the principles of convenience and economy. Dust prevention of shelter is to cover dry bulk cargo vehicles with rain cloth and other shelters to reduce the impact of wind on the cargo and alleviate the problem of ground dust caused by the scattering of cargo during transportation. In addition, the pier can be considered to be built in a remote location far away from the residential area (for example, a large sea-coal and ore pier) and more environmentally friendly machinery should be selected as far as possible under the premise of meeting operating conditions. For example, continuous ship unloaders usually cause less dust pollution than intermittent ones.

3.4.4　不同货种港口物流作业的特别要求

3.4.4　Special Requirements for Port Logistics Operations of Different Cargo Types

（1）煤炭港口的特别要求

（1）Special Requirements for Coal Ports

配煤功能是煤炭港口相对于其他港口一项特有的功能,是根据用户的不同用途和不同要求对煤炭在堆场进行各种质量的混合从而实现产品的再造。主要的配煤工艺有四种,分别是:交替卸车垛位配煤工艺、船舱混装配煤工艺、双取料机配煤工艺以及取装—直取配煤工艺。交替卸车垛位配煤作业前,首先要绘制卸车工艺垛型图和取料工艺图,必须分别以图为依据完成卸车配煤作业和取料配煤作业,在配煤过程中港务公司应当进行质量抽检。船舱混装配煤作业首先要绘制装船舱型工艺图,以图为依据通过装船卸船的作业实现配煤功能。双取料机配煤作业通过两台取料机取煤,通过同一条带式输送机在装船过程中实现配煤功能。取装—直取配煤作业是车船直取和堆场取料同时进行,在装船过程中完成配煤。传统的配煤计算方式需要依赖人工,但随着科技的进步,人们可以通过编程实现配煤计算,从而在减轻了人工压力的同时,有效地降低成本。

The coal blending function is a unique function of the coal port compared to other ports. It is to mix various qualities of coal in the yard according to the different uses and different requirements of the users to realize the remanufacturing of the products. There are four central coal blending processes, namely: alternate unloading and stacking position coal blending process, cabin mixed assembling coal blending process, dual reclaimer coal blending process and taking and loading-direct coal blending process. Before the alternate unloading and stacking position coal blending operation, the unloading process stacking diagram and the reclaiming process diagram must be drawn first, and the unloading coal blending operation and the reclaiming coal blending operation must be completed based on the diagrams. In the coal blending process, the port lines should conduct quality inspections. For the operation of cabin mixed coal assembling, the cabin-type process diagram must be drawn first, and the coal blending function shall be realized through the operation of loading and unloading on the basis of the diagram. The coal blending operation with dual reclaimer takes coal through two reclaimers, and realizes the coal blending function during the loading through the same belt conveyor. Taking and loading-direct coal blending operation is that the vehicle and ship direct taking and yard reclaiming are carried out simultaneously, and the coal blending is completed during the loading process. Traditional coal blending calculation methods need to rely on labour, but with the advancement of science and technology, people can realize coal blending calculation through programming, reducing labour pressure and effectively reducing costs.

煤炭的堆场作业除了要注意配煤的操作问题外,还要格外注意煤炭的自燃问题。煤炭自燃会引起火灾并释放有毒有害气体,伤害人体器官,造成缺氧窒息引发事故。预防煤炭自燃问题十分重要。煤炭堆场防自燃通常可以采用水消法、压实法、采出法等。水消法是指在煤堆周围安装水喷淋设备。根据研究分析,煤在自燃前全水分为 5%~7%,当煤的含水量达到 12% 时不会发生自燃,所以通过向煤堆洒水可以有效避免自燃。在夏季时,为避免煤堆吸收过多热量,还可以在煤堆上喷洒石灰水。压实法是在对煤作业时将煤按 6 m、10 m、14 m 分层堆放,借助推土机和挖掘机分别进行层层压实和垛边压实,当煤堆内部温度高于 60 ℃ 时,进行煤堆二层开路压实以释放热量,以减少煤与氧气的接触面积从而达到预防自燃的目的。采出法是通过将煤打翻配合喷淋进行灭火,因为煤堆的自燃,通常是从距离表层2~4 m 煤的内部开始,所以此方法能有效控制煤的自燃。

In addition to coal blending, the coal yard operations must also pay special attention to the spontaneous combustion of coal. Spontaneous combustion of coal can cause fires and release toxic and harmful gases, harm human organs, cause hypoxia and suffocation, and cause accidents. It is essential to prevent spontaneous combustion of the coal. The prevention of spontaneous combustion in coal yards can usually adopt water elimination method, compaction method, and mining method. The water elimination method refers to the installation of water spray equipment around the coal pile. According to research and analysis, the total moisture content of coal before spontaneous combustion is 5% to 7%. When the water content of coal reaches 12%, spontaneous combustion will not occur, so spontaneous combustion can be effectively avoided by spraying water on the coal pile. In summer, to prevent the coal pile from absorbing too much heat, it is also possible to spray lime water on the coal pile. The compaction method is to stack the coal in layers of 6 m, 10 m, and 14 m during coal operation and use bulldozers and excavators to perform layer-by-layer compaction and stack edge compaction. When the internal temperature of the coal pile is above 60 ℃, the second layer of the coal pile is open-circuited and compacted to release heat to reduce the contact area between coal and oxygen to achieve the purpose of preventing spontaneous combustion. The mining method is to extinguish the fire by overturning the coal with spraying. Because the spontaneous combustion of the coal pile usually starts from the inside of the coal 2 ~ 4 m away from the surface, this method can effectively control the spontaneous combustion of the coal.

除煤炭本身,在煤的基础上经过高温形成的焦炭通常在作业过程中会采用和煤炭类似的作业流程和储存办法,但也有需要特别注意的地方。由于焦炭的单位价值普遍高于煤炭,并且粒度越大使用价值也越高。所以在焦炭的运输过程中,应当格外注意减少操作过程引起的破碎、轻泡的问题。同时,和煤炭相比,焦炭的运输量相对较少。出于经济方面的考量,通常不会将焦炭港口设置为大规模的专用港口。为有效避免焦炭破碎造成的损失,在装卸搬运的过程中应当降低作业机械的高度,减少货物下落距离,以较为轻柔缓慢的动作进行作业。

In addition to the coal itself, coke formed on the basis of coal at high temperatures usually adopts similar operating procedures and storage methods to coal during the operation, but there are also some places require special attention. Because the unit value of coke is generally higher than that of coal, and the larger the particle size, the higher the use-value. Therefore, during the transportation of coke, special attention should be paid to reducing the problems of crushing and light foaming caused by the operation process. At the same time, compared with coal, the transportation volume of coke is relatively tiny. Due to economic considerations, coke ports are usually not set up as large-scale dedicated ports. In order to effectively avoid the loss caused by the crushing of coke, the height of the operating machinery should be lowered during the loading, unloading and handling process to reduce the falling distance of the cargos, and the operation should be carried out in a gentle and slow motion.

(2)铁矿石港口的特别要求
(2) Special Requirements for Iron Ore Ports

铁矿石一般密度为 4.8 t/m³,且和煤炭、散粮相比颗粒更大。因此,铁矿石码头在装卸时通常会选用与煤炭码头和散粮码头不同的间歇式卸船机械。间歇式卸船机械利用抓斗抓取物料卸船,工作循环周期中有一个空返回程。铁矿石港口常用的代表机械为桥式抓斗卸船机,其额定生产率为 400 ~ 5 000 t/h,可靠性和适应性更强,但在使用过程中更容易产生磨损。

Iron ore generally has a density of 4.8 t/m³, and its particles are more significant than coal and bulk grain. Therefore, the iron ore pier usually uses intermittent ship unloading machinery different from the coal pier and the bulk grain pier when loading and unloading. Intermittent ship unloading machinery uses grabs to grab materials and unload the ship. There is an empty return in the working cycle. The representative machinery commonly used in iron ore ports is the bridge grab ship unloader, with rated productivity of 400 ~ 5,000 t/h, more reliable and adaptable, but more prone to wear during use.

除此之外,铁矿石自身的属性也对铁矿石码头堆场的地面结构提出了更高的要求,要在普通堆场地面的基础上进行特别的强化处理,通常的方式有三种:①选用经过加强夯实的块石地基,可以利于水分的渗透以保证矿石堆的干燥,缺点是容易引起取矿不干净的问题;②选用水泥地基堆场,此方式仅适用于北方,在南方地区使用容易产生积水问题;③块石与水泥块相拼,块与块之间留缝。这种方式是前两种方式的结合,缺点是成本高,易破碎。

In addition, the properties of iron ore itself also put forward higher requirements on the ground structure of the iron ore pier yard. Special strengthening treatment should be carried out based on the common yard ground. There are three usual methods:①The use of strengthened and compacted block stone foundation can facilitate the penetration of water to ensure the dryness of the ore pile, but the disadvantage is that it is easy to cause the problem of unclean ore extraction;②Cement foundation yard is used, this method is only suitable for the north, and it is prone to water accumulation when used in the south;③The block stone and the cement block are joined together, leaving a gap between the blocks. This method is a combination of the first two methods. The disadvantage is that it is costly and easily broken.

(3)散粮港口的特别要求
(3)Special Requirements for Bulk Grain Ports

与煤炭港口和铁矿石港口不同,在散粮的运输过程中,会经常使用筒仓来作为贮存散装物料的仓库。筒仓按照储存货物的种类不同,可以分为农业筒仓和工业筒仓两大类。本部分所涉及的筒仓主要是农业筒仓,用来贮存粮食、饲料等粒状和粉状物料。虽然筒仓的建造成本通常会比房式仓略高,但运输过程中的作业成本更低,所以筒仓已成为最主要的粮仓形式之一。港口储存散粮一般会选择立筒仓,筒仓直径一般为6~8 m。它占地面积小、截面通常为圆形,因此储存空间大,并且密闭防火性能良好。

Unlike coal ports and iron ore ports, silos are often used as warehouses for storing bulk materials during the transportation of bulk grain. According to the different types of cargos stored, silos can be divided into two categories: agricultural silos and industrial silos. The silos involved in this section are mainly agricultural silos, which are used to store granular and powdery materials such as grain and feed. Although the construction cost of a silo is usually slightly higher than that of a house-type silo, the operation cost during the transportation is lower, so the silo has become one of the most essential forms of the granary. For bulk grain storage in ports, a group of vertical silos are generally selected, and the diameter of the silos is generally 6~8 m. It occupies a small area and the cross-section is usually round, so it has an ample storage space and has good airtight fireproof performance.

由于粮食的食用性,在运输过程中要格外注重保护粮食质量。在利用立筒仓储存粮食时,通常会遇到粮食发热和害虫入侵的问题,影响粮食储存的质量。针对粮食储存中常见的发热问题,可以采取机械通风的方法创造低温环境,改善储粮性能:均衡温湿通风可以分多次共进行6~10 h,每次通风总风量置换粮堆内部空隙。停机2~3遍,经过1~3天内部温湿度平衡后再次开机。冬季通风降温过程分三个阶段。首个阶段将粮温降到15~20 ℃,第二阶段降到5~10 ℃,第三阶段降到0~5 ℃。通风后要注意做好密闭等保温工作。针对粮食储存中常见的害虫入侵的问题,主要从两方面采取措施:一方面要加强筒仓的消毒工作,可以用80%敌敌畏以0.1~0.2 g/m³、0.2~0.3 g/m³的消毒用药量对空仓和器材进行消毒,按总用量加水10~20倍稀释后进行喷洒,再经过3天的密闭和1天的通风处理达到杀虫目的。另一方面,还可以使用化学药剂熏蒸技术,一般选用有效成分大于等于56%的磷化铝片剂和有效成分大于等于85%的磷化铝粉剂为主要来源的磷化氢作为熏蒸的化学药剂,将药剂投放于粮食表面,针对害虫重点聚集处重点打围投放,然后通过自然解潮、整仓环流(熏蒸的气体在粮面以上的空间和粮堆组成的整个仓房内的循环)的熏蒸作业方式,达到杀虫的目的。此外,应当做好不定期扦样筛查工作。在扦样的过程中应当遵循上、中、下均取,散装运输设备不少于8个均匀布点的原则,用扦样器扦取样品完成对粮食的筛查,以保证粮食的质量。

Due to the edible nature of food, special attention must be paid to protecting the food quality during transportation. When using vertical silos to store grain, it usually encounters the problems of heat generation and pest invasion, which affect the quality of grain storage. Given the expected heat problems in grain storage, mechanical ventilation can be used to create a low-temperature environment and improve grain storage performance; balanced temperature and humidity ventilation can be divided into multiple times for a total of 6~10 h, and the total air volume of each ventilation replaces the internal voids of the grain pile. Stop it for 2~3 times, and start it again after 1~3 days of internal temperature and humidity balance. The winter ventilation and cooling process is divided into three stages. In the first stage, the temperature of the grain is lowered to 15 ~20 ℃, in the second stage to 5~10 ℃, and in the third stage to 0 ~ 5 ℃. After ventilating, pay attention to heat preservation work such as airtight. In response to the common pest invasion problem in grain storage, measures are mainly taken from two aspects: On the one hand, it is necessary to strengthen the disinfection of the silo. You can use 80% dichlorvos to disinfect the empty warehouse and equipment at a disinfection dosage of 0.1~0.2 g/m³ and 0.2~ 0.3 g/m³. Add water 10~20 times the total amount. Spray it after dilution, and then pass airtight for three days and ventilate for one day to achieve the purpose of killing insects. On the other hand, chemical fumigation technology can also be used. Generally, aluminium phosphide tablets with effective ingredients ≥ 56% and aluminium phosphide powder with effective ingredients ≥ 85% are selected as the primary source of phosphine as the fumigation chemicals. The medicament is placed on the surface of the grain, focusing on the focus of the pests gathering place, and then through the natural damp relief, the whole warehouse circulation (the fumigation gas circulating in the space above the grain surface and the entire warehouse composed of grain piles) fumigation operation method to achieve the purpose of killing insects. In addition, irregular sample screening should be done well. In the process of sampling, it should follow the principle that the top, middle and bottom should be taken equally, and the bulk transportation equipment should be at least eight evenly distributed points. Sampler should be used to screen the grain to ensure the quality of the grain.

◆ 3.5 石油天然气货港口物流运作流程与管理

3.5 Logistics Operation Process and Management of Oil and Gas Cargo Ports

3.5.1 石油天然气货港口概述
3.5.1 Overview of Oil and Gas Cargo Ports

石油天然气货,主要为散装液体货物,是指无须包装,通过管道、泵进行装卸,直接装入货舱、槽罐进行运输的各种液体状的货物。石油天然气货主要分为:石油及其产品、液化石油气、液体化学品等。其中石油及其产品、液化石油气和液化天然气都是重要的能源,尤其是石油类货物,在世界海运量中占有相当大的比重,也是我国重要的进出口货源。石油天然气货具体分类如表 3.2 所示。

表 3.2　不同种类石油天然气货的概念与分类

种类	产品	分类
石油制品	汽油	分航空、车用和溶剂汽油等多种
	煤油	分为灯用煤油、动力煤油和矿灯煤油
	柴油	分为轻柴油和重柴油
	燃料油	又叫重油或锅炉油,是原油蒸馏出汽油、煤油、柴油后,经精制除杂直接蒸馏得到的油品,可作为船舶、工业和工厂锅炉的燃料
	润滑油	提取了汽油、煤油、柴油后剩下的重质油,采取减压蒸馏法制成的液体油品,精制后的润滑油可以用各种不同比例调配各种黏度的润滑油
	化工油类	如纯苯、甲苯、石蜡、地蜡等产品
	建筑油类	如液体沥青、硬沥青等产品
液化气	液化石油气(LPG)	主要成分为丙烷,是丙烷、丁烷及其混合物的总称
	液化天然气(LNG)	主要成分为甲烷,其他还有乙烷、丙烷、丁烷等
	液化化学品气	是指除了上述两类液化气外,凡是在常温下为气态,经冷冻或加压的方法,以液态形式进行运输的化学物质,包括无机化合物或单质以及各类有机化合物

(资料来源:孙铮,张明齐.港口企业装卸实务[M].北京:对外经济贸易大学出版社,2010.)

Oil and gas cargos, mainly bulk liquid cargos, are various liquid-like cargos that are loaded and unloaded through pipes and pumps without packaging, and directly into cargo cabins and tanks for transportation. Oil and gas cargos are mainly divided into petroleum and its products, liquefied petroleum gas, liquid chemicals, etc. Among them, petroleum and its products, liquefied petroleum gas, and liquefied natural gas are important energy sources, especially petroleum cargo, which occupies a considerable proportion in the world shipping volume and is also an important source of import and export cargo in China. The specific classification of oil and gas cargo is shown in Table 3.2.

Table 3.2　Concept and classification of different types of oil and gas cargos

Category	Product	Classification
Petroleum products	Gasoline	There are various types of gasoline such as aviation, automotive, and solvent gasoline
	Kerosene	It is divided into lamp kerosene, power kerosene, and mining lamp kerosene
	Diesel	It is divided into light diesel and heavy diesel
	Fuel oil	Also called heavy oil or boiler oil, it is the oil obtained by distilling gasoline, kerosene, and diesel oil from crude oil and then distilled directly by refining and removing impurities, which can be used as fuel for ships, industrial and factory boilers
	Lubricant	The heavy oil left after extracting gasoline, kerosene, and diesel oil is made into liquid oil by taking the method of reduced pressure distillation, and the refined lubricant can be used in various proportions to allocate various viscosity lubricants
	Chemical oil	Products such as pure benzene, toluene, paraffin, and floor wax, etc.
	Construction oil	Products such as liquid asphalt, hard asphalt, etc.
Liquefied gas	Liquefied Petroleum Gas (LPG)	The main component is propane, which is a general term for propane, butane, and their mixtures
	Liquefied natural gas (LNG)	The main component is methane, other than ethane, propane, butane, etc.
	Liquefied chemical gas	It refers to all chemical substances, including inorganic compounds or monomers and all kinds of organic compounds, that are gaseous at room temperature and are transported in liquid form by freezing or pressurization, except for the two types of liquefied gases mentioned above

　　石油天然气货港口作业具有连续、密闭、运量大、效率高的特点。主要发展趋势是：吨级大型化和专业化、装卸货种多样化、装卸工艺流程自动化、安全及环保要求高。我国在石油天然气货港口的设计、建造及运营上已形成相对完善的标准。石油天然气货港口通常的必要设施有：泊位、装卸油平台、输油管、油罐区和维修车间等。停靠石油天然气货港口的船舶，以原油船为例，通常航行于国际航线，船舶吨位大、吃水深，同时考虑危险品性质，因此石油天然气货港口都布置在天然水深较大的新区，并且远离城市和其他港区。海上卸油设备、油船和岸上设施之间的布置形式分为单点系泊、多点系泊、固定码头形式和栈桥形式。

　　The operation of oil and gas cargo ports has the characteristics of continuous, confined, large capacity, and high efficiency. The main development trend is large tonnage and specialization, loading and unloading cargo diversification, loading and unloading process automation, safety, and high environmental requirements. China has formed relatively perfect standards in the design, construction, and operation of oil and gas cargo ports. The necessary facilities in oil and gas cargo ports are berths, oil loading and unloading platforms, oil pipelines, oil tank areas, maintenance workshops, etc. Ships calling at oil and gas cargo ports, taking crude oil tankers for an example, are usually sailing in international routes with large tonnage and deep draught, and considering the nature of dangerous cargo. Therefore, the oil and gas cargo ports are arranged in new areas with large natural water depth and far away from cities and other port areas. The arrangement between offshore oil unloading equipment, tankers, and shore facilities is divided into the single-point mooring, multi-point mooring, fixed quay form, and trestle form.

石油天然气货港口主要进行油船货物装卸及油罐车货物装卸。

The oil and gas cargo ports mainly carry out loading and unloading operation for oil tankers and tanker trucks.

（1）油船货物装卸
（1）Loading and Unloading Operations for Oil Tankers

油船货物装卸主要分为：港口直接装卸、通过海上泊地装卸和水上直接装卸三种：①港口直接装卸。目前国内大部分石油天然气货港口采用这种方式。港口前沿安装数台输油管，连接油船与港口，采用岸上油泵或自流方法进行石油装卸。②通过海上泊地装卸。它是通过离开陆地的水深处设置的靠船设施来对大型油船进行装卸。油船的海上泊地按其构造形式及输油管方式可分为靠船墩方式、栈桥方式、单点系泊方式和多点系泊方式。③水上直接装卸。油船都备有高效率的油泵，可完成船—船、船—驳的水水直接中转装卸。

Loading and unloading operations for oil tankers are mainly divided into three types: direct loading and unloading at the port, loading and unloading by sea berth, and direct loading and unloading on the water: ①Direct loading and unloading at the port. Currently most domestic oil and gas cargo ports use this method. Several oil pipelines are installed at the quayside of the port to connect the oil tanker and the port, and oil loading and unloading are carried out by the onshore oil pump or self-flow method. ②Loading and unloading by sea berth. It is loaded and unloaded large oil tankers through the berthing facilities set up in the water depth away from land. Oil tanker berth at sea according to its construction form and the way the oil pipeline can be divided into the way against the pier, trestle bridge, single point mooring, and multi-point mooring way. ③Direct loading and unloading on the water. The oil tankers are equipped with the high-efficiency oil pump. It can complete the direct transit loading and unloading of water among ships or from ships to the barges.

（2）油罐车货物装卸
（2）Loading and Unloading Operations for Tanker Trucks

油罐车的罐装方法有泵装和自流装车。自流装车是在有条件的地方,利用地形高差自流罐装。油罐车卸车分原油及重油卸车和轻油卸车两种方式。原油及重油卸车时,采用密闭自流下卸方式、敞开自流下卸方式或泵抽下卸方式;轻油卸车均采用上卸方式,设卸油台,与装油台类似。上卸方式又分为虹吸自流卸油和泵抽卸油两种。

Tanking methods of tanker trucks are pump loading and self-flow loading. Self-flow loading is in places with conditions, taking the advantage of terrain height difference to achieve self-flow tanking. Unloading tanker truck is divided into crude oil and heavy oil unloading, and light oil unloading in two ways. When unloading crude oil and heavy oil, adopt closed self-flow unloading method, open self-flow unloading method or pumping unloading method; Light oil unloading all uses the upper unloading method, and sets up unloading platform that is similar to the loading platform. The upper unloading method is divided into two kinds of oil unloading: siphon self-flow unloading and pumping unloading.

3.5.2 石油天然气货港口物流运作与流程
3.5.2 Logistics Operations and Processes of Oil and Gas Cargo Ports

石油天然气货港口的物流活动的关键在于装卸活动。大量石油主要采用油罐储存。石油的运输,根据具体情况不同,主要采用油船、油罐车和长输油管线进行运输,需要在专业化石油港口进行装卸。因此,我们在本节着重介绍石油天然气货港口的装卸环节的相关理论。本节主要针对石油天然气货港口物流作业的一般流程进行介绍。

The key to logistics activities in oil and gas cargo ports lies in loading and unloading activities. Large quantities of oil are mainly stored in tanks. The transportation of oil, depending on the specific situation, is carried out mainly by tankers, tanker trucks, and long pipelines, which require loading and unloading at specialized oil ports. Therefore, we focus in this section on the theory related to the loading and unloading aspects of oil and gas cargo ports. This section focuses on the general flow of logistics operations in oil and gas cargo ports.

石油天然气货港口的装卸作业主要有:卸船进罐、装船、船—船直取、车—船直取和调和作业等,另外还有泄空、置换及吹扫等附属工艺作业。石油天然气货港内装卸流程大致可分如下五种:

Oil and gas cargo port loading and unloading operations are mainly: unloading into the tank, loading, ship-ship direct taking, vehicle-ship direct taking, and blending operations, in addition to air release, replacement and blowing, and other ancillary process operations. The loading and unloading process in the oil and gas cargo port can be roughly divided into five types as follows.

（1）卸船进罐作业

（1）Ship Unloading into the Tank Operation

该作业主要利用船泵的压力接卸,将船中所载油品直接泵入港区储罐。这种流程要求平面与高程设计中以满足船泵按正常流量卸油时的扬程、大于进罐的全管路系统水头损失为前提。卸船过程中的中间加压,受到自控手段和机泵参数配合等的限制,目前已建成的工程多采用"旁接油罐加压"方案,即在原有过程中增设中间罐和接力泵。这种方案需增设油罐,存在占地大、能耗高的弊端,并且对设备控制以及管理等方面都提出了很高的要求。装卸设施性能的提高,为提高港口卸船效率提供了可能。尤其是大型油船配泵的扬程较高、流量大,码头上的设备相应配套,卸船效率大大提高,缩短了油船靠泊时间,提高了泊位通过能力。卸船效率主要由船泵和陆上接收设施的能力决定。

The operation mainly uses the pressure of the ship pump to receive and unload the oil contained in the ship and pump it directly into the port storage tank. This process requires the plane and elevation design to meet the head of the ship pump according to the normal flow of oil discharge, greater than the head loss of the whole pipeline system into the tank as the premise. The intermediate pressurization in the unloading process is restricted by the means of automatic control and the parameters of the machine and pump, etc. At present, the completed project mostly adopts the scheme of "bypass tank pressurization", i.e. the intermediate tank and relay pump is added in the original process. This solution requires the installation of additional tanks, which has the disadvantages of large foot print and high energy consumption and puts forward high requirements for equipment control and management. The improved performance of loading and unloading facilities provides the possibility to improve the efficiency of port unloading. In particular, large oil tankers with high head and high flow rate of pumps and corresponding equipment on the quay have greatly improved the unloading efficiency, shortened the berthing time of oil tankers, and increased the berthing capacity. The unloading efficiency is mainly determined by the capacity of ship pumps and land-based receiving facilities.

（2）装船作业

（2）Ship Loading Operation

装船作业按照地形条件,有两种装船方式:一种是港区设置高位储罐,借助有利的地形,重力流装载,这种方式更加节能,可以降低装船成本;另一种方式是设置装船泵,将储罐内油品泵送至船舱。通常,港口的罐区和装船码头之间距离较远,两者之间的自动控制、通信联络和联动操作极为重要。在输油过程中,当罐区、码头和油船等环节中发生故障时,必须迅速停泵、关阀,停止输油作业,避免发生事故。目前,国内大型石油天然气货港口均实现了以上控制功能。

According to the terrain conditions, there are two ways of ship loading: One is to set up high storage tanks in the port area, with the help of favorable terrain, gravity-flow loading, which is more energy-saving and can reduce the cost of loading; The other way is to set up a loading pump, which is pump the oil in the storage tanks to the ship's hold. Usually, the distance between the tank area and the ship loading terminal is far, so the automatic control, communication, and linkage operation between them are very important. In the process of oil transmission, when a failure occurs in the tank area, terminal and tanker, the pump must be quickly stopped and the valve must be closed to stop the oil transmission operation to avoid accidents. At present, the above control functions are realized in domestic large oil and gas cargo ports.

（3）"船—船直取"作业
(3) "Ship-Ship Direct Taking" Operation

将卸货船舶中的货油通过合理的工艺流程,直接装运到预先靠泊的空载装货船舶里。该作业流程不仅可以提高港口的泊位利用率,减少对港口设施的占用,降低能源消耗,缩短船舶在港时间,减少费用,而且有利于港口生产安全。这种工艺方式应用在栈桥式两侧靠船的情况中更加合适。

The cargo oil from the unloading vessel is directly loaded into the empty loading vessel which is berthing in advance through a reasonable process. This operation process not only can improve the utilization rate of berths in the port, reduce the occupation of port facilities, reduce energy consumption, shorten the time of ships in port, reduce costs, but also is conducive to port production safety. This process is more suitable in the case of berthing ships on both sides of the trestle.

（4）"车—船直取"作业
(4) "Vehicle-Ship Direct Taking" Operation

这种工艺适用于油罐车、油船联合作业的情况。通过合理调度,将到港油罐车内油品直接装载到油船中或将油船中油品直接装载到油罐车中。但由于装卸效率受到限制,大型油品码头上很少采用这种方式。

This process applies to the joint operation of tanker truck and tanker. Through reasonable scheduling, the oil in the tanker truck will be loaded directly into the tanker or the oil in the tanker will be loaded directly into the tanker truck. However, due to the limitation of loading and unloading efficiency, this method is rarely used in large oil terminals.

（5）燃料油调和装船流程
(5) Fuel Oil Blending and Loading Process

一般通过油泵将燃料油从油罐中泵出,装载入调和罐进行调和操作。调和结束,通过油泵为船舶供应。

Generally, the fuel oil is pumped out from the tank through the oil pump, loaded into the blending tank for blending operation. After the blending is finished, the blending fuel oil is supplied to the ship through the oil pump.

◆ 3.6　汽车货港口物流运作流程与管理

3.6　Logistics Operation Process and Management of Automobile Cargo Ports

3.6.1　汽车货港口概述
3.6.1　Overview of Automobile Cargo Ports

（1）商品汽车分类
（1）Classification of Commodity Automobiles

商品汽车通常指可以用于买卖交易的汽车。根据商品汽车的用途,可以将其分为乘用车和商用车两大类。乘用车的具体用途主要表现在可以载运乘客以及乘客的随身行李;商用车的作用主要体现在商业用途,比如运送人员和货物。

Commodity automobile generally refers to the car used for trade and sale. According to the use, commodity automobile can be divided into passenger vehicles and commercial vehicles two categories. Passenger vehicles are mainly used to carry passengers and their carry-on luggage; Commercial vehicles are mainly used for commercial purposes to transport personnel or cargo.

①乘用车:它是指在设计和技术特性上主要用于载运乘客及其随身行李和临时物品的汽车,其包括驾驶人座位在内最多有不超过9个座位。

①Passenger vehicle: it refers to the vehicles mainly used to carry passengers and their carry-on luggage and temporary items in terms of design and technical characteristics, which has no more than 9 seats, including the driver's seat.

②商用车:它是指在设计和技术特性上用于运送人员和货物的汽车,分为客车、半挂牵引车、货车三类。

②Commercial vehicle: it refers to the vehicles used to transport personnel and cargo in terms of design and technical characteristics, which are divided into three categories: passenger cars, semi-trailer tractors and trucks.

a. 客车:在设计和技术特性上用于载运乘客及其随身行李的商用车,包括驾驶人座位在内座位数超过9座。客车有单层的或双层的,又分为小型客车、城市客车、长途客车、旅游客车等。

a. Passenger car: A commercial vehicle designed and technical characteristics to carry passengers and their carry-on luggage, with more than 9 seats including the driver's seat. Passenger cars are single- or double-decker. It is also divided into small passenger car, city passenger car, long-distance passenger car, tourist passenger car and so on.

b. 半挂牵引车:装备有特殊装置用于牵引半挂车的商用车。

b. Semi-trailer tractor: Commercial vehicle specially equipped to pull a semi-trailer.

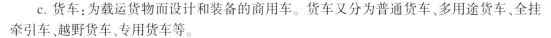

c. 货车：为载运货物而设计和装备的商用车。货车又分为普通货车、多用途货车、全挂牵引车、越野货车、专用货车等。

c. Truck：A commercial vehicle designed and equipped to carry goods. Trucks are divided into ordinary trucks, multi-purpose trucks, full tractors, off-road trucks, special trucks and so on.

（2）汽车货港口的特点
(2) Characteristics of Automobile Cargo Ports

以下是汽车货港口的主要设施：泊位、码头前沿、堆场、中控室、汽车处理中心、检查口、通信设施。堆场可以说是汽车货港口重要的作业资源，堆场作业是汽车货港口作业的重要环节。随着汽车货港口吞吐量的增加，堆场出现很多问题，如车位资源紧缺。码头堆场的传统操作方式无法适应现代化的变化，出现堆场车位利用率不高、倒车较多等问题。

The following is the main implementation of the automobile cargo port：berth, quayside of the terminal, storage yard, central control room, automobile processing center, inspection port, communication facilities. In the automobile cargo port, the storage yard can be said to be a very important operation resource, and the storage yard operation can also be said to be one of the most important links in the automobile cargo port operation. Due to the increasing throughput of automobile cargo port, there are many problems in the storage yard, such as the scarcity of parking space resources. The most serious problem is that the traditional operation mode of the terminal yard cannot adapt to the change of modernization, and the utilization rate of the yard parking space is not high and the reversing is more.

汽车货具有易受损的特性，汽车货港口在货物堆存要求等方面与集装箱码头、散杂货码头等其他装卸码头有所不同。汽车作为高附加值商品，在物流活动中要求营运方具备安全的操作环境、先进的作业技术以及更强的个性化服务功能。

Automobile cargo has the characteristics of being vulnerable to damage, and automobile cargo ports are different from container terminal, bulk grocery terminal and other loading and unloading terminal in terms of cargo storage requirements. As a high value-added commodity, automobiles require operators to have a safe operating environment, advanced operation technology and stronger personalized service functions in logistics activities.

3.6.2 汽车货港口物流运作与流程
3.6.2 Logistics Operation and Process of Automobile Cargo Ports

（1）商品汽车装卸船工艺流程概述
(1) Overview of Loading and Unloading Process of Commodity Automobile

商品汽车在汽车货港口的装卸作业采用滚装运输的方式，即通过码头作业人员逐辆驾驶进行上下船作业的水路运输方式。整个装卸操作工艺分为两种：一种为单步式装卸工艺，其特点是作业司机驾驶汽车从码头直接驶入舱内，并在指定位置进行定位，对作业司机来说不存在分工问题,作业司机负责商品车装卸作业过程中车辆装卸作业的全部操作。但在实际生产过程中,会出现在舱内定位时由于后车需频繁等候前车定位完毕后才可进行定位作业,这样会存在造成整条作业线路的拥堵,进而影响周转速度。为了减少舱内等待时间,需要妥善安排好作业线路上的汽车货。相比单步式装卸操作工艺,分步式操作工艺的特点是将车辆装卸过程分为短驳和定位两个步骤,装卸作业司机相应地分为短驳司机和定位司机。因为定位与短驳作业对司机和指挥人员的现场作业要求有所区别,所以将作业过程分步实施,对装卸作业人员进行分工,这样做既降低了作业人员操作的复杂程度,又有利于提高生产作业的安全水平。

In the loading and unloading operation of the automobile cargo port, usually the commodity automobile use the way of roll-on transportation, that is to say, the terminal operators drive one by one to get on and off the ship operation. The whole loading and unloading operation process is divided into two kinds: one is a single-step loading and unloading process. The character of the loading and unloading process is that the driver drives the car directly into the cabin from the terminal and positions it in the designated position. There is no division of labor problem for the driver, and the driver is responsible for all the operation of the vehicle loading and unloading operation during the loading and unloading operation of the commodity automobile. However, in the actual production process, there will be the positioning of the cabin after the vehicle needs to wait frequently for the positioning of the vehicle can be carried out, which will cause the congestion of the whole operation line, and then affect the turnover speed. In order to reduce the waiting time in the cabin, we need to properly arrange the automobile cargo on the operation line. Compared with the single-step loading and unloading operation process, the step-by-step operation process is that the vehicle loading and unloading process is divided into two steps: short barge and positioning. The loading and unloading drivers are divided into short barge driver and positioning driver. Because positioning and short barge operation are different in the site operation requirements of drivers and commanders, the operation process is carried out step by step, and the loading and unloading operators are divided, which not only reduces the complexity of the operation, but also is conducive to improving the safety level of production operation.

以上仅是对码头进行船舶装卸作业的操作工艺流程进行的分类,而从汽车货港口整体的生产方案来说,根据生产过程中车辆在码头的候装和停放位置的不同,其生产作业方案又可以具体分为两类:一是卸船时,商品车直接由滚装船卸载至堆存场地;装船时,由堆存场地直接装载至船舶。二是卸船时,商品车先由滚装船卸载至码头前沿临时堆放,待卸船完毕后由码头前沿移至堆存场地;装船时,商品车先由堆存场地移至码头前沿再由码头前沿装载至滚装船。第一类装卸生产方案是我国汽车货港口最常采用的作业流程,分为装船作业前、装船作业中、装船作业后三个部分。

The above is only the classification of the operation process of ship loading and unloading operations at the terminal. However, in terms of the overall production plan of the automobile cargo port, according to the positions of vehicles waiting for loading and unloading and parking at the terminal are different, and the production operation plan can be divided into the following two categories. Scheme（Ⅰ）：During unloading，the commercial vehicle is directly unloaded from the roll-loading ship to the storage site；and during loading，directly loaded to the ship from the storage site. Scheme（Ⅱ）：During unloading，the commercial vehicle shall be unloaded from the roll-loading ship to the quayside for temporary stacking，and moved from the quayside of the terminal to the loading site；and during loading，the commercial vehicle is unloaded from the storage site to the quayside and then loaded to the roll-loading vessel from the quayside. Scheme（Ⅰ）is the most commonly used operation process in China's automobile cargo ports，which is divided into three parts：before loading operation，during loading operation and after loading operation.

（2）商品汽车装船工艺流程

（2）Loading Process of Commodity Automobile

①装船作业前

①Before the Loading Operation

就出口待装船商品汽车在装船前的作业流程而言，在装船工作组织方面：码头要组织各相关部门召开船前会协调安排装船事宜。单船指导员作业前根据作业计划将作业内容布置给作业队，并在开工前组织作业队召开会议，再次向全体作业人员布置作业内容。

In terms of the operation process of export commodity automobile for shipment，the organization of shipment work：the relevant departments shall be organized to coordinate and arrange the shipment matters. The ship instructor shall arrange the operation content to the operation team according to the operation plan before operation，organize the team meeting before commencement，and assign the operation contents to all the operators again.

在具体作业方面：装船前，作业人员需检查滚装船的跳板放下的高度，确认船舶跳板的落地前沿已经铺上橡胶垫子，避免商品车的头部和底部由于跳板弹起受到损害；利用交通锥等对作业区域进行必要封闭，使作业区域与其他区域有效隔开，保证作业区域的安全；作业人员准备好电瓶、电瓶线、燃油、渡板、信号旗（灯）等作业用品。这些作业用品中，有些用于一般性正常作业环节，而有些用于非正常车辆作业环节；在舱内布置行走作业路线，全体作业人员和交通车进行试走，从而减少作业中的无序性和随意性，提高作业的安全性和可靠性。

For specific operation：Before loading，the operator shall check the height of the landing board and confirm that the landing front has been covered with rubber mat to avoid damage to the head and bottom of the commercial vehicle；Use the traffic cone to separate the operation area from other areas to ensure the safety of the operation area；The operator shall prepare battery，battery line，fuel oil，ferry board，signal flag（lamp）and other operating supplies. Among these supplies，some are used for general normal operation，while some are used for abnormal vehicle operation；Arrange walking route in the cabin，all operators and vehicles test the operation route，thus reduce the disorder and randomness in operation and improve the safety and reliability.

②装船作业中

②During the Loading Operation

关于装船作业按照第一类装卸生产方案可具体分为如下三大环节:从堆场到舱内临时停放区域的短驳环节、舱内临时停放区域到指定积载位置的定位环节、定位停车后的车辆固定环节。

According to the scheme（Ⅰ）, it can be divided into the following three links: the short barge link from the storage yard to the temporary parking area in the cabin, the positioning link from the temporary parking area in the cabin to the designated load position, and the fixed link of the vehicle after parking.

短驳环节又可细分为车辆堆场启动环节、堆场至船舱内临时停放区域的行驶环节、船舱内停车环节三大部分。

The short barge link can be subdivided into three parts: the starting link of the vehicle in the storage yard, the driving link from the yard to the temporary parking area in the cabin, and the parking link in the cabin.

车辆在堆场的启动环节:短驳司机先确认装船车辆的车种、目的港等基本信息。在堆场启动商品汽车前应先检查车辆周围,确认汽车没有损坏才可动车,如有车损必须先向堆场员或内里报告确认登记后才可动车。打开车门时注意钥匙不能碰到商品车钥匙孔外的其他部分,进入驾驶室后按规定顺序启动车辆。短驳司机根据指挥(交通车司机的手势、哨子信号)松手刹车缓慢启动车辆,禁止突然加速或转向。对于车身较长的商品车或特种车辆启动要特别注意,待车辆完全出位后再打方向盘,避免内外轮碰撞。

The starting link of the vehicle in the storage yard: the short barge driver shall first confirm the basic information of the vehicle type and destination port of the loading vehicle. Before starting the commercial vehicle in the storage yard, check the vehicle around the bullet train to confirm that the vehicle is not damaged. If there is any damage, you must report to the storage yard officer or the internal manager for registration before the bullet train. When opening the door, note that the key can not touch other parts outside the keyhole of the commercial vehicle. After entering the cab in the specified order, start the vehicle. The short barge driver loosens the brake according to the command（the vehicle driver's gestures, whistle signal）and slowly starts the vehicle, prohibiting sudden acceleration or steering. For the long commercial vehicles or special vehicles, pay special attention to start after the vehicle completely out of the steering wheel, to avoid internal and external wheel collision.

堆场至船舱内临时停放区域的行驶环节:按照装卸作业开始前确认的行驶路线行驶,一般要求在港内道路的行驶速度保持在 35 km/h 以内;船舱和堆场内的行驶速度需控制在 20 km/h 以内;转弯或通过跳板时要求车速控制在 5 km/h 以内。行驶过程中先行车要随时注意后续车的行驶状态,后续车必须注意先行车的行驶状态,它们需要及时调整行驶速度,保持安全距离。当车速为 20 km/h 时,前后两车间距应该保持在 15 m 左右(不同汽车货港口对速度限制和安全间距的要求略有不同)。

Driving link from the yard to the temporary parking area in the cabin: according to the driving route confirmed before the loading and unloading operation, the driving speed on the port road is generally kept within 35 km/h; the cabin and the yard should be controlled within 20 km/h; the speed should be controlled within 5 km/h when turning or passing the springboard. In the process of driving, the car in front must always pay attention to the driving state of the rear car, and the car behind should also observe the driving state of the vehicle in front. They should adjust the driving speed in time and maintain a distance to determine the safety of the site. When the speed is 20 km/h, the distance between the front and rear vehicles should be kept at about 15 m (the speed limit and safety spacing requirements are slightly different for different automobile cargo ports).

定位环节也可细分为：舱内启动车环节、舱内定位环节、定位后停车环节三大部分。

The positioning link can also be subdivided into three parts：the starting link in the cabin, the positioning link in the cabin, and the parking link after positioning.

舱内启动车环节：定位司机需事先确认目的港和积载位置及确认车头和车轮的方向，打开车门上车，按规定顺序启动车辆，根据定位信号员指挥松手刹车，缓慢启动车辆，禁止突然加速及转向。

The starting link in the cabin：the positioning driver should confirm the location of the destination port and the accumulated load in advance and confirm the direction of the front and wheel, open the door to get on the car, start the vehicle in the prescribed order, release the brake according to the positioning signal officer, slowly start the vehicle, and prohibit sudden acceleration and steering.

舱内定位环节：不同类型的车辆所需使用的定位方法不同。目前主要使用两种定位方法：一种是针对轿车、小型客车、皮卡等各种小型车辆的三步定位法；另一种是针对无助力转向的大客车、货车、特种机械等舱内无法调头的车辆的直接定位法。其中，三步定位法要求定位信号员站在待定位车辆副驾驶室侧后/侧前方进行指挥，指示车辆后退/前进，车尾/车头到达定位位置后，再指示司机调整方向盘并后退/前进，待车身完全回正后指示司机回直方向盘（至于车辆是采用后退倒车定位还是前进顺车定位，目前根据汽车货港口的行业惯例，外贸船装船采用倒车定位，内贸船装船采用顺车定位）。定位信号员再站到车辆预订位位置驾驶室侧后方，指示车辆后退/前进以完全到达定位位置，完成定位操作。在三步定位法中需要特别注意的是：车辆移动和方向盘转动操作不能同时进行。直接定位法则是定位司机在倒车定位过程中，按照定位信号员的指挥，实现车辆的定位，车辆进入定位位置前，应处在定位位置正前方。后方视野较差车辆定位时应在车头增设定位信号员，协同车尾信号员进行指挥。无论何种定位方法，定位操作车辆速度一般要求不超过 5 km/h。

The positioning link in the cabin：different types of vehicles need to use different positioning methods. At present, two positioning methods are mainly used：One is the three-step positioning method for various small vehicles such as cars, small buses and pickup trucks；The other is the direct positioning method for the vehicles in buses, trucks and special machinery that cannot turn around without power steering. Among them, three-step positioning method requires positioning signal officer in the vehicle to locate the deputy cab side after/side front command, indicating the vehicle back/forward, rear/front, instruct the driver to adjust the steering wheel and back/forward, after the body is completely back to the steering wheel (as for the vehicle is backward reverse positioning or forward car positioning, currently according to the car port industry practice, foreign trade ship with reverse positioning, domestic trade ship adopts the car positioning). Position the positioning signal officer to the rear of the cab at the vehicle reservation position. Indicates the vehicle to move back/forward to fully reach the positioning position and complete the positioning operation. In the three-step positioning method, special attention is needed that the vehicle movement and steering wheel rotation operation cannot be carried out simultaneously. Direct positioning law is to locate the driver in the process of reversing positioning, according to the command of the positioning signal officer, to achieve the positioning of the vehicle. The vehicle into the positioning position should be directly in front of the positioning position. When the vehicle with poor rear vision is located, a positioning signal officer should be added in the front, and cooperate with the rear signal officer to command. Regardless of the positioning method, the positioning operation vehicle speed is generally required not to exceed 5 km/h.

定位后停车环节：定位司机需按规定操作顺序停车，定位司机下车时应防止脚部碰到车门内饰，离开驾驶舱后，将原来的保护用品（如车衣）复原。定位信号员确认车内钥匙及挡位摆放正确，刹车锁止后，关闭车门。关于定位停车需要注意的是：车辆定位停在坡道上时，应在车辆驻车制动后，在坡道低端的轮胎下放置三角形垫木；坡道尽量优先停放自动挡车辆。定位司机在船舱内定位停车要确保车与车间的合理距离。

The parking link after positioning: the positioning driver should stop according to the prescribed operation order, prevent the positioning driver from touching the door interior when getting off the car. After leaving the cockpit, restore the original protective supplies (such as car clothes). The positioning signal officer confirms that the interior keys and gear are placed correctly, and the door is closed after the brake is locked. Regarding positioning parking, it should be noted that: when the vehicle is parked on a slope, a triangular pad should be placed under the tire at the lower end of the slope after the vehicle has parked and applied the brakes; Prioritize parking automatic transmission vehicles on ramps. The driver should ensure a reasonable distance between the vehicle and the workshop when parking in the cabin.

最后绑扎系固环节应当注意，滚装船舶因干舷较高，受风面大，在海上航行时易出现摇摆。为防止因船体摇摆造成积载在舱内的车辆移动进而引起车辆相碰撞导致车损，对装载的车辆进行有效的绑扎固定是滚装运输装船作业中不可或缺的环节。

Finally, it should be paid to the binding link that the roll-on ship has high freeboard and large wind surface, which is easy to swing in the sea sailing. In order to prevent the movement of the vehicle loaded in the cabin and cause vehicle collision and vehicle damage, the effective binding and fixation of the loading vehicles is an indispensable link in the roll-on transportation and loading operation.

③装船作业后

③After the Loading Operation

装船作业后的工作主要是作业现场的恢复清理和码头作业用品的收回入库,如车辆绑扎固定后通道上多余绑扎材料应该及时清理并放置和固定在舱壁边或通道边等不影响车辆装卸的位置;电瓶线、燃油、渡板、信号旗(灯)等作业用品需收回码头库内。

The main tasks after the loading operation are the restoration and cleaning of the work site and the retrieval and storage of terminal operation supplies. If there are excess binding materials on the channel after the vehicle is tied and fixed, they should be promptly cleaned and placed and fixed at positions such as the cabin wall or channel edge that do not affect the loading and unloading of vehicles; Battery cables, fuel, ferry boards, signal flags（lights）and other operational supplies need to be retrieved from the terminal warehouse.

（3）商品汽车卸船工艺流程
（3）Unloading Process of Commercial Vehicles

商品汽车卸船工艺流程仍然以我国专业汽车货港口最常采用的第一类作业流程方案为基础进行讨论。同时,由于对商品汽车的装船工艺流程已做了十分详尽的介绍,卸船是装船的反向作业,其工艺流程特别是工艺要求方面与装船作业有很多相同或相似的地方,因此,关于商品汽车卸船工艺流程仅着重介绍卸船工艺中的移位环节:卸船车辆完成拆除绑扎作业后,定位司机便可进行移位作业。定位司机应先确认好临时停放场所,确认卸货港、车轮方向、绑扎带已拆除干净,检查车辆有无残损,如有残损必须报告作业组长。定位司机打开车门上车按规定顺序启动车辆。然后在信号员的指挥下进行车辆移位,定位司机需在定位信号员指挥下缓慢启动车辆,禁止突然加速,移位操作车辆应低速行驶,按照移位信号员指挥棒的方向打方向盘移动车辆到舱内临时停放区域。在移位作业时需要注意的是:当启动舱内斜坡上的车辆上坡时应在坡道低端的轮胎下方放置三角形热木,防止车辆溜坡;当启动车身较长的商品汽车及特种车辆时,要待车辆完全出位后再打方向盘,避免由于内轮差导致碰撞。

The unloading process of commercial vehicles is still discussed based on the operation process scheme（Ⅰ）most commonly used in professional automobile cargo ports in China. At the same time, due to the commodity vehicle loading process has been made a very detailed introduction, unloading is loading reverse operation, the process especially the loading requirements have many the same or similar places, therefore, about the commodity vehicle unloading process only introduces the shift process: after the unloading vehicle complete the binding operation, the positioning driver can shift operations. The positioning driver shall first confirm the temporary parking place, confirm that the unloading port, wheel direction and binding belt have been removed, and check the vehicle for any residual damage, which must be reported to the operation leader. The positioning driver open the door and start the vehicle in the specified order. Then shift the vehicle under the command of the signal officer, the positioning driver should slowly start the vehicle under the command of the positioning signal officer, prohibit sudden acceleration, the shift operation vehicle should be driven at low speed, according to the direction of the baton of the shift signalator to move the vehicle to the temporary parking area in the cabin. When shifting the job, it should be noted that when the vehicle on the slope of the starter compartment should be placed below the tires at the low end of the ramp, prevent vehicle sliding; When starting commercial cars and special vehicles with long body, take the steering wheel to avoid collision due to the inner wheel difference.

◆ 3.7　冷冻货港口物流运作流程与管理

3.7　Logistics Operation Process and Management of Frozen Cargo Ports

3.7.1　冷冻货港口概述
3.7.1　Overview of Frozen Cargo Ports

（1）冷冻货港口简介
（1）Frozen Cargo Port Description

冷冻货是指为了保持品质而使其从生产、运输、消费的过程中始终处于低温态的货物。冷冻货物与普通货物相区别的是冷冻货物需要制冷系统,这对与冷冻货物相关的基础设施、运输工具及技术有更高的要求;冷库、冷藏车、冷藏船、冷藏箱的购置成本相对于普通货物的基础设施和运输工具更高,其在运营过程中的能源消耗也更多;而先进的冷藏技术可以延长冷藏货的保质期,减缓冷冻货的腐烂速度。按照其装载的工具不同,冷冻货可以分为两种:一种是通过冷藏集装箱运输的适箱冷冻货;一种是通过冷藏船运输的非适箱冷冻货。总体来说,冷冻货的特征如下:

Frozen cargo refers to goods that are always at a low-temperature state in the process of production, transportation, consumption in order to maintain quality. The difference between refrigerated cargo and ordinary cargo is that refrigerated cargo requires refrigeration systems, which places higher requirements on the infrastructure, means of transport and technology associated with frozen cargo: the purchase cost of cold stores, refrigerated vehicles, refrigerated vessels, and refrigerated containers is higher than that of infrastructure and means of transport for ordinary cargo. It also consumes more energy in the process of operation, and advanced refrigeration technology can extend the shelf life of frozen cargo, slow down the rate of decay of frozen cargo. According to the means of loading, frozen cargo can be divided into two categories: one is refrigerated cargo transported by refrigerated container, the other is non-refrigerated cargo transported

by refrigerated vessel. In general, the characteristics of frozen cargo are as follows:

①易腐性

①Perishability

冷冻货物通常是具有易腐特征的食品,其保质期往往较短,在运输过程中的时间过长会造成产品品质的稳定性下降,甚至造成冷冻货的腐烂。对于这类货物,在运输过程中能够保持的温度环境越低,原品质就能够维持得越长久。即冷冻货的产品质量随时间变动而变化的过程中,"温度"是其主要的影响因素。

Frozen cargo usually has perishable characteristics of food, their shelf life is often short. The time in the transport process too long will cause the stability of product quality to decline, and even cause frozen cargo to rot. For such cargo, the lower the temperature environment that can be maintained during transportation, the longer the original quality can be maintained. That is, "temperature" is the main factor that affects the quality of frozen cargo in the process of changing with time.

②运输时效性

②Timeliness of Transport

因为冷冻货容易腐烂,在低温状态下虽然可以保持冷冻货的新鲜度,但要付出极高的制冷成本,所以冷冻货需要尽快地从产地到消费者手中,对时效性要求较高。为了减少冷冻货在运输过程中腐烂变质而影响销售,冷冻货销售商往往会在冷冻货被运至销售端时,设定一个"时间窗的限制"。

Because the frozen cargo is perishable, at low temperature although can maintain the freshness of frozen cargo, the high refrigeration costs have to be paid, so frozen cargo needs to let consumers get it from the origin as soon as possible, timeliness requirements are higher. To reduce the deterioration of frozen cargo in the transport process and affect sales, frozen cargo sellers often set a "window of a time limit" before shipping to the end of sales.

③所需设施设备的特殊性

③The Special Nature of the Facilities and Equipment Required

冷冻货运对运输、储存设施设备有着特别的要求。如需要冷藏集装箱、冷藏船或冷藏车运输,在冷库或专门的冷藏箱堆场储存。冷冻货在运输过程中,冷藏车、冷藏船需要消耗更多的能源来保证制冷到适宜的温度使冷冻货保鲜。

Frozen freight transportation has special requirements for transportation and storage facilities and equipment, such as refrigerated containers, refrigerated vessels, or refrigerated vehicles are required to transport the cargo, cold stores or special refrigerated container yards are required to store them. During the transportation of frozen cargo, the refrigerated trucks and vessel need to consume more energy to ensure the refrigeration to the proper temperature to keep the frozen cargo fresh.

④所需信息化程度高

④The Required Level of Information is High

将射频识别技术、全球定位系统、地理信息系统及条码技术等各种先进技术应用于对冷冻货所处环境的温度、pH 值及含氧量等情况进行实时跟踪与监控,能够有效降低产品损失率,减小配送的风险,改善配送效率。

The application of RFID (Radio Frequency Identification Technology), GPS, GIS, and bar code technology to the real-time tracking and monitoring of the temperature, pH value, and oxygen content of the frozen cargo can effectively reduce the rate of product loss, reduce the risk of distribution and improve the efficiency of distribution.

(2)设施的特殊要求

(2) Special Requirements for Facilities

港口作为冷链物流体系中的重要节点,可为大宗冷冻和冰鲜货物提供运输和仓储服务。装卸和运输低效等会引起冷冻货物环境温度发生变化,从而影响货物品质。所以冷藏相关实施设备应满足如下要求:

As an important node in the cold chain logistics system, the port can provide transportation and storage service for bulk frozen and chilled cargo. The inefficient handling and transportation will cause the change of the ambient temperature of the frozen cargo, which will affect the quality of the cargo. Therefore, refrigeration-related implementation equipment should meet the following requirements:

①泊位

①Berth

专业化冷藏船泊位需满足码头冷藏散货的装卸要求,一般为 5 000 吨级以上,装卸时使用门座式起重机。

Specialized refrigerated berth should meet the loading and unloading requirements of port refrigerated bulk cargo, generally more than 5,000 tons, using the portal crane when loading and unloading.

②港口冷库

②Port Cold Storage

非适箱的冷冻货经冷藏船舶卸载后,可运输至冷藏船后方的冷库进行中转。中转冷库是肉类、水产品和果蔬等冷冻和冰鲜货物在岸边卸船后发往腹地或直接转口时的临时存储设施。

Non-containerized frozen cargo can be unloaded by a refrigerated vessel and transported to the cold store behind the refrigerated vessel for transshipment. Transit cold storage is a temporary storage facility for frozen and chilled cargo such as meat, aquatic products, and fruits and vegetables when they are unloaded at the shore and sent to the hinterland or for direct transit.

③冷藏集装箱堆场

③Refrigerated Container Yard

集装箱码头在冷藏集装箱堆场进行海运冷藏集装箱装卸、交接、堆存以及保管等作业。堆场堆存冷藏箱类型包括冷藏重箱、空箱,货物来源和去向较为复杂,既包括进出口货物,又包括保税暂存及转口货物。

The container terminal carries out the operations of loading, unloading, handing over, stacking, and storage of the sea refrigerated containers in the refrigerated container yard. The types of storage refrigerated containers include reefer heavy containers, empty containers. The origin and destination of the cargo are more complicated, including import and export cargo, bonded temporary storage and re-export cargo.

④冷冻产品检验中心

④Frozen Products Inspection Center

海关与检验检疫部门通过在封闭和低温环境下的联合查验,保证进出口货物的质量,减少冷冻产品的通关时间,降低冷链过程中的"断链"风险。

The customs and the inspection and quarantine department can guarantee the quality of the import and export cargo, reduce the customs clearance time of the frozen products, and reduce the risk of "broken chain" in the process of the cold chain through the joint inspection under the closed and low-temperature environment.

⑤生鲜食品分拨配送中心

⑤Fresh Food Distribution Center

对港区内企业运出货物进行分拨、拼车以及对运入货物进行分拣,从而有效提高冷藏车辆实载率和服务水平,降低物流成本。

To improve the loading rate and service level of refrigerated vehicles and reduce the logistics cost, the enterprises in the port area carry out the distribution, carpooling, and sorting of the incoming cargo.

⑥综合服务区港区

⑥Integrated Services Port Area

冷链物流信息、管理与办公中枢,为关、检、港及其他相关部门提供办公场所,为相关企业提供物流信息服务。

Cold chain logistics information, management, and office hub, for customs, inspection, port, and other relevant departments to provide office space, for the relevant enterprises to provide logistics information services.

3.7.2 冷冻货港口物流运作与流程
3.7.2 Logistics Operation and Process of the Frozen Cargo Ports

按照冷冻货储运环境及装载形式不同,将港口分为两种:一种是服务于适箱货的集装箱专业化港口,包含与冷藏集装箱相关的全流程设施设备,如冷藏箱堆场;另一种是服务于多类型非适箱货的港口冷冻货专用港口,如远洋渔业专用码头。港口冷冻系统作业流程主要包括集装箱码头冷冻货物作业流程和冷冻货物专用码头流程两个方面。

Port is divided into two types according to the different storage and transportation environment and loading forms of the refrigerated cargo: One is the specialized container port serving the containerized cargo, it includes all-process facilities related to refrigerated containers, such as refrigerated container yards; The other is a special port for refrigerated cargo that serves many types of non-containable cargo, such as a special terminal for deep-sea fisheries. The operation flow of the port refrigeration system mainly includes two aspects: the operation flow of refrigerated cargo in the container terminal and that of the refrigerated cargo special terminal.

集装箱码头冷冻货物作业流程：冷藏集装箱在集装箱码头的装卸和运输方式与普通集装箱类似，但堆场作业具有特殊性，即装卸过程中需要有机械工人进入目标箱区进行电源插拔的辅助操作。

The operation flow of refrigerated cargo in a container terminal: The loading, unloading, and transportation of refrigerated containers at container terminals are similar to those of ordinary containers, but the yard operation is special—during loading and unloading, a mechanic must enter the target container area to perform the auxiliary operation of the power plug.

（1）进口冷藏集装箱作业流程
（1）The Operation Flow of Import Refrigerated Container

卸船前先检查冷藏箱制冷温度和箱体状况，如一切正常则切断电源，并卷好电源线和插头，进行卸船。冷藏集装箱经岸桥从船上吊下放置在集卡或自动牵引车上，被送到冷藏箱专用堆场后由场桥卸下。在场桥装卸完毕后需要工作人员进入箱区进行插电源的辅助操作，使冷冻机按规定温度进入工作状态。并对冷藏箱制冷机组的运行情况监测，对于监控系统中箱内温度异常的冷藏箱，还需工作人员进行现场检查和核对。部分被抽到检测的冷藏箱被送到检验区进行检验检疫和海关检验，确认没有问题后再送到堆场存放。冷藏集装箱在堆场停留一段时间后，外集卡进入港口提箱，工作人员拔掉箱区相关集装箱的电源后，冷藏箱由场桥运至外集卡后离港。

Before discharging, check the refrigerating temperature and the condition of the refrigerated container is needed. If everything is normal, cut off the power supply, roll up the power cord and plug, then unload the vessel. The refrigerated containers are lowered from the vessel by a quayside bridge, placed on the trucks or the automatic tractor, and delivered to the special storage yard of the refrigerated containers. After loading and unloading the bridge at the site, the workers need to enter the container area to plug in the power supply for auxiliary operation, so that the refrigerator is in accordance with the specified temperature into the working state. It also monitors the operation of the refrigeration unit of the refrigerating container. For the refrigerating container with abnormal temperature in the monitoring system, the workers need to check it on the spot. Some of the refrigerated containers drawn for testing are sent to the inspection area for inspection quarantine and customs inspection and then sent to the depot for storage after confirmation that there are no problems. After the refrigerated container stays in the yard for some time, the external trucks enter the port suitcase, the staff unplug the power supply of the relevant container in the container area, and the refrigerated container is transported from the yard bridge to the external trucks and leaving the port.

（2）出口冷藏集装箱作业流程

（2）Export Refrigerated Container Operation Process

出口冷藏集装箱由外集卡运输至港口，并按照要求到达冷藏集装箱堆场指定位置排队等待卸箱，由场桥搬运至对应箱位进行堆存，卸箱作业完成后外集卡离开堆场。部分被抽到检验的集装箱被送至检验处进行检验检疫和海关检验，没有问题后再被送到堆场进行堆存。港口工作人员在集装箱卸箱作业完毕后对冷藏集装箱进行插电，并确认箱内温度及其他指标正常。集装箱船到港后，冷藏集装箱由港口工作人员进行断电后，被内集卡运输至码头前沿并短暂堆存等待，通过岸桥将其搬运至船舶的指定箱位处，最后由船舶工作人员进行插电作业并检验，除认真检查箱体和冷冻机设备进行交接外，还要认真检查冷藏箱设定的温度，包括装箱单指定的温度、冷藏箱设定的温度和冷藏箱记录的温度，这三个温度应一致无误，在码头堆放期间应使冷冻机按规定温度处于正常工作状态。冷藏箱装船前应检查温度状况，在正常工作状态下切断电源，并卷好电源线和插头，然后由内集卡运至码头前沿短暂堆存后由岸桥运至船舶，完成冷藏集装箱港口出口作业。在上述过程中，需尽量避免冷藏集装箱制冷中断，以保证冷冻货物始终处于适宜的温度环境中。

The export refrigerated container is transported from the external trucks to the port and arrives at the designated location of the refrigerated container yard according to the requirements to queue for unloading, then transported from the yard bridge to the corresponding container location for storage. After the unloading operation is completed, the external trucks leave the yard. Some of the containers selected for inspection were sent to the inspection office and quarantine and customs for inspection, if no problems were found out, they would be sent to the yard for storage. After the completion of the reefer container plug, port staff conduct the unloading operation and ensure that the temperature and other indicators are normal. After the Knock Nevis arrives at the port, the reefer containers are cut off by the port staff, transported to the quayside of the port by the internal trucks and stored for a short period, then transported to the designated position of the vessel by the quay bridge, in the end, the vessel staff will conduct the plug-in operation and inspection. In addition to carefully checking the container body and the equipment of the refrigerator for handover, they will also carefully check the temperature set by the refrigerator container, including the temperature specified in the packing list, the temperature set by the refrigerator, and the temperature recorded by the refrigerator, these three temperatures should be consistent and the refrigerator should be kept in normal working condition according to the stipulated temperature during stacking at the port. The refrigerated containers shall be checked for temperature conditions before shipment, the power supply shall be cut off under normal working conditions, the power cord and plug shall be rolled, and then transported from the inner container to the quayside of the port for a short period of storage and from the quay bridge to the vessel, finish the export operation of a refrigerated container port. In the above process, the refrigeration interruption of the refrigerated container should be avoided as far as possible, to ensure that the refrigerated cargos are always in a suitable temperature environment.

（3）冷冻货物专用码头作业流程
(3) The Operation Flow of the Special Port for Frozen Cargo

冷链专用码头指以冷藏运输船为主要停靠船型,将托盘和冷库作为存储单元和场地,以门机为码头前沿装卸设备,对特定货种进行相应冷链物流操作的专用码头。与通用件杂货码头装卸工艺相似,港口冷库作为港内中转冷储场所,也可与冷库外冷藏集装箱及堆场配合进行出货操作。

Special cold chain ports refer to special ports that take refrigerated transport ships as the main berthing vessels, use pallets and cold storage as storage units and sites, and use door crates as loading and unloading equipment at the quayside of port to carry out corresponding cold chain logistics operations for specific types of cargo. Similar to the general cargo terminal loading and unloading process, the cold storage in the port serves as the cold storage place for in-port transfer, and can also cooperate with the cold storage container and storage yard for shipment operation.

国际干线和长途冷链运输中,冷冻货在冷藏船泊位通过门座式起重机等卸下后,由内集卡水平运输,到达冷库接卸区后,通过叉车以托盘形式放入冷库内货架进行仓储;或运输至临港保税冷库进行加工和贮存,后中转至其他地区;或经港口集疏运系统运输至腹地冷链物流中心,再分拨配送至目标客户。作为各种水工建筑物和冷链设施及设备的综合体,冷冻货专用码头是冷链物流的一个重要环节。

In international trunk line and long-distance cold chain transportation, the frozen cargo are unloaded by the door type crane at the refrigerated berth and transported horizontally by the internal trucks. After arriving at the cold storage receiving and unloading area, they are put into the shelf of the cold storage in the form of pallet by forklift trucks for storage or transported to the bonded cold storage for processing and storage, and then transferred to other regions. Some also are set to the hinterland cold chain logistics center through the port collection and distribution system, and then distributed to target customers. As a complex of various hydraulic structures and cold chain facilities and equipment, the special cold cargo terminal is an important link of cold chain logistics.

关于冷冻货物专用码头生产作业,大体流程为:冷藏船到港后停在合适的泊位处,为船舶分配合适的门座式起重机进行卸船,货物通过港口牵引车挂车进行水平运输到达冷库接卸区后,通过叉车以托盘形式放入冷库内货架。随后对冷冻货物进行查验,并对其进行预处理或精深加工,加工之后的货物在堆场进行冷储,根据客户需求等待外集卡来提货将其运出港口进行贸易中转或城市配送

As for the production operation of the special terminal for frozen cargo, the general process is as follows: the refrigerated vessel stops at an appropriate berth after arriving at the port, and the vessel is assigned an appropriate gantry crane to unload the ship. The cargo are transported horizontally by the port tractor trailer to the reception and unloading area of the cold storage, and then put into the shelf of the cold storage in the form of pallet by forklift trucks. Then the frozen cargo are inspected and pre-processed or intensively processed. The processed cargo are cold stored in the storage yard, and wait for the external trucks to pick up the cargo and transport them out of the port for trade transfer or urban distribution according to customer demand.

3.7.3 冷冻货港口物流管理特殊要求
3.7.3 Special Requirements for Logistics Management of Frozen Cargo Ports

集装箱泊位应满足冷藏集装箱的装卸要求。泊位吨级从 1 000 吨级至 15 万吨级不等。从港方而言,希望尽可能少的泊位资源,装卸尽可能多的货物;对船方而言,希望泊位资源充足,从而减少船舶在港等待泊位的时间。基于经济效益视角,如果泊位数越多,码头建设费用和运营管理成本越高,造成岸线资源的浪费;反之,冷藏船等待靠泊时间就越长,除了船舶自身费用外,待泊时船舱冷藏设备制冷效率下降,给船东带来更大的经济损失。港方和船方的总费用主要为码头建设费用(码头基础设施投资根据设施平均使用寿命,按平均年限法进行折旧估算)、运营阶段冷藏船等待靠泊产生的成本和冷藏船在相应泊位进行装卸产生的成本。

Container berths should meet the loading and unloading requirements of reefer containers. Berths range in tonnage from 1,000 to 150,000 tons. From the perspective of the port side, it hopes to have as few berth resources as possible and load and unload as much cargo as possible. For the ship, it is hoped that the berth resources are sufficient, so as to reduce the time for the vessel to wait for the berth in the port. From the perspective of economic benefit, the more berths there are, the higher the construction cost and operation management cost will be, resulting in the waste of shoreline resources. On the contrary, the longer the waiting time for the reefer ship, in addition to the ship's own cost, the cooling efficiency of the ship's refrigerated equipment decreases when waiting for the berth, bringing greater economic loss to the shipowner. The total cost of the port and the ship mainly consists of the port construction cost (the investment in port infrastructure is estimated by the average life method based on the average service life of the facility), the cost of waiting for the berthing of the refrigerated vessel in the operation stage and the cost of loading and unloading of the refrigerated vessel at the corresponding berth.

冷藏箱专用堆场箱位间应留有一定间距。一方面,设置冷藏箱专用插座或电源支架,保证冷藏箱重箱堆存能力;另一方面,为机械设备和工作人员插座留下空间,保证装卸箱作业安全和查验箱号方便。冷藏箱专用堆场一般采用冷藏箱温度集中监测系统及设施,并设置 PTI 检验区以进行冷藏箱运输前的检验。堆场内部存储货物均为堆垛形式,堆码高度一般不超过 2 层,对于设施较为先进和齐全的冷藏箱堆场,其堆高视具体条件可适当增加;港口冷库一般采用贯通式货架、窄巷道式货架和穿梭式货架等重型类货架,一般为 3 层以上,也是一种立体存储系统。冷藏箱堆场也需要设有专门的供电装置,一般包括电源支架或地面插座设施,可为冷藏集装箱制冷提供电源和送配电设施;港口冷库多通过对制冷机组供电、利用冷却剂蒸发吸收库内热量进行制冷。

There should be a certain space between containers in the special storage yard for reefers. On the one hand, the special socket or power supply bracket of the refrigerator is set up to ensure the storage capacity of the heavy container of the refrigerator. On the other hand, the space is left for the socket of the mechanical equipment and staff to ensure the safety of the operation of loading and unloading containers and the convenience of checking the container number. Refrigerated storage yard generally adopts centralized temperature monitoring system and facilities, and sets PTI inspection area for the inspection of refrigerated containers before transportation. All the cargos stored in the yard are in the form of stacking, and the stacking height is generally no more than 2 layers. For the refrigerator yard with more advanced and complete facilities, the stacking height can be appropriately increased according to the specific conditions. Port cold storage generally uses heavy shelves such as through-type shelves, narrow lane shelves, and shuttle shelves, which is also a three-dimensional storage system. Refrigerated container yard also needs a special power supply device, generally including power supply bracket or ground socket facilities, which can provide power supply and distribution facilities for refrigerated container refrigeration. Port cold storage mainly uses the refrigeration unit power supply and coolant evaporation to absorb the heat in the storage for refrigeration.

码头核验区的设置需满足要求。即当装载冷冻货的冷藏集装箱运抵港口时,需通过报关和报检等程序并经批准后才予以放行。在集装箱通关时,监管部门不能对所有通关集装箱进行查验,通常选择部分通关箱进行抽查。被抽查到的集装箱到达海关查验的相关区域,根据地磅的实际称重和已知的报关数据对比,初步判定是否需进行下一步查验。如需进行进一步检查,先根据 X 光机的机检结果判定是否需开箱查验,根据最后的查验结果决定该集装箱是否顺利完成通关,如若不满足条件则对其进行罚没。当开箱的货物需做检疫处理时,完成熏蒸及其他相关操作并根据最后查验结果决定该集装箱是否顺利完成通关。检验区的主要设施如下:

The setting of the terminal verification area shall meet the requirements. That is, when the reefer container loaded with frozen cargo arrives at the port, it needs to go through customs declaration and inspection procedures and be approved before it is released. In the container clearance, the supervision department can not check all the containers, usually select part of the clearance containers for a spot check. After the selected containers arrive at the relevant area of customs inspection, according to the actual weighing of the odometer and the known customs declaration data, preliminarily determine whether to carry out the containers to the next inspection. If further inspection is required, the inspection results of the X-ray machine should be used to determine whether the container needs to be opened for inspection, and the final inspection results should be used to determine whether the container has completed customs clearance. If the conditions are not met, they will be confiscated. When unpacked cargo need to be quarantined, fumigation and other related operations shall be completed and the final inspection results shall be used to determine whether the container is successfully cleared through customs. The main facili-

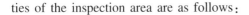

ties of the inspection area are as follows:

（1）查验平台
（1）Inspection Platform

查验平台分为海关功能查验区查验平台和联检查验功能区查验平台两种。海关功能查验区查验平台主要实现查验集装箱的开箱操作,是海关功能区查验平台为海关查验的场地。进入集中查验区的集装箱,若仅被海关布控查验时,该箱被送至海关功能区查验平台进行查验。联检功能区查验平台为海关和出入境检验检疫局共同查验的工作场地,主要包含集装箱的开箱平台和出入境检验检疫的卫生除害场地等。当进入集中查验区的集装箱需海关和出入境检验检疫局共同开箱查验时,需将该集装箱运送至联检功能区查验平台。

The inspection platforms are divided into two types: customs functional inspection area inspection platform and joint inspection functional area inspection platform. Customs functional inspection area inspection platform mainly realizes the unpacking operation of inspection containers and is the venue for customs inspection. If the container entering the centralized inspection area is only subject to customs control and inspection, the container will be sent to the customs functional inspection area inspection platform. The inspection platform in the joint inspection functional area is the work site jointly inspected by the customs and the entry-exit inspection and quarantine bureau, mainly including the container unpacking platform and the entry-exit inspection and quarantine sanitary and pesticide removal site. When containers entering the centralized inspection area need to be opened for inspection jointly by the Customs and the entry-exit inspection and quarantine bureau, the containers shall be transported to the joint inspection area inspection platform.

（2）检验检疫落地查验场地
（2）Inspection and Quarantine Landing Inspection Site

出入境检验检疫局需查验的集装箱在出入境检验检疫功能区查验场地的作业场所由人工开箱查验。进入集中查验区的集装箱,若仅被检验检疫布控且需开箱查验,则该箱会被送至出入境检验检疫功能区落地查验场地进行查验。

Containers to be inspected by entry-exit inspection shall be opened for inspection manually at the inspection site in the inspection function zone. If the container entering the centralized inspection area is only controlled by the inspection and quarantine and needs to be opened for inspection, the container will be sent to the landing inspection site in the entry-exit inspection and quarantine functional area for inspection.

（3）堆箱场地及待提区
（3）Stacking Site and Pick-up Area

当需要查验的集装箱在完成开箱查验作业时,若查验平台的卡位资源被占用,则该箱将放置于堆箱场地中等待查验资源的释放。若集装箱完成开箱查验作业,则该集装箱将放置于待提区中,等待送离集中查验区。

When the container to be checked is unpacked, if the slot resources of the inspection platform are occupied, the container will be placed in the packing site to wait for the release of the inspection resources. If the container has completed the unpacking inspection, the container will be placed in the pick-up area, waiting to be sent out of the centralized inspection area.

(4) 罚没仓库

(4) Confiscate the Warehouse

在上述不同类别的查验过程中,当集装箱的查验结果不合格时,海关和出入境检验检疫局将集装箱中货物予以没收,并存放于罚没仓库中,等待销毁或进行其他方式的处理。

In the above different types of inspection, when the inspection result of the container is not qualified, the customs and the entry-exit inspection and quarantine bureau will confiscate the cargo in the container and store them in the confiscation warehouse for destruction or other treatment.

第4章 港口物流发展新技术

Chapter 4 | New Technologies for Port Logistics Development

❖ 4.1 智慧港口技术与实践

4.1 Technology and Practice of Smart Port

4.1.1 智慧港口的内涵与发展
4.1.1 Connotation and Development of Smart Port

作为水路与陆路货物运输的换装节点,港口是多种运输方式的交汇,是多方数据信息的有机融合。智慧港口的建设是提高港口作业效率与稳定性、实现港口与供应链上下游企业协同运作的关键因素之一。利用物联网、大数据、云计算、现代优化技术,港口构建了智慧港口平台与决策系统,从而提升了港口运行效率与服务水平。

As a reloading node for water and land transportation, the port is the intersection for multiple transportation modes and the fusion of multi-party information. The construction of smart ports plays a crucial role to improve the efficiency and stability of port operations and realize the coordinated operation of ports and upper and lower enterprises of the supply chain. Internet of things, big data, cloud computing, and modern optimization technologies are used to build the smart port platform and decision-making system, which can improve port operation efficiency and service levels.

智慧港口理念来源于智慧地球、智慧城市等概念,是在港口发展新理念和科技催生下产生的新概念。智慧是机械运作与智能决策的深层结合,不断创新生产服务与管理模式。综合国内外智慧港口的定义,将智慧港口定义为:通过如物联网和云计算等新兴信息技术建立智能化港口信息平台,实现港口物流过程的实时检测与控制;运用先进港口调度技术与智能决策方法,提高港口运营决策的科学性;通过港口各作业环节与客户、海关、政府部门等外部环节的协调与一体化运作,建设智能、高效的现代化口岸系统。

The smart port is derived from smart earth and smart city, a new concept created by port development and technology. Smart is the deep combination of mechanical operation and intelligent decision-making, and constantly innovates the production service and management mode. Based on the existing domestic and foreign definitions, the smart port is defined as follow: Establishing a smart port information platform to achieve real-time detection and control of the port logistics process, through new information technologies such as the internet of things and cloud computing, etc.; Using advanced dispatching technology and intelligent decision-making methods to improve the scientificity of port operation decision; Building an intelligent and efficient modern port system through coordination and integrated operation of the internal and external (customers, customs and government agencies) port operations.

　　智慧港口主要包含智慧口岸、智慧码头、智慧商务和智慧物流等,实现了口岸通关一体化、作业自动化、服务便利化以及物流可视化等,如图 4.1 所示。智慧港口是港口发展的主要方向,是智慧交通和智慧城市的重要组成部分,对国家的创新驱动和转型可持续发展具有重要意义。在新一轮信息技术变革下,智慧港口将引领世界港口发展。

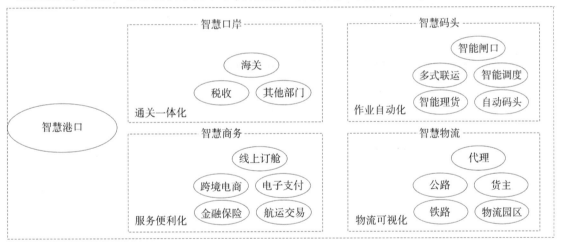

图 4.1　智慧港口功能构成

The smart port mainly includes a smart port, smart terminal, smart commerce, and smart logistics, which realizes port clearance integration, operation automation, service facilitation, and logistics visualization of the port, as shown in Figure 4.1. The smart port is the main development direction and an important part of smart transportation and smart cities, which is extremely important to innovation and sustainable development. Under the new round of information technology changes, the smart port will lead the world ports development.

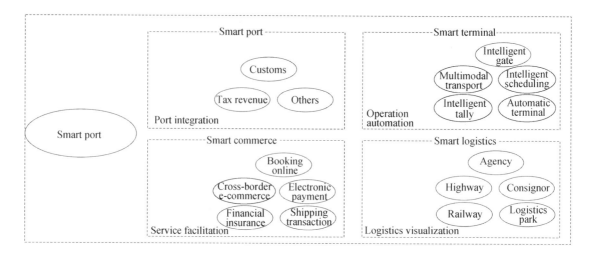

Figure 4.1 Function composition of smart port

随着相关技术与理论研究的不断发展,港口逐渐从资源控制转向资源管理、从内部流程优化转向外部连接互动、从客户价值提升转向生态系统价值最大化。智慧港口发展逐渐呈现出以下趋势:

With the continuous development of related technology and theory, ports have gradually shifted from resource control to resource management, from internal process optimization to external connection interaction, and from customer value enhancement to ecosystem value maximization. The development of the smart port gradually shows the following trends:

(1)港口物流服务协同化
(1)Coordination of Port Logistics Service

跨行业、跨部门、跨区域的高效率物流协作是智慧港口的重点,可有效提升价值链的整体效率、服务质量和客户体验。

Smart port focuses on efficient logistics collaboration across industries, departments, and regions, which can improve efficiency, service quality, and customer experience.

(2)港口运营智能化
(2)Intelligence of Port Operations

运营智能化是智慧港口的灵魂,是以数据驱动为核心的港口智能化运营管理。

Intelligent operation plays a key role in the smart port, which is a port intelligent management based on data-driven.

(3)港口贸易便利化
(3)Facilitation of Port Trade

基于数字化、智能化技术强化港口物流资源整合,优化资源配置,提升港口物流效率与服务水平,促进贸易便利化。

Strengthen the integration of port logistics resources based on digital and intelligent technologies; optimize resource allocation; improve port logistics efficiency and service levels; promote trade facilitation.

（4）数据服务社会化
（4）Socialization of Data Service

依托港口先天优势，利用大数据技术挖掘数据潜在价值，借助云计算、大数据及移动互联网等技术探索数据应用，利用区块链技术推动传统航运业的快速健康发展，提供高价值的商业机会和决策支持，提高港口数据应用的社会价值。

According to the inherent port advantages, use big data technology to discover the potential data value. Use cloud computing, big data, and mobile internet to explore data applications. Use blockchain technology to promote the rapid and healthy development of the traditional shipping industry. Provide high-value business opportunities and decision support, and increase the social value of port data.

（5）业务模式开放化
（5）Openness of Business Model

围绕数字化和开放式创新，加快港口与金融、产业互联网的结合，提升港口综合软实力，提高港口业务模式创新的开放化。

Focus on digitization and open innovation, accelerate the combination of ports with finance and industrial internet, improve the comprehensive soft power of ports, and increase the openness of port business model innovation.

（6）港口生态圈和谐化
（6）Harmony of the Port Ecosystem

加深资源共享，最大化提升资源利用率，形成开放共享、互联互通的良好港口生态圈，是智慧港口运作的基本保障。

Improve resource sharing, maximize improve resource utilization, form a good port ecosystem for open sharing and connectivity, is the basic guarantees for smart port operations.

在智慧港口发展中，借助数字化、智能化等现代信息技术，积极开展世界贸易一体化，从而完成开放协作、高度互联、绿色经济的港口生态圈构建。政府部门加强政策引导，建立完善的监管体系，引领港口的高层次发展；港口企业基于港口生态圈视角完善智慧港口顶层设计，完善内外协作与业务创新，提升增值服务比例，推动模式创新；利益各方坚持"开放共享、多赢互惠、信息互通、合作共赢"的原则，加强资源整合和优化配置，最大化港口价值网络的整体利益。

During the development of the smart port, with modern information technologies such as digitalization and intelligence, implement the world trade integration actively and thus establish an open, collaborative, interconnected, green, and economic port ecosystem. The government should strengthen policy guidance, establish a sound policy and regulatory system, and lead the port industry to a higher level. Port enterprises should improve the top-level design of smart ports based on the port ecosystem, strengthen internal and external collaboration and business innovation, increase the proportion of value-added services, and promote model innovation. All the interested parties should adhere to the principle of " open sharing, reciprocity, information exchange, and win-win cooperation", improve resource integration and optimize allocation, and maximize the overall benefits of the port value network.

4.1.2 智慧港口关键技术及创新性
4.1.2 Key Technologies and Innovation of Smart Port

为应对逐步提高的大宗散货进出口系统生产率及集装箱装卸的物流系统效率,智慧港口基于一系列智能技术,实现了港口运作环节及信息服务的智能化。智慧港口的建设包含全程信息跟踪技术、基于射频识别的智能识别技术、运行工具重量检测技术以及智能决策支持技术等多项关键技术。

In order to cope with the gradual improvement of the productivity of bulk cargo import and export systems and the efficiency of container loading and unloading logistics systems, the smart port has realized the intellectualization of port operation links and information services based on a series of intelligent technologies. The construction of smart ports involves several key technologies such as whole-process information tracking technology, RFID-based intelligent identification technology, weight detection technology of running tools , and intelligent decision support technology.

(1)全程信息跟踪技术
(1) Whole-process Information Tracking Technology
全程信息跟踪技术主要包括遥感、地理信息系统、全球定位系统。通过该技术获得如实时地理位置、预计到达时间等船舶信息,为船舶在港区的动态调度提供基本依据。

Whole-process information tracking technology mainly includes remote sensing (RS), geographic information system (GIS), and global positioning system (GPS). The technology obtains ship information such as geographical location and expected arrival time, providing a basis for ship dynamic dispatch in the port.

(2)基于射频识别的智能识别技术
(2) RFID-based Intelligent Identification Technology
集装箱智能识别系统储存了大量信息,可防止篡改,并可以准确记录操作的时间和地点。它通过设备终端管理交通流,提高外集卡进出港效率与港口设备配置效率,提升港口整体服务水平。

The container intelligent identification system stores a lot of information to prevent tampering and accurately record the time and place of operation. It manage the traffic flow through the equipment terminal, improve the efficiency of external trucks entering and leaving the port and port equipment configuration, and strengthen the overall port service level.

（3）运行工具重量检测技术
(3) Weight Detection Technology of Running Tools

它通过与其他智能运输技术结合获得船舶的特定实时信息，为港口设备配置提供依据。该技术还可在港内自动检查船舶，自动检测货物超载和船舶平衡情况，提高了港口作业与货物运输的安全性，有利于港口运作效率的提升。

It is combined with other intelligent transportation technologies to obtain specific real-time ship information, which provides a basis for port equipment configuration. The technology can automatically inspect vessels in the port and detect cargo overload and vessel balance, and thus strengthening the safety of port operations and cargo transportation and improving port operation efficiency.

（4）智能决策支持技术
(4) Intelligent Decision Support Technology

它依托大数据技术，通过云计算技术和辅助系统完成科学决策。它基于港口实时数据、人工智能、现代优化技术，可提高作业调度的智能化水平，改变生产调度决策依赖人为经验的局面，提高码头作业资源的利用效率。

It relies on big data technologies and completes scientific decisions by cloud computing technology and auxiliary system. Based on real-time port data, artificial intelligence, and modern optimization technology to improve the intelligent level of operation dispatching, change the situation that production scheduling decisions rely on human experience, and improve the efficiency of terminal operation resource utilization.

新一代港口建立了完善而便捷的数据库及数据交换系统，实现了部门、地区、行业间的信息交流。智慧港口的建设方便了管理部门的统一管理，实现了行业的信息共享，有效整合了海关内外的信息资源。

The new generation of ports have established a comprehensive and convenient database and exchange system to realize the information exchange among departments, regions, and industries. The construction of a smart port has facilitated unified management, realized industry information sharing, and effectively integrated the information resources inside and outside the customs.

4.1.3 工业物联网与港口作业管理
4.1.3 Management of Industrial Internet of Things and Port Operations

物联网是以互联网为基础，通过射频识别、红外感应器、全球定位系统、激光扫描等信息传感设备连接物流与互联网,实现了信息的实时采集、传输及发布。

Based on the internet, the internet of things (IoT) connects logistics with the internet through radio frequency identification (RFID), infrared sensors, GPS, laser scanning, and other information sensing equipment to achieve real-time information collection, transmission, and release.

工业物联网技术即将物联网技术应用于工业领域。工业物联网技术在工业生产中融入具有感知监控功能的传感控制器,以完成数据的实时采集,进而提高工业制造和产品制造的质量,最终实现传统工业的智能化转变。

The industrial internet of things is the IoT technology applied in the industrial field. Industrial IoT technology integrates sensors and controllers with sensing and monitoring capabilities in the industrial production process to complete the real-time data collection and thus improve the quality of industrial manufacturing and product manufacturing, and finally realize the intelligent transformation for traditional industries.

港口作为水路与陆路运输的交接点,集聚了大量的先进机械设备,物流管理流程复杂。随着港口作业业务量的增加,原有业务流程与管理手段无法满足现有需求,为提高管理效率、降低运营成本,物联网技术逐渐应用于港口生产运作。港口借助物联网感知、互联、智慧的技术特征,加强港口装备、船货信息及港口物流资源和参与方之间的互联互通,如图 4.2 所示。随着射频识别、无线传感网络及其他技术的研发应用,鹿特丹港、汉堡港等港口陆续建成智能化港口,国内宁波港、青岛港、盐田港、大连港等相继建成港口物联网或智能港口项目。

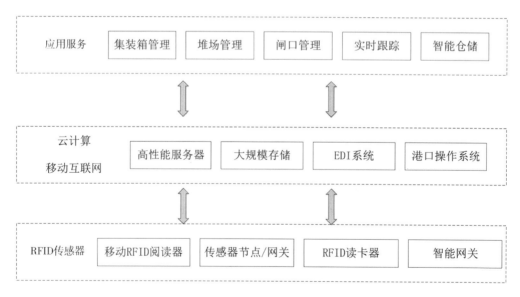

图 4.2　物联网智慧港口建设体系

As a connection point between water and land transportation, the port gathers a large number of advanced machinery and equipment, and the logistics management process is complicated. With the increase of the port operation business volume, the original business processes and management methods can not meet the existing needs. To improve management efficiency and reduce operating costs, IoT technology is gradually applied to port production operations. With the help of the technical features of perception, interconnection, and wisdom of the IoT, ports strengthen interconnection between port equipment, cargo information, port logistics resources, and participants, as shown in Figure 4.2. With the development and application of RFID, wireless sensor networks, and other technologies, ports such as Rotterdam Port and Hamburg Port have successively implemented intelligent ports. In China, Ningbo Port, Qingdao Port, Yantian Port, and Dalian Port have completed the IoT or smart port projects.

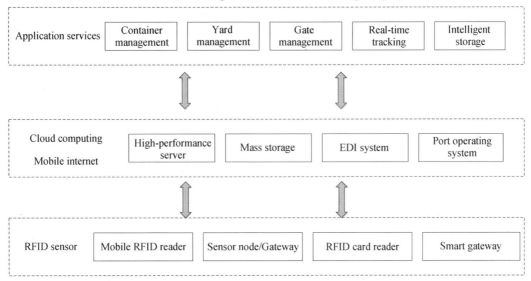

Figure 4.2　Smart port construction system based on the IoT

通过物联网技术显著提升港口信息建设水平,能够明显改善港口经营模式,提升港口供给量与可控性。然而,物联网技术设计的信息量大、流程复杂,其对信息的稳定及数据的传输速率具有较高的要求。由于高速率、低时延、高可靠、大连接等几大特性,5G 已成为各大领域在研究工业物联网时关注的重点。

Through IoT technology, the level of port information construction can be significantly improved, the port business model can be significantly improved, and the supply and controllability of the port can be improved. However, the design of IoT technology has a large amount of information and complex process, which has high requirements for information stability and data transmission rate. Due to the advantages of high speed, low delay, high reliability, and large connection, 5G has become the focus of attention in various fields when studying the industrial IoT.

4.1.4　基于移动物联网的港口集卡预约系统
4.1.4　Port Trucks Appointment System Based on Mobile Internet of Things

预约集港是指通过限定不同时间段内的集卡到达数量降低高峰时段集卡的到达数量,

其可有效缓解码头集卡拥堵,提高码头作业效率。外集卡的预约流程如图4.3所示。通过码头与港外堆场间的联系,码头提供多个预约时段及其预约份额;堆场依据自身运力选择预约时段并给出对应集装箱量;码头根据整体预约情形确定最终集港计划并通知堆场;最后,由堆场依据计划安排集港。

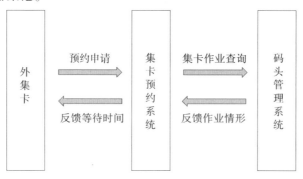

图4.3　外集卡预约流程

The appointment truck collection refers to reducing the number of truck arrivals during peak hours by limiting that in different periods, which can effectively alleviate congestion and improve the efficiency of the terminal operations. The external truck appointment process is shown in Figure 4. 3. Through the connection between the terminal and the external yard, the terminal provides multiple appointment periods and their appointment shares. The yard chooses the appointment period and the container volume based on transportation capacity. The terminal determines the final truck collection plan and informs the yard. Finally, the yard arranges the truck collection according to the plan.

Figure 4.3　External truck appointment process

预约集港模式精细、可控性强,码头可在集港前精准掌握各时段的集装箱量及箱源分布,利于码头的堆场机械调度,进而有效提高堆场利用效率。港外堆场预先得知码头收箱能力,可合理安排自身运力,避免集卡高峰时段闸口和运力的浪费,提高集卡周转率,提升堆场经营效益。堆场作业效率和集卡周转效率的提高有利于堆场和集卡能耗的降低,进而降低污染排放,促进环保港口的建设。

The appointment truck collection mode is fine and controllable. The terminal can accurately grasp the volume and distribution of the container at various times before collection, which is conducive to yard equipment scheduling and yard utilization efficiency. The external yard gets the container collection capacity in advance, rationally arranges transportation capacity, avoids waste of gates and transportation capacity at peak time, and improves the truck turnover and operation efficiency. The improvement of yard operation efficiency and the truck turnover efficiency will reduce energy consumption and pollution emissions and thus promote the construction of environmentally friendly ports.

4.1.5　典型案例介绍
4.1.5　Typical Case Introduction

面对港口运营成本上升和航运联盟化、大型化趋势,新加坡港、鹿特丹港、汉堡港、上海港等港口积极探索向下一代港口的转型。

In the face of rising port operating costs and the trend of shipping alliances and large-scale ships, ports such as Singapore Port, Rotterdam Port, Hamburg Port, and Shanghai Port are actively exploring the transition to the next generation port.

（1）新加坡港
（1）Singapore Port

新加坡港(如图 4.4 所示)位于新加坡南部的沿海,西临马六甲海峡的东南侧,南临新加坡海峡的北侧,是世界最大的集装箱港口之一。同时,其还是新加坡全国政治、经济、文化及交通的中心。2019 年其完成集装箱吞吐量 3 720 万 TEU,仅次于上海港位居世界第二位。目前,其正积极以其智慧港口大士港的建设为核心,打造智慧集装箱港口,以应对日益激烈的全球港口竞争。为实现"表现力、生产力、可持续发展"三大目标,新加坡港征集新一代集装箱港口的创新技术方案,从运营效率、可执行力、绿色环保等方面建设智慧港口。第一,提升智能化运营,完善集装箱自动跟踪配载、堆场实时控制和船舶装卸,保证安全生产和服务水平的稳定性。第二,构建并优化网络化运输体系,整合港口物流链资源,加强港口物流价值链服务。第三,提升业务模式创新,建立联通互享的信息系统,实现信息集成。第四,提出大数据治港概念,整合物流信息资源,优化物流流程,提高服务能力。其五,构建良好的港口生态圈,与物流各方建立合作关系,实现贸易的便利化运作。

Singapore Port (as shown in Figure 4.4) is located on the south coast of Singapore, southeast of Malacca Strait in the west, and north of Singapore Strait in the south. It is one of the largest container ports in the world. It is also the center of Singapore's national political, economic, cultural, and transportation. In 2019, it completed a container throughput of 37.2 million TEU, ranking second in the world after Shanghai Port. At present, it is actively building a smart container port with the construction of its smart port (i.e., Tuas Port) as the core to cope with the increasingly fierce global port competition. In order to achieve the three goals of "expressiveness, productivity, and sustainable development", Singapore Port solicits innovative technology solutions for a new generation of container ports to build a smart port in terms of operation efficiency, enforceability, and green environmental protection. First, promote intelligent terminal operations. Realize automatic container tracking, real-time yard control, and ship operation. Ensure the stability of production safety and service levels. Second, build and optimize the network transportation system, integrate port logistics value chain resources, and strengthen port logistics chain services. Third, innovate business models, build interconnected information systems, and achieve information integration. Fourth, use big data to manage ports, integrate logistics information resources, optimize logistics processes, and improve service capability. Fifth, build a good port ecosystem, establish cooperative relationships with port logistics parties, and achieve trade facilitation.

图 4.4　新加坡港

Figure 4.4　Singapore Port

（图片来源：新加坡港务局. Port of Singapore［EB/OL］. https：// www. mpa. gov. sg/web/portal/home/port-of-singapore.）

（2）鹿特丹港

（2）Rotterdam Port

作为曾经的世界第一港口,鹿特丹港(如图 4.5 所示)是最早开始建设自动化码头的港口。1993 年,世界上第一个集装箱自动化码头便在鹿特丹港的 ECT 三角洲码头投产。近年来,鹿特丹港也不断加速自动化码头建设,如鹿特丹世界门户港码头等自动化码头的相继投产建成。2020 年鹿特丹港的集装箱吞吐量达 1 435 万 TEU。作为欧洲最大的贸易港,鹿特丹港以全球枢纽港和欧洲临港产业集聚区为目标,积极完善智慧港口。第一,构建便捷可靠的港口集疏运系统,完善港口腹地的运输,优化内陆多式联运网络。第二,促进码头运营智能化,通过建立自动化码头提升港口运作效率与服务质量。第三,整合物流相关方的资源,完善物流服务的协同衔接,构建便利化的国际贸易体系。第四,建立国际化的运输信息系统,完善港口相关各方间的信息互通与共享,提高港口物流链一体化服务水平。第五,加强与港口物流各方合作,促进政企合作。

As once the world's largest port, Rotterdam Port (as shown in Figure 4.5) was the first port to build an automatic terminal. In 1993, the world's first automated container terminal was put into operation at ECT Delta Wharf in Rotterdam Port. In recent years, Rotterdam Port has also been accelerating the construction of automatic terminals, such as Rotterdam World Gateway (RWG) terminal, and other automatic terminals have been put into operation and completed one after another. In 2020, the container throughput of Rotterdam Port will reach 14.35 million TEU. As the largest trading port in Europe, Rotterdam Port actively improves the smart port with the goal of global hub port and European port industrial agglomeration area. First, build a convenient and reliable port collection and distribution system, strengthen hinterland transportation, and optimize the inland multimodal transport network. Second, promote the intelligent terminal operation, improve port operation efficiency, and service quality by establishing automated terminals. Third, strengthen the integration of port logistics resources, promote business collaboration of port logistics services, and facilitate international trade facilitation. Fourth, build an international transportation information system, realize the information communication and sharing between relevant parties in the port, and improve the integrated service level of the port logistics chain. Fifth, strengthen cooperation with port logistics parties and promote cooperation between government and enterprises.

图 4.5　鹿特丹港

Figure 4.5　Rotterdam Port

（图片来源：Danny Cornelissen. Aerial photo Theemswegtrace［EB/OL］. https：// www.portofrotterdam.com/ en/pressroom/photo-gallery.）

（3）汉堡港

（3）Hamburg Port

汉堡港（如图4.6所示）作为德国最大港口及欧洲第三大港口,因其优越的地理位置已成为欧洲最重要的中转海港与交通枢纽。其共有双小车岸边集装箱装卸桥14台,可对超大型集装箱船舶进行装卸作业。堆场及水平运输系统主要由双轨道龙门吊装卸堆垛系统及自动导引车组成。2020年汉堡港集装箱吞吐量达853万TEU。汉堡港的智慧港口建设目标是安全、高效、协同、绿色、可持续发展。第一,提高港口的资源利用率,完善港口物流基础设施建设,优化自身的自动化生产力。第二,构建自动化码头和物流服务基地,完善运营的智能化水平及运作效率。第三,完善港口腹地的多式联运体系,构建智能交通系统,强化其中转枢纽的地位。第四,构建完善的控制平台和大数据系统,为客户提供一体化服务。第五,积极推进港口生态圈建设。

As the largest port in Germany and the third-largest port in Europe, Hamburg Port（as shown in Figure 4.6) has become the most essential transit port and transport hub in Europe because of its superior geographical location. There are 14 double trolley container loading and unloading bridges on the shore, which can load and unload super large container ships. The storage yard and horizontal transportation system are mainly composed of double-track gantry crane loading and unloading stacking systems and AGV. In 2020, the container throughput of Hamburg Port will reach 8.53 million TEU. The construction goal of the smart port of Hamburg Port is safety, high efficiency, coordination, green, and sustainable development. First, improve resource utilization, strengthen port logistics infrastructure construction, and enhance port automation productivity. Second, build automated terminals and logistics service bases to improve the intelligent level and operation efficiency. Third, improve the hinterland multimodal transport system, build the intelligent transportation system, and strengthen the transit hub position of the Hamburg Port. Fourth, establish a modern control platform and big data system to provide integrated services for customers. Fifth, promote the construction of the port ecosystem.

图 4.6　汉堡港

Figure 4.6　Hamburg Port

(图片来源：Michael Lindner. Port of Hamburg［EB/OL］. https：// www. hafen-hamburg. de/en/press/？ all = 0&media = 89990&media_created = 0&media_type = 5091.)

（4）上海港
（4）Shanghai Port

上海港(如图 4.7 所示)是世界最大港口,其由长江口南岸港区、杭州湾北岸港区、黄浦江港区、洋山深水港区组成。其自动化码头洋山港四期码头于 2017 年建成投产,共有 7 个集装箱泊位,可满足各类大小船只停泊需要。作为全球最大的单体自动化集装箱码头,其吞吐量可达 630 万 TEU。上海港依托开放式创新和新技术带来的新动能和新格局,积极完善智慧港口的建设。第一,完善设备的自动操作、调度的智能化和数据信息交互可视化,提升运营效率。第二,改变传统的装卸封闭模式,实现供应链上下游的协同与高效作业,完善物流资源的整体化。第三,提高业态的创新性,积极扩大自身业务范围。第四,加强港口的信息化、精益化和系统化建设,构建大数据平台服务系统,完善集疏运的协同化,建设物流相关方的完善商业环境,促进高附加值产业的聚集。第五,建设协同化的港口生态圈,提升贸易的便利化。

Shanghai Port (as shown in Figure 4.7) is the world's largest port, which is composed of the south bank port area of the Yangtze River Estuary, the north bank port area of Hangzhou Bay, the port area of Huangpu River, and Yangshan deep-water port area. Its automated terminal Yangshan Port Phase IV terminal was completed and put into operation in 2017, with 7 container berths, which can meet the berthing needs of vessels of all sizes. As the worlds's largest single automated container terminal, its throughput can reach 6.3 million TEU. Relying on the new driving forces and new pattern brought by open innovation and new technology, Shanghai Port actively improves the construction of the Smart Port. First, improve operational efficiency through equipment operation automation, intelligent port dispatching, and information visualization. Second, break through the traditional closed operation mode, turn to the efficient and coordinated operation of the supply chain, and promote the integration of port logistics resources. Third, innovate business models and expand business scope. Fourth, strengthen information, lean, and systematic construction of the port, build a big data platform service system, improve the coordination of collection and distribution, build the perfect business environment for logistics participants, promote the gathering of high value-added industries. Fifth, build a closely coordinated port ecosystem and promote trade facilitation.

图 4.7　上海港
Figure 4.7　Shanghai Port

(图片来源:张晓鸣.上海港集装箱吞吐量今年将再创新高[EB/OL]. https://wenhui.whb.cn/third/baidu/202111/04/432197.html.)

(5)青岛港
(5)Qingdao Port

青岛港集装箱码头始建于1982年。目前,青岛港(如图4.8所示)是世界第六大港,其自动化码头分别于 2017 年及 2019 年投产运营,2019 年其集装箱吞吐量完成 2 183 万标准箱,位居世界第七位。作为大型港口之一,青岛港重视智慧码头建设,有效借助互联网资源与云技术,扩大港口服务内容及业务服务能力,以全程线上服务为核心,完善物流用户、产品、服务三者协同的物流服务生态圈。青岛港以自身优势为基础完成价值创新,以区域性物流生态圈的战略制定及领导为目标,规划和控制生态系统,有效提升地区智慧港口竞争力和贸易便利化水平。

Container terminals of Qingdao Port were founded in 1982, Qingdao Port (as shown in Figure 4.8) is now the sixth-largest port in the world, and its automated terminals were put into operation in 2017 and 2019 respectively. In 2019, its container throughput reached 21.83 million TEU, ranking seventh in the world. As one of the largest ports around the world, Qingdao Port attaches importance to the construction of the smart port and expands port service content and business service capabilities based on the Internet and cloud technologies. With the main feature of online service, Qingdao Port builds a port logistics service ecosystem that gathers logistics users, products, and services. Combined its resource endowment to complete value innovation, Qingdao Port becomes the maker and leader of the regional logistics ecosystem strategy. It can formulate and control the ecosystem, and enhance the competitiveness of regional smart ports and trade facilitation level.

图 4.8 青岛港

Figure 4.8 Qingdao Port

(图片来源:张进刚.山东港口青岛港:繁忙节日景象展现工业之美[EB/OL]. https://www.xuexi.cn/lgpage/detail/index.html? id=6156021900314397019&item_id=6156021900314397019.)

◈ 4.2　自动化集装箱码头

4.2　Automated Container Terminal

4.2.1　自动化集装箱码头的概念与分类
4.2.1　Concept and Classification of Automated Container Terminal

随着全球经济贸易的飞速发展,海运已经逐渐成为世界货物运输的最主要途径,占据国际贸易量的四分之三以上。港口作为海上货物中转与装卸的重要节点,其整体作业水平直接影响货物的周转效率。集装箱码头是集装箱货物在水陆联运过程中的重要枢纽中心,完成集装箱的装卸和运输等作业。近年来,随着港口集装箱吞吐量的快速增长,传统集装箱码头逐渐无法应对船舶大型化、人工成本上升及复杂天气因素所带来的挑战。针对上述问题,各大集装箱码头综合采用计算机、传感、自动化控制等其他技术,完成对生产全过程的优化控制、对码头装卸和运输设备的实时智能化调度。自动化集装箱码头成为集装箱码头发展的必然趋势。

With the rapid development of the global economy and trade, shipping has gradually become the most critical world cargo transportation, accounting for more than three-quarters of international trade volume. As an essential node of maritime cargo transfer, the port operation level directly affects the cargo turnover efficiency. The container terminal is the important hub of container cargo in the process of water and land combined transportation, completing the loading, unloading and transportation of containers. In recent years, with the rapid growth of port container throughput, traditional container terminals are gradually unable to cope with the challenges of large-scale vessels, rising labor costs, and complex weather factors. In view of the above problems, the major container terminals comprehensively adopt computer, sensing, automatic control and other technologies to complete the optimal control of the whole production process, the real-time intelligent dispatching of the loading, unloading and transportation equipment at the terminal. Automated Container Terminal (ACT) has become an inevitable trend in container terminal development.

自动化集装箱码头的概念是于1993年在鹿特丹港启用ECT三角洲码头后提出的。它指的是与堆场作业以及与堆场海侧的交互作业已自动化的码头。起初,自动化集装箱码头的概念是围绕着港内堆场作业进行定义的,但这只是自动化码头发展的起步阶段。集装箱码头发展总的趋势是向更高水平的自动化发展的,涉及更多人工作业的替代与更高的作业效率。实践证明,自动化集装箱码头能显著提升运营效率,缩短船舶靠泊时间,提高港口吞吐量,保证货物装卸质量,提高港口经济和社会效益,并提供个性化服务。

The concept of ACT was put forward after the ECT Delta Wharf was opened in Rotterdam Port in 1993. It refers to the terminal whose interactive operation with the yard and the seaside of the yard has been automated. At first, the concept of ACT was defined around the yard operation in the port, but this is the only initial stage of the development of automated terminals. The general trend of container terminal development is to a higher level of automation, which involves substituting more manual operations and higher operation efficiency. The operation practice proves that the ACT can significantly improve operational efficiency, shorten the ship berthing time, increase port throughput, ensure the cargo handling quality, improve port economic and social benefits, and provide personalized services.

自动化集装箱系统主要分为水平运输、岸边装卸和堆场装卸。

The ACT system is mainly divided into the horizontal transportation, quayside loading and unloading, yard loading and unloading.

（1）自动导引车和自动跨运车是集装箱码头重要的水平运输设备。

（1）Automated guided vehicles（AGV）and automated lifting vehicles（ALV）are important horizontal transportation equipment in container terminals.

AGV 和 ALV 是自动化码头的主要水平运输设备，两者如图 4.9 所示，其性能对比如表 4.1 所示。自动化集装箱码头的装卸系统形式通常由水平运输设备决定，以作业设备的特点为基础，综合考虑建设的目标、投资、成本等因素。

AGV and ALV are the main horizontal transportation equipment of the ACT, which are shown in Figure 4.9, and their performance comparison is shown in Table 4.1. The form of the loading and unloading system of the ACT is usually determined by horizontal transportation equipment, based on the characteristics of operation equipment and considering the construction objectives, investment, cost, and other factors.

(a) 自动导引车

(a) AGV

(b) 自动跨运车

(b) ALV

图 4.9　自动化水平运输设备图示

Figure 4.9　Diagram of automatic horizontal transportation equipment

（图片来源：上海振华重工.全球首创！ZPMC 打造自主驾驶无人跨运车［EB/OL］. https://www.sohu.com/a/216835759_440748.）

表 4.1　ALV 与 AGV 的对比

设备	适用规模	装卸效率	灵活性	环保节能	设备维护	总设备投资
AGV	多泊位	高	高	电力驱动,无污染排放,能耗低	低	高
ALV	多泊位	低	更高	内燃驱动,有污染排放,能耗高	高	更高

Table 4.1　Comparison of ALV and AGV

Equipment	Scale	Efficiency	Flexibility	Energy conservation	Equipment maintenance	Investment
AGV	Multiple Berths	High	High	Electric-driven;Pollution-free; Low consumption	Low	High
ALV	Multiple Berths	Low	Higher	Fuel-driven; Pollution discharged; High consumption	High	Higher

AGV 由磁钉导航,通过电池驱动,在中控室的计算机调度下,按规定的导引路径完成自动行驶,具备无人驾驶、自动导航、定位精确、路径优化及安全避障等优势。作业方面,AGV 可分为普通 AGV 和提升式 AGV。以进口集装箱作业为例,在 AGV 与场桥作业交互的环节,普通 AGV 会将集装箱运送至堆场作业交互区后等待场桥将集装箱卸下后可执行下一集装箱运输任务。采用提升式 AGV 的自动化码头系统在堆场的海侧交互区设置固定的集装箱支架,由 AGV 自带的升降平台完成集装箱支架取、放箱,AGV 无须等待场桥设备作业,从而提高 AGV 作业效率。续航方面,荷兰鹿特丹港的 RWG、APMT MV2 码头、美国长滩港的 LBCT 码头和上海港洋山四期自动化码头采用的均是换电式 AGV。当电量不足时,AGV 需要驶入换电站进行电池更换,这大大影响了码头的作业效率。青岛港新前湾自动化码头应用的是一种循环充电式 AGV。循环充电能源补充方式的设计理念是利用 AGV 与堆场海侧交互区支架进行集装箱交互的时间,进行电能补充,从而实现码头 24 h 全天不间断运作。

AGV is guided by magnetic nails and driven by batteries. Under the computer dispatching in the central control room, the AGV completes automatic driving according to the specified guidance path. AGV has intelligent functions such as automatic driving, automatic navigation, accurate positioning, route optimization, and obstacle avoidance. In terms of function, AGV is divided into ordinary AGV and lifting AGV. Taking the imported container operation as an example, during the interaction between AGV and yard crane operation, ordinary AGV transports the container to the exchange area of the yard and waits for the yard crane to unload the container before conducting the next task. In the automatic terminal system with lifting AGV, fixed container supports are set in the seaside exchange area of the yard. The lifting platform provided by

AGV is used to load/unload the container to/from the support. Since AGV does not need to wait for the operation of yard cranes, the efficiency of AGV is improved. In terms of endurance, RWG terminal and APMT MV2 terminal at Rotterdam Port in the Netherlands, LBCT terminal at Long Beach Port in the United States, and Yangshan phase Ⅳ automatic terminal at Shanghai Port all adopt a power exchange AGV. When the power is insufficient, AGV needs to drive into the replacement power station for battery replacement, which greatly affects the operation efficiency of the terminal. New Qianwan automatic terminal of Qingdao Port applies a kind of circulating charging AGV. The design concept of cyclic charging energy supplement mode is to supplement the electric energy by using the time of container interaction between AGV and the support in the seaside exchange area of the yard to realize the 24-hour uninterrupted operation of the terminal.

ALV 是在跨运车基础上开发的集装箱。与提升式 AGV 类似，ALV 可直接自行从码头交换区提箱和卸箱，无须等待岸桥或场桥对集装箱进行作业。这极大地减少了岸桥、场桥和水平运输设备之间的对位操作，降低了作业设备之间操作的不连贯性和不协调性，从而减少设备的双向等待时间，使设备得到更加充分的利用，提高了码头整体装卸效率。

ALV is a kind of container transport equipment developed on the basis of straddle carrier. Similar to the lifting AGV, ALV can directly load/unload the container to/from the exchange areas of the yard without waiting for the quay cranes or yard cranes to handle the containers. This dramatically reduces the alignment operation among quay cranes, yard cranes, and horizontal transportation equipment and reduces the inconsistency and disharmony of operation between operation equipment, so as to reduce the two-way waiting time of equipment, make more full use of the equipment and improve the entire efficiency of the terminal.

（2）岸边装卸系统主要包括单小车岸桥和双小车岸桥。

（2）Quayside loading and unloading system mainly includes single trolley quay crane and double trolley quay crane.

码头岸桥负责船舶集装箱的装卸作业，与船舶服务和等待时间直接相关，对岸桥有效的利用能够显著提高港口的作业效率。单小车岸桥指的是码头起重机只有一个小车，该小车沿着起重机的臂部移动，一次性将集装箱从船舶转移到车辆上或从车辆转移到船舶上。单小车岸桥适用于采用 ALV 的自动化码头工艺系统，ALV 能够有效协调岸桥装卸作业与水平运输作业，提高单小车岸桥作业效率。

Quay cranes are responsible for the loading and unloading containers from vessels, which is directly related to vessel service and waiting time. The effective use of quay cranes can significantly improve the operation efficiency of the terminal. Single trolley quay crane has only one trolley, which moves along the crane's arm to transfer the container from the vessel to the vehicle or from the vehicle to the vessel at one time. Single trolley quay cranes are applicable to the automatic terminal process system with ALV. ALV can effectively coordinate the loading and unloading operations of quay cranes and horizontal transportation operations, and improve the operation efficiency of single trolley quay cranes.

青岛港新前湾自动化码头和上海港洋山四期码头应用的是一种双小车岸桥。双小车岸桥在主体上装备了两个小车和一个转运平台，即陆侧副小车与海侧主小车的缓存交接区。以卸船作业为例，岸桥主小车将船舶上集装箱转移到转运平台上，岸桥副小车再将转运平台上的集装箱转移到在岸桥作业交互区等待的车辆上。双小车岸桥的出现克服了单小车岸桥因吊具从大型船舶上提起集装箱时必须行进的垂直距离较长而造成的效率低下的问题。

New Qianwan automatic terminal of Qingdao Port and Yangshan Phase Ⅳ terminal of Shanghai Port apply double trolley quay cranes. The double trolley quay crane is equipped with two trolleys and a transfer platform on the main body, (i.e., the buffer handover area between the auxiliary trolley on the landside and the main trolley on the seaside). Taking ship unloading operation as an example, the main trolley of the quay crane transfers the containers on the ship to the transfer platform, and the auxiliary trolley of the quay crane transfers the containers on the transfer platform to the vehicles waiting in the interaction area. The appearance of double trolley quay cranes overcomes the low efficiency caused by the long vertical distance that must be travelled when the spreader lifts the container from the large vessel.

由于船舶结构各不相同、港口作业受天气影响较大等原因，自动化码头岸桥作业是难以进行自动化的环节，无论是单小车岸桥还是双小车岸桥，都是工作人员在远程中控室完成吊具装卸箱作业。目前，主要的岸桥远程控制系统由瑞士 ABB 公司开发。

Due to the different vessel structures and the significant impact of weather on port operations, it is difficult to automate the quay crane operation in ACTs. Whether it is a single trolley quay crane or a double trolley quay crane, the staff completes the spreader loading and unloading in the remote central control room. At present, the primary quay crane control system is developed by ABB in Switzerland.

（3）集装箱堆场作业系统多采用 ARMG（自动轨道吊）和 ARTG（自动轮胎吊）。ARMG 依据固定的轨道在堆场内行驶，其作业的移动范围较为局限；而 ARTG 可在码头内完成灵活的行驶，有较高的机动性，可实现不同堆场间以及同一堆场不同箱区间的集装箱转移。与 ARTG 相比，ARMG 具备更高的稳定性，可更好地实现全自动化作业，因此自动化码头多采用 ARMG 来完成堆场作业。

（3）Container yard operation system mainly uses ARMG (automatic rail-mounted gantry crane) and ARTG (automatic rubber-typed gantry crane). ARMG travels on a fixed track in the terminal and has a limited movement area. ARTG has a more flexible driving route and strong maneuverability, which is conducive to container transfer operations between different yards or different container sections of the same yard. Compared with the ARTG, ARMG has higher stability and can realize automatic operation. ARMG is used to complete yard operations in most ACTs.

　　一些港口通过部署两台 ARMG 来提高港口的作业效率。目前,自动化码头应用的双 ARMG 系统有两种,分别为可穿越式双 ARMG 系统和不可穿越式双 ARMG 系统。前者表示两个彼此无法通过的相同大小的 ARMG,后者表示两个可以相互通过的大小不同的 ARMG(外部 ARMG 和内部 ARMG)。作业流程方面,在可穿越式双 ARMG 系统中,外部 ARMG 和内部 ARMG 均能服务堆场海、陆侧交互区的作业。然而,当外部 ARMG 的吊具在某一贝中装卸集装箱时,内部 ARMG 既不能穿过该贝,也不能在同一贝中执行装卸作业。在不可穿越式双 ARMG 系统中,两个 ARMG 不能互相通过。因此,堆场陆侧和海侧集装箱装卸作业被分离开来,海侧的所有任务均由海侧 ARMG 处理,陆侧的所有任务均由另一个陆侧 ARMG 处理。上述作业是海侧 ARMG 和陆侧 ARMG 的一种非合作作业模式,考虑到不可跨越式双 ARMG 之间的冲突问题,通常会优先考虑海侧 ARMG 的作业效率。此外,不可穿越式双 ARMG 作业系统还有一个合作作业模式。合作作业模式要求堆场的箱区划分成"交换"区域、海侧堆存区域以及陆侧堆存区域。以出口箱作业为例,陆侧 ARMG 将集装箱从集卡上卸下后放置陆侧堆存区域进行堆存。船舶靠港后进行装箱作业时,陆侧 ARMG 将该集装箱移动至"交换"区域,海侧 ARMG 将该箱装载至 AGV 上,由 AGV 和岸桥完成后续作业。

　　Some ports deploy two ARMGs to improve the operation efficiency. At present, there are two types of two ARMGs systems applied in ACTs, namely two crossover ARMGs systems and two non-crossover ARMGs systems. The former represents two ARMGs of the same size that cannot pass through each other, and the latter represents two ARMGs of different sizes that can pass through each other (i.e., outer ARMG and inner ARMG). In terms of operation process, both outer ARMG and inner ARMG can serve the operations in seaside and landside interaction areas of the yard in the two crossover ARMGs systems. However, when the outer ARMG is loading or unloading containers in a bay, the inner ARMG can neither pass through the bay nor work in the same bay. In the two non-crossover ARMGs systems, two ARMGs cannot pass through each other. Therefore, the loading and unloading operations on the landside and seaside of the yard are separated. The seaside containers are handled by the seaside ARMG, and the landside containers are handled by another landside ARMG. The above operation is a non-cooperative operation mode of seaside ARMG and landside ARMG. Considering the conflict between the two non-crossover ARMGs, the operation efficiency of seaside ARMG will usually be given priority. In addition, the two non-crossover ARMGs system also has a cooperative operation mode. The cooperative operation mode requires that the block of the yard be divided into the "exchange" area, the seaside storage area, and the landside storage area. Taking the operation of exported containers as an example, the landside ARMG unloads exported containers from trucks and stores them in the landside storage area of the block. When the ship arrives at the terminal and carries out the loading operation, exported containers are carried to the "handover" area by the landside ARMG and then loaded onto the AGVs by the seaside ARMG. Moreover, the subsequent operations are carried out by AGVs and the quay cranes.

4.2.2 自动化集装箱码头工艺与作业流程
4.2.2 Technology and Operation Process of ACT

（1）自动化集装箱码头布局形式
（1）Layout of ACT

码头堆场平面布局主要包括垂直和水平两种形式。其中,自动化集装箱码头多采用堆场垂直布局,传统人工码头多采用堆场平行布局。堆场垂直布局形式为堆场与岸线垂直布置,如图4.10所示。AGV/ALV 不进入堆场,堆场内集装箱作业依靠场桥设备完成。AGV/ALV 行驶路径短,作业循环时间短,水平运输效率高。采用堆场垂直布局的代表性港口有:青岛港新前湾自动化码头和上海港洋山四期码头。然而,由于不同港口面临的内外部环境不同,其所适应的码头堆场布局也有所区别。以广州南沙港自动化码头为例,广州港南沙码头具有缺少港外堆场,堆场纵深大,业务上主要以内贸水水中转为主的特点。结合该特点,该码头采用堆场水平布局,集装箱的送、提可以在堆场任何位置,如图4.11所示。此外,广西港钦州自动化集装箱码头在堆场垂直布局的基础上,应用了一种全新码头 U 形工艺,通过实现堆场"点到点"侧面装卸,以减少对场桥资源的占用情况,如图4.12所示。

The layout of the terminal yard mainly includes vertical and horizontal forms. The ACT mainly adopts the vertical layout of the yard, while the traditional container terminal mostly adopts the parallel layout of the yard. The vertical layout is that the yard is perpendicular to the quayside, as shown in Figure 4.10. The AGV/ALV operations do not enter the yard, and thus operations in the yard are completed by yard cranes. The AGV/ALV operation has a short driving path, a short cycle time and high horizontal transportation efficiency. The representative ports with vertical layout of stacking area, New Qianwan automatic terminal of Qingdao Port and Yangshan Phase Ⅳ terminal of Shanghai Port adopt the vertical layout of the yard. However, due to the different internal and external environments faced by different ports, their suitable layouts are also different. Take Nansha ACT of Guangzhou Port as an example, which has the characteristics of lack of yard outside the port, large depth of yard, and main conversion of domestic trade water-to-water. Combined with this feature, the terminal adopts the parallel layout of the yard, and the delivery and extraction of containers can be at any position of the yard, as shown in Figure 4.11. In addition, based on the vertical layout of the yard, Qinzhou ACT of Guangxi Port applies a new U-shaped design to reduce the occupation of yard crane resources by realizing "point-to-point" side loading and unloading of the yard, as shown in Figure 4.12.

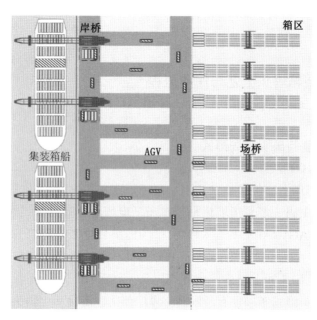

图 4.10　堆场垂直布局

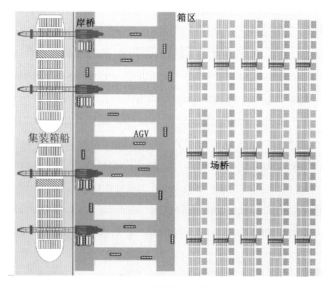

图 4.11　堆场水平布局

图 4.12 堆场垂直布局 U 形工艺

(图片来源:钦州市发展和改革委员会. 带您了解钦州首个自动化集装箱码头[EB/OL].
http://zwgk.qinzhou.gov.cn/auto2521/gzdt_2874/202009/t20200915_3378201.html.)

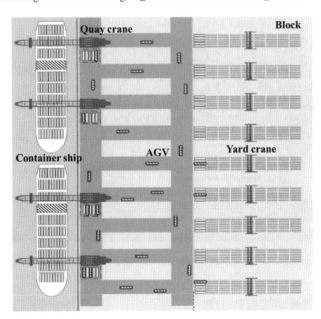

Figure 4.10 Vertical layout of the yard

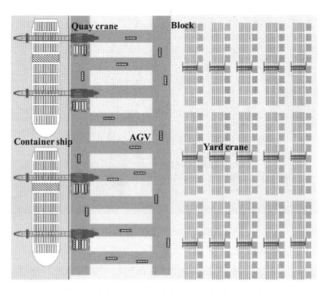

Figure 4.11　Parallel layout of the yard

Figure 4.12　Vertical layout of the yard with U-shaped design

（2）自动化集装箱码头装卸工艺
（2）Loading and Unloading Process of ACT

随着集装箱运输的快速发展,新型集装箱码头装卸设备和工艺不断涌现。目前,国际上主要采用的自动化集装箱码头装卸工艺如下:①荷兰鹿特丹港 Euromax 码头、德国汉堡港 HHLA CTA 码头采用的 AGV+ARMG 模式;②日本名古屋港 Tobishima 码头采用的 AGV+ARTG 模式;③荷兰鹿特丹港 APM MV2 码头采用的 ALV+ARMG 模式。在国内,以自动化集装箱装卸设备技术发展的成熟度及系统整体应用情况来看,"双小车岸桥+AGV+ARMG"的码头装卸工艺方案,自动化程度最高、技术最为成熟、应用最为广泛。青岛港新前湾自动化集装箱码头、上海港洋山港四期码头均采用该种装卸工艺模式。此外,广州港南沙自动化集装箱码头采用集成激光导航和北斗定位技术的 IGA 进行水平搬运作业。IGA 运动轨迹不受磁钉约束,作业更加灵活。此外,天津港北疆港区 C 段自动化集装箱码头对集卡进行改进,开发了一套港内作业的无人集卡设备。

With the rapid development of container transportation, new loading and unloading equipment and technologies of container terminals are emerging. At present, the main loading and unloading processes of ACT adopted internationally are as follows: ① AGV + ARMG mode adopted by Euromax terminal of Rotterdam Port in the Netherlands and HHLA CTA terminal of Hamburg Port in Germany; ②AGV + ARTG mode adopted by Tobishima terminal of Nagoya Port in Japan; ③ALV + ARMG mode adopted by APM MV2 terminal in Rotterdam Port in Netherlands. In China, according to the maturity of the technical development of loading and unloading equipment of ACT and the overall application of the system, the terminal loading and unloading process scheme of "double trolley quay crane + AGV + ARMG" has the highest degree of automation, the most mature technology and the most widely used. The loading and unloading process mode is adopted for New Qianwan ACT of Qingdao Port and Yangshan Phase Ⅳ terminal of Shanghai Port. In addition, the Nansha ACT of Guangzhou Port adopts intelligent guided vehicle (IGA), integrating laser navigation and Beidou positioning technology for horizontal transportation operations. As IGA's motion trajectory is not constrained by magnetic nails, it is more flexible. In addition, the Section C area of Beijiang ACT in Tianjin Port has improved the container truck and developed a set of unmanned container truck equipment for operation in the port.

(3) 自动化集装箱码头作业流程
(3) Operation Process of ACT

自动化集装箱码头作业流程如图 4.13 所示。对于集装箱进口流程,船舶到港前,码头人员以船公司提供的船舶计划为基础完成泊位计划,预先确定进口箱的堆场堆存位置、对应装卸设备,制订船舶的卸船顺序表及堆场的堆存计划。当船靠泊后,岸桥完成卸船作业,码头的集装箱运输设备将进口箱依照指定的路径运至堆场,场桥按指定的堆存计划将进口箱堆放入对应箱位。

The operation process of ACT is shown in Figure 4.13. For the container import process, before the ship arrives, the terminal staff makes a berth plan based on the shipping plan provided by the shipping company. Determine the yard storage position and operating equipment for the import containers, and prepare the unloading sequence and yard plan. After the ship berths, the quay crane unloads the ship. The container transport equipment of the wharf transports the import container to the yard, and the yard crane stores the imported container to the block according to the yard plan.

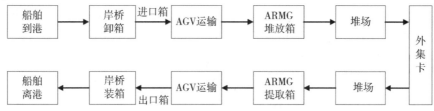

图 4.13　自动化集装箱码头作业流程

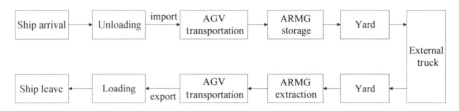

Figure 4.13　The operation process of ACT

对于集装箱出口流程,在装船开始前,码头的配载员依据配船图、装箱单、场站收据等进行集装箱配载,制订装船的作业计划。在装船过程中,堆场以装船的顺序单为依据完成集装箱运输,场桥将出口箱放置于集卡上,集卡将出口箱运至码头前沿,岸桥将出口箱放置于船舶的对应位置。当堆场的出口箱均装上船舶,则装船过程完成,船舶离港。

In terms of the container export process, the terminal stowage staff completes the loading plan according to the stowage plan, packing list, and receipts before the loading operation. During the loading operation, the yard issues containers according to the ship loading plan. The yard crane transfers the exported container to the transportation truck, the transportation truck carries the exported container to the quayside, and the quay crane loads the exported container to the designated location of the vessel. After the loading operation of all exported containers, the loading operation is completed, and the ship leaves the port.

4.2.3　自动化码头典型案例
4.2.3　Typical Cases of ACT

（1）荷兰鹿特丹港
（1）Rotterdam Port in the Netherlands

荷兰鹿特丹港自动化码头采用半自动化单小车岸桥,岸桥在对箱时需人工操作,其余操作均无须人工干预。堆场采用全自动化堆场轨道吊 ARMG,堆场箱区配备单台 ARMG。应用 AGV 作为码头前沿与堆场之间的水平运输设备,行驶路线为环形固定线路,单次仅支持一个集装箱装卸作业。AGV 使用网格系统完成导航与控制,配备超声波探测装置及防碰撞装置。

Rotterdam Port in the Netherlands adopts a semi-automatic single trolley quay crane. The quay crane needs a manual operation, and the remaining operations do not require manual intervention. The ARMG is used in the yard, and the block is equipped with a single ARMG. The AGV is used as the horizontal transportation equipment between quayside and yard. The AGV route is a ring-shaped fixed-line, and only one container loading and unloading operation is supported at a time. The AGV uses a grid system for navigation and control, equipped with ultrasonic detection devices and anti-collision devices.

（2）厦门远海全自动化集装箱码头

（2）Xiamen Ocean Gate Fully Automated Container Terminal

2016 年，作为国内首个全自动化集装箱码头，厦门远海自动化集装箱码头实现了集装箱码头的自动化改造并投产运营，打破了国内自动化码头发展的空白。码头采用"自动化双小车岸桥+AGV+自动化轨道吊"的全自动化工艺系统，支持自动化岸桥、传统岸桥同船混合作业，其全景如图 4.14 所示。码头堆场采用平行岸线布局，堆场端部进行集装箱交换。码头 AGV 为电力驱动，通过磁钉定位，在堆场交互区车道配备有 AGV 伴侣。同时，厦门远海自动化码头也在积极探索 5G 技术等在设备远程控制、智能集卡等领域的实践应用。厦门远海自动化码头的建成为传统码头的智能化升级改造、建设智慧港口提供了良好的范本，引领国内自动化码头建设步入快速发展的道路。

In 2016, as the first fully automated container terminal in China, Xiamen Ocean Gate Automated Container Terminal realized the automation transformation of the container terminal and put it into operation, breaking the gap in the development of automated terminals in China. The terminal adopts a fully automated process system of "automated double trolley quay crane + AGV + automatic rail-mounted gantry crane", which supports the mixed operation of automated quay crane and traditional quay crane on the same vessel, and its panorama is shown in Figure 4.14. The terminal yard is laid out in parallel with the shoreline, and containers are exchanged at the end of the yard. The AGVs are electrically driven, positioned by magnetic pegs, and equipped with AGV mates in the lanes of the yard interaction area. At the same time, Xiamen Ocean Gate Automated Container Terminal is also actively exploring the practical application of 5G technology and other technologies in areas such as remote control of equipment and intelligent collector trucks. The completion of Xiamen Ocean Gate Automated Container Terminal provides a good model for the intelligent upgrading and transformation of traditional terminals and the construction of smart ports, leading the construction of domestic automated terminals into the road of rapid development.

图 4.14　厦门远海全自动化码头全景图

Figure 4.14　The panorama of ACT in Xiamen Ocean Gate

（图片来源：郭滢，樊志远，桂平，等.《航拍中国》（第二季）第 6 集福建［EB/OL］. https：//tv.cctv.com/2019/04/08/VIDEdHKOZu1ROUWdewiZ87wR190408.shtml？spm＝C55924871139.PY8jbb3G6NT9.0.0.）

（3）青岛港前湾四期全自动化集装箱码头
（3）Qianwan Phase Ⅳ Fully ACT of Qingdao Port

青岛港全自动化码头以青岛港自主知识产权实现全智能决策、全系统管理,系统运行稳定可靠,开辟了全自动化集装箱码头作业的新时代,其全景如图 4.15 所示。青岛港自动化码头建设成本低、周期短、起点高,技术方案可实现全智能、高效率和零排放。首创 L-AGV循环充电技术,续航时间无限制;岸桥由中央控制室操控,采用机器人自动拆装集装箱扭锁系统;自动化轨道吊"一键锚钉"系统,场桥轨道吊可在两分钟内完成固定。

Qingdao Port realizes intelligent decision-making and system-wide management with independent intellectual property rights. The system runs stably and reliably, opening up a new era of fully ACT operations, and the panorama is shown in Figure 4.15. The construction cost of Qingdao Port is low, the cycle is short, and the starting point is high. The technical solution can realize full intelligence, high efficiency, and zero emissions. Qingdao Port pioneered the L-AGV cycle charging technology with unlimited battery life. The quay crane is controlled by the central control room, and the robot automatically disassembles the container lock system. The "one-click anchor" system can fix the automated yard crane in two minutes.

图 4.15 青岛港自动化码头全景图

Figure 4.15 The panorama of Qingdao Port

（图片来源:青岛港.青岛港简介［EB/OL］. https://www.qdport.com/#/zyyw.）

（4）上海港洋山四期全自动化集装箱码头
（4）Yangshan Phase Ⅳ Fully ACT of Shanghai Port

上海洋山四期自动化码头以"高可靠,高效率,绿色环保,世界最先进、世界最大规模"为目标,致力于成为港口行业中的全球科技进步引领者,建设全自动化集装箱码头;技术方案方面具备智慧港口、绿色港口、科技港口、效率港口等特点;规划设计方面具有全自主规划、全自主设计、软硬件自主研发及软硬件自主集成调试等特点,其全景如图 4.16 所示。码头配有 SPSS 船型扫描系统,OCR 识别系统,可实现双小车岸桥自动作业;AGV 配备避让系统和智能单机导航系统,可自动避让障碍;堆场配有高度集成的信息系统,配备 AGV 伴侣的缓存区,可减缓 AGV 与场桥的耦合时间,提高系统作业效率。

The goal of Shanghai Port is to build an fully ACT with "high reliability,high efficiency, green environmental protection,the most advanced and the largest of the world". Shanghai Port is committed to becoming a technology leader in the global port industry and building a fully automated container terminal. In terms of technical solutions,Shanghai Port has the characteristics of smart ports,green ports,technology ports,and efficient ports. In terms of planning and design, it has the characteristics of independent planning,independent design,independent software and hardware research and development,and independent software,and hardware integrated debugging. The panorama is shown in Figure 4.16. The terminal is equipped with the SPSS scanning system and OCR identification system,which can realize the automatic operation of the double trolley quay crane. AGV is equipped with an avoidance system and an intelligent stand-alone navigation system,which can avoid obstacles automatically. The yard is equipped with a highly integrated information system and a transfer area of the AGV-mate to reduce the coupling time between the AGV and the yard crane and improve the operation efficiency.

图 4.16　上海洋山港自动化码头全景图

Figure 4.16　The panorama of Shanghai Port

(图片来源:上港集团.迈入洋山四期产能扩大新阶段[EB/OL]. http://www.portshanghai.com.cn/yszt/1998. jhtml.)

❖ 4.3　港口多式联运新技术

4.3　New Technology of Port Multimodal Transport

4.3.1　港口多式联运技术概述
4.3.1　Overview of Port Multimodal Transport Technology

多式联运指的是单一合同下,涉及两种及以上不同交通工具的运输过程。与传统的单一运输方式相比,多式联运具有产业链条长、资源利用高效、综合效益高的特点,通过的发挥不同运输方式的优点,达到简化货运环节,实现合理运输的目的,达到降本增效的目的。以港口为核心的多式联运系统由海海联运、海河联运、海公联运、海铁联运、海空联运等构成。多式联运将传统的海运港到港运输发展为门到门运输,实现了多种运输方式之间的无缝连接,充分发挥各种运输方式的优势,具备手续简便、安全可靠、提早结汇等优点。以港口为依托,研究多式联运并完善区港联动,将临港产业与物流产业进行有机结合,加强国际贸易,能够有效促进港口经济的飞速发展。

Multimodal transport refers to the transportation process involving at least two different modes of transportation under a single contract. Compared with traditional single-mode transportation, multimodal transport has the characteristics of a long industrial chain, efficient resource utilization, and high comprehensive benefits. By giving full play to the advantages of different transportation modes, it can simplify freight links, realize reasonable transportation and achieve the purpose of cost reduction and efficiency increase. The multimodal transport system with the port as the core consists of sea-sea transport, sea-river transport, sea-road transport, sea-rail transport, sea-air transport, and so on. Multimodal transport develops the traditional port-to-port transportation into door-to-door transportation, realizes the seamless connection between various transportation modes, gives full play to the advantages of various transportation modes, and has the advantages of simple procedures, safety and reliability, early settlement of foreign exchange, and so on. Relying on the port, studying multimodal transport and improving regional port linkage, organically combining port industry and logistics industry, and strengthening international trade can effectively promote the rapid development of the port economy.

港口多式联运的运营依托现代化的信息平台。港口多式联运的货物主要为集装箱货物。目前,集装箱运输正在向着智能化和信息化的方向发展。为此,需要构建以现代化信息技术为核心建设多式联运信息平台,构建一套安全可信的集装箱追踪监管、信息共享与应用服务平台,完成物流节点的数据源与信息整合,确保相关信息的准确、真实和可靠,有效促进物流的快速稳定发展,实现物流业的降本增效。为此,各政府机构和企业也在不断探索卫星通信、物联网、大数据平台等新一代信息技术在多式联运中的应用。比如,广西壮族自治区研发了北斗车船终端和应用系统,形成了一批应用成效显著的北斗多式联运解决方案。此外,条形码、射频识别(FRID)、传感器、全球定位系统等物联网新技术已经普遍应用于多式联运中的各个环节。

Port multimodal transport relies on a modern information platform. The cargo of port multimodal transport is mainly container cargo. At present, container transportation is developing towards intelligence and informatization. Therefore, it is necessary to build a multimodal transport information platform with modern information technology as the core, build a set of safe and reliable container tracking supervision, information sharing, and application service platform, complete the data source and information integration of logistics nodes, ensure the accuracy, authenticity, and reliability of relevant information, effectively promote the rapid and stable development of logistics and realize cost reduction and efficiency increase of logistics industry. Therefore, government agencies and enterprises are also constantly exploring the application of new-generation information technologies such as satellite communication, the IoT, and big data platforms in multimodal transport. For example, Guangxi Province has developed Beidou vehicle and vessel terminals and application systems, forming several Beidou multimodal transport solutions with remarkable application results. In addition, the new technologies of the IoT such as bar code, radio frequency identification (FRID), sensors, and GPS have been widely used in all links of multimodal transport.

4.3.2 港口多式联运运作形式
4.3.2 Operation Mode of Port Multimodal Transport

作为一种有效的运输组织方式,多式联运主要由两种或两种以上的运输工具进行衔接与转运,完成整个运输过程。多式联运主要具有三种形式:驮背式运输是使用较广的形式,指卡车拖车或集装箱放置于铁路平板车的公铁联运;卡车渡运、火车渡船和集装箱船等形式大多适用于水路长途运输,将卡车拖车、铁路车或集装箱放置于驳船或船舶进行长途运输,从而提高经济性;航空货运与卡车运输的组合运输是溢价包裹递送服务常用的一种形式。

Multimodal transport is an effective transport organization method, which is mainly connected and transshipped by two or more transport equipment to complete the entire transport process. There are three main forms of multimodal transport. Piggyback transportation is a kind of road-train transportation that sets truck or container on railway flatbed, a widely used transportation form. Multimodal transport such as truck ferry, train ferry, or container vessel is mainly used for long-distance water transportation, which places trucks, trains, or containers on the ship to improve economic efficiency. The combination of air and truck is commonly used in premium package delivery services.

港口多式联运指以国际海上运输为主要干线运输的国际多式联运。公海联运为进出口货物由公路运至海港,并直接由船舶运出或货物由船舶运输至海港后由公路运出,只需"一次申报、一次查验、一次放行"可完成整个运输过程的形式。海河联运可有效减少运输环节和驳船次数,减少成本,降低损耗,利于港口腹地的扩张,吸引众多货源。海铁联运是进出口货物由铁路运至沿海海港直接由船舶运出或货物由船舶运至海港后由铁路运出,只需一次通关申报的运输方式。

Port multimodal transport is the international multimodal transport with international maritime transport as the main trunk line. Sea-road transportation is how the cargos are transported by road to seaports or seaports to the road directly, which only needs "one declaration, one inspection, one release". Sea-river transportation can effectively reduce transportation links, costs, and wastes, which is conducive to expanding of the port hinterland and attraction of cargo. Sea rail intermodal transport refers to the transportation of import and export goods by railway to coastal ports directly by ship, or the transportation of goods by ship to ports and then by railway,

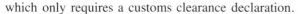

which only requires a customs clearance declaration.

海铁联运是港口多式联运的重要组成部分,是以海运或铁路集装箱为运输单元,铁路、海运有机结合,将货物运抵相应地点的多式联运物流形式。海铁联运承运人根据多式联运合同和托运人的指令,将集装箱货物一票到底运输至目的交付地点。中国的海铁联运主要以"集装箱在铁路通道运输为主干,以沿海港口、内陆无水港或陆港为重要货物换装节点,铁路、水路、公路实现一体化运作"的形式为主。

Rail-sea intermodal transport is an important part of port multimodal transportation. It is a logistics model that delivers goods to a designated location and a multimodal transport mode combining railway and sea, using containers as the transportation unit. According to the multimodal transport contract and the shipper's instructions, the carrier of rail-sea intermodal transport transports the container to the destination delivery place. The rail-sea intermodal transport in China is "Containers are mainly transported by railway. Port and inland dry port or land ports are important reloading nodes. Integrate railway, waterway, and highway".

4.3.3 联合国国际货物多式联运公约
4.3.3 United Nations Convention on the International Multimodal Transport of Goods

《联合国国际货物多式联运公约》于 1980 年 5 月 24 日在日内瓦的联合国国际联会第二次会议上通过,共包含 40 条和一个附件。公约规定了多式联运合同双方当事人的法律地位、多式联运合同和多式联运单据、联运人的赔偿责任、发货人的赔偿责任,以及索赔和诉讼等,是国际上首部以统一国际货物多式联运合同法律规定为目标的国际公约。公约适用于不同运输方式以各种排列组合的形式所开展的国际货物多式联运,且不论其中是否包含海运区段。公约对世界广泛开展的国际货物多式联运具有极强的指导作用和参考价值,对各国的相关立法和之后的国际公约制定具有一定的借鉴价值。

The United Nations Convention on the International Multimodal Transport of Goods was adopted on 24 May 1980 at the second meeting of the United Nations International Federation in Geneva and contains 40 articles and an annex. The Convention sets out the legal status of the parties to the multimodal transport contract, the multimodal transport contract and multimodal transport documents, the liability of the intermodal carrier, the liability of the consignor, as well as claims and litigation, and is the first international convention with the objective of unifying the legal provisions of multimodal contracts for the international carriage of goods. The Convention applies to international multimodal transport of goods carried out by different modes of transport in various combinations, whether or not they include a maritime sector. The Convention has a strong guiding role and reference value for the international multimodal transport of goods that is widely carried out in the world, and has a certain reference value for the relevant legislation of various countries and the formulation of subsequent international conventions.

作为世界上首部多式联运公约,该公约加深了人们对于多式联运运输模式的认知,促进了多式联运的推广,有利于国际社会对多式联运合同和法规的研究与探索,促进了各国相关立法的步伐。公约中的许多条款对于各国的业务实践具有极强的指导意义和可操作性,其中的许多概念与规定也被实践所接纳采用,如公约对于国际多式联运、多式联运单证、多式联运经营人、多式联运合同等的定义。公约中部分规定所遵循的原则和宗旨已经在实质上基本被国际社会所接受和采纳,对于国际运输实践和各国司法实践具有积极的引导作用。

As the world's first multimodal transport convention, it has deepened people's knowledge of multimodal transport modes, promoted the promotion of multimodal transport, facilitated the international community's research and exploration of multimodal transport contracts and regulations, and promoted the pace of relevant national legislation. Many of the provisions of the Convention are of great guidance and operability for national business practices, and many of the concepts and provisions in the Convention have been adopted in practice, such as the definitions of international multimodal transport, multimodal transport documents, multimodal transport operators and multimodal transport contracts. Some of the provisions of the Convention are based on principles and purposes that have been largely accepted and adopted by the international community, and have a positive guiding effect on international transport practice and national judicial practice.

多式联运公约是国际范围内在多式联运立法领域的第一次有益的探索,但该公约第36条第1款规定,当公约得到30个国家批准或加入后12个月开始生效,而该公约至今仍然无法达到它所规定的生效条件。如今在研究和探索多式联运法律制度时,《鹿特丹规则》也是一部重要的多式联运公约。《鹿特丹规则》全称为《联合国全程或部分海上国际货物运输合同公约》,又称《联合国运输法公约》。《鹿特丹规则》由联合国贸易发展法委员会运输法工作组于2008年12月12日审议通过,并在荷兰鹿特丹正式签署发布。该公约的适用范围是"海运+其他",因此公约不仅调整海上货物运输合同的关系,同时也规范包含海运区段在内的国际货物多式联运合同关系。在对多式联运法律制度不断探索的过程中,在持续关注《鹿特丹规则》的同时,也应加深对于《联合国国际货物多式联运公约》的探讨研究。

The Multimodal Transport Convention was the first useful exploration in the field of multimodal transport legislation on an international scale, but article 36, paragraph 1 of the Convention stipulates that it shall enter into force 12 months after it has been ratified or acceded to by 30 countries, and the Convention has so far been unable to meet the conditions for its entry into force. Today, the "Rotterdam Rules" are also an important multimodal transport convention when studying and exploring the legal system of multimodal transport. The full name of the "Rotterdam Rules" is the "United Nations Convention on Contracts for the International Carriage of Goods Wholly or Partly by Sea", also known as the "United Nations Convention on Transport Law. The Rotterdam Rules" were adopted by the UNCITRAL Working Group on Transport Law on 12 December 2008 and signed and published in Rotterdam, the Netherlands. The scope of application of the Convention is "maritime + other", so the Convention not only regulates the relationship between contracts for the carriage of goods by sea, but also the relation-

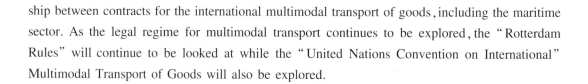

ship between contracts for the international multimodal transport of goods, including the maritime sector. As the legal regime for multimodal transport continues to be explored, the "Rotterdam Rules" will continue to be looked at while the "United Nations Convention on International" Multimodal Transport of Goods will also be explored.

4.3.4 中国港口多式联运示范工程
4.3.4 Port Multimodal Transport Demonstration Project in China

（1）大连港多式联运示范工程
（1）Dalian Port Multimodal Transport Demonstration Project

大连港始终坚持以铁兴港的发展战略，是连接东北物流大通道和南北沿海物流大通道的重要枢纽。大连港拥有良好的地理位置、先进的港口基础设施、大量的航道资源及先进的智能化服务，为其在多式联运发展上提供了较强的支持。2016年以来，大连港依托"一带一路"建设和中国对多式联运发展的支持，成功开通"三星"班列和"辽满欧"商品车过境班列，并建立了如"海运+冷藏班列+公路短驳"模式。来自中日韩各地的汽车零件、机械设备、日用小商品等，均可通过海铁联运通道运往欧洲。2017年，大连港监管的中欧过境班列达438列，2018年，大连港海铁联运货运量达39.3万TEU。目前，大连口岸已建立辐射东北三省及蒙东全境的内陆集疏运体系网络，并有望在未来连通俄罗斯等欧洲国家及地区。大连港已逐渐成为中国主要的集装箱海铁联运和海上中转港口之一。

Dalian Port insists on the development strategy of railway port revitalization. It is an important hub connecting the Northeast Logistics Corridor and the Northsouth Coastal Logistics Corridor. Dalian port has the advantages of good geographical location, advanced port infrastructure, abundant waterway resources and intelligent smart services, which provide strong supports for its development in multimodal transport. Relied on "One belt, one road" construction and China's support for multimodal transport development, since 2016, Dalian Port successively opened the "Samsung" and "Liao-Man-Europe" commodity trains and established the mode of "sea transportation + refrigerated train + short highway barge". Auto parts, machinery, and commodities from Japan, Korea, and China can be transported to Europe through rail-sea intermodal transport. In 2017, Dalian Port supervised 438 China-Europe transit trains. In 2018, the rail-sea intermodal transport volume of Dalian Port reached 393,000 TEU. Nowadays, Dalian Port has established a network of inland collection and distribution systems that radiates northeast China and eastern Mongolia and is expected to connect Russia and other European countries and regions in the future. It has gradually become a major container train transportation and maritime transit port.

（2）宁波舟山港多式联运示范工程
（2）Ningbo-Zhoushan Port Multimodal Transport Demonstration Project

宁波舟山港是我国主要枢纽港之一，共拥有19个港区，200多条航线。2019年宁波舟山港完成货物吞吐量10.8亿 t,位居世界港口第一位;完成集装箱吞吐量2 753万 TEU,排名全球前三。宁波舟山港的海铁联运始于2009年,相较于其他港口起步较晚。但其借助其优秀的区位优势及设施条件,宁波舟山港海铁联运保持高速增长。2019年,宁波舟山港海铁联运吞吐量达到了80.2万 TEU。目前,宁波舟山港已开行14条固定班列,辐射全国15个省(市、区)46个地级市。宁波舟山港海铁联运的整体发展趋势为快速向内陆延伸。相较于其他港口,宁波舟山港海铁联运的最大特点是货物以外贸为主。随着政策红利的显露和运价分担机制的逐渐完善,宁波舟山港海铁联运持续发展,逐步确立了其海铁联运南方第一大港的地位。

Ningbo-Zhoushan Port is one of the center hub ports in China, with 19 port areas and more than 200 routes. In 2019, Ningbo-Zhoushan Port completed a cargo throughput of 1.08 billion tons, ranking first in the world. The container throughput reached 27.53 million TEU, ranking the top three in the world. The sea-rail transport in Ningbo-Zhoushan Port started in 2009 and started later than other ports. However, with its excellent location advantages and facilities, Ningbo-Zhoushan Port sea-rail transport has maintained rapid growth. In 2019, the sea-rail transport throughput of Ningbo-Zhoushan Port reached 802,000 TEU. At present, Ningbo-Zhoushan Port has opened 14 fixed trains, radiating 46 prefecture-level cities in 15 provinces (cities, districts) across the country. The overall development trend of Ningbo-Zhoushan Port sea-rail transport is to extend inland rapidly. Compared with other ports, the biggest feature of sea-rail transport of Ningbo-Zhoushan Port is that the goods are mainly foreign trade. With the exposure of policy dividends and the gradual improvement of freight rate sharing mechanism, sea-rail transport of Ningbo-Zhoushan Port has developed continuously and gradually established its position as the largest port in the south.

(3)天津港多式联运示范工程
(3)Tianjin Port Multimodal Transport Demonstration Project

天津港是我国北方最大的综合性港口,拥有3条通往内陆口岸的集装箱海铁联运通道。其位于渤海湾西侧,可连接东北亚与中西亚,是亚欧大陆桥东方起点。同时天津港配有良好的基础设施,各类泊位总数160个。2019年天津港集装箱吞吐量达1 730万 TEU,其中海铁联运运量达64.7万 TEU。天津港海铁联运陆上通道的建设逐渐加强,有利于集疏运体系的不断完善,加强海、空、铁多种运输的高效整合。中铁天津集装箱中心站开通运营后,天津港联通二连浩特、阿拉山口、霍尔果斯、满洲里等过境口岸,连接“一带一路”沿线的亚欧各地,完善新的国际集装箱运输快速通道,加强国内集装箱发运与接卸能力。

Tianjin Port is the largest comprehensive port in North China, with three container rail-sea intermodal transport channels leading to inland ports. It is located in the west of Bohai Bay, connecting Northeast Asia and central and Western Asia. It is the eastern starting point of the Eurasian Continental Bridge. At the same time, Tianjin Port is equipped with good infrastructure, with 160 berths. In 2019, the container throughput of Tianjin Port reached 17.3 million TEU, including 647,000 TEU of rail-sea intermodal transport. In Tianjin Port, the construction of the rail-sea intermodal transport land channel is gradually strengthened, conducive to the continuous improvement of the collection and distribution system and the efficient integration of sea, air, and rail transportation. After the opening and operation of the China Railway Tianjin Container Terminal, Tianjin Port connects the Erenhot, Alashankou, Huoerguosi, and Manchuria and other transit ports, connects Asia and Europe along the "One belt, one road", and improves the new international container transport rapid transit, and strengthens the capacity of domestic container shipping and unloading.

（4）青岛港多式联运示范工程
(4) Qingdao Port Multimodal Transport Demonstration Project

青岛港位于我国渤海湾港口群与长三角港口区的中心地带, 是世界第七大港, 是我国综合交通运输体系的重要枢纽。目前, 青岛港已经汇聚集装箱航线 160 余条, 开通海铁联运班列 40 余条, 形成了"一市一线、一地一港、覆盖山东、面向世界"的网络布局。青岛港拥有海关总署批复建立的全国沿海首家多式联运海关监管中心——中铁联集青岛中心站海关监管场所, 使货物到达中心站即可视为到达码头前沿, 实现了"一站式"海铁联运操作。同时, 青岛港的"跨境集装箱海铁联运示范工程"已实现了海铁联运的无缝对接。目前, 青岛港正努力构建海铁联运的全程现代物流体系, 达到串联日韩、东盟、中亚、欧洲四大地区的目标, 实现东中西互联互通。

Qingdao Port is located in the center of China's Bohai Bay Port Cluster and the Yangtze River Delta port area. It is the seventh largest port in the world and an essential hub of China's comprehensive transportation system. At present, Qingdao Port has gathered more than 160 container routes and opened more than 40 rail-sea intermodal transport trains, forming a network layout of "one city, one line, one place and one port, covering Shandong and facing the world". Qingdao Port has the first customs supervision place of China Railway Lianji Qingdao central station, the National Coastal intermodal customs supervision center approved by the General Administration of customs, which makes the arrival of cargo at the central station can be regarded as reaching the quayside of the port and realizes the "one-stop" rail-sea intermodal transport operation. Meanwhile, the "cross border container rail-sea intermodal transport demonstration project" of Qingdao Port has realized the seamless connection of sea rail intermodal transport. At present, Qingdao Port is trying to build a whole process modern logistics system of rail-sea intermodal transport, reaching the goal of connecting Japan and the Republic of Korea, ASEAN, Central Asia, and Europe, and realizing the interconnection between the East and the West.

第5章 港口物流发展政策与措施

Chapter 5 | Policy and Measures for Port Logistics Development

◈ 5.1 港口管理模式与激励政策

5.1 Port Management Model and Incentive Policy

5.1.1 港口管理模式分类
5.1.1 Category of Port Management Model

港口管理模式具有显著的差异性,在不同的国家之间、在同一国家的多个港口之间、在同一港口的不同发展时期之间,港口管理的模式不尽相同。根据其经营管理主体,可将港口管理模式大体上分为三类:(1)由政府机构或国有企业管理港口;(2)由政府机构、国有企业和私有企业共同管理港口;(3)由私有企业管理港口。

There are significant differences in port management models. The specific forms of port management models are quite different between the ports in different countries and different ports in a country, and different periods of a port. According to port management entities, the port management model could be divided broadly into three categories: (1) Ports managed by government agencies or state-owned enterprises; (2) Ports jointly managed by government agencies, state-owned enterprises and private enterprises; (3) Ports managed by private enterprises.

政府机构或国有企业管理港口:由政府或国有企业直接投资并经营管理,缺乏竞争和发展动力,易造成资源浪费,运营效率和服务质量较低的问题,增加政府财政负担。

Ports managed by government agencies or state-owned enterprises: government agencies or state-owned enterprises directly invest in and manage a port. It is easy to cause waste of resources and lower operational efficiency and service quality, owing to a lack of competition and development motivation.

政府机构、国有企业和私有企业共同管理港口：该模式最普遍，按照市场规律管理港口。可进一步细分为由中央直接控制、管理的集中管理模式与将港口的管理权移交给地方政府或独立港口管理部门的分散管理模式。

Ports managed jointly by government agencies, state-owned enterprises and private enterprises: this is the most common case, which manages ports following market rules. This case could be further divided into a centralized management model that is directly controlled and managed by the central government and a decentralized management model that transfers port management to local governments or independent port management departments.

私有企业管理港口：减少国家直接参与港口的运营管理，市场化程度大，运营效率高。虽然存在港口管理私有化的趋势，但由于该行业投资大、资金周转慢等原因，完全由私人企业经营管理的港口并不多。

Ports managed by private enterprises: this case reduces direct governmental participation in port operation and management, with a significant degree of marketization and high operational efficiency. Although there is a trend of port privatization, there are not many ports entirely managed by private enterprises, due to the significant investment and the slow capital turnover.

5.1.2 世界主要港口管理模式
5.1.2 Management Model of Main Global Ports

（1）世界主要港口管理模式（如表 5.1 所示）

（1）Management Model of Main Global Ports（as Shown in Table 5.1）

表 5.1　世界主要港口管理模式

管理模式	国家/地区	代表港口
政府机构或国有企业管理港口	德国、荷兰、比利时	汉堡港、不来梅港、鹿特丹港、安特卫普港
政府机构、国有企业和私有企业共同管理港口	集中管理：新加坡、斯里兰卡、肯尼亚	新加坡港
	分散管理：日本、澳大利亚、加拿大、中国台湾	高雄港
私有企业管理港口	英国、中国香港	香港港

Table 5.1　Management model of main global ports

Management model	Country/Region	Representative ports
Port managed by government agencies or state-owned enterprises	Germany, Netherlands, Belgium	Hamburg Port, Bremen Port, Rotterdam Port, Antwerp Port

续表

Management model	Country/Region		Representative ports
Port managed jointly by government agencies, state-owned enterprises and private enterprises	Centralized management model: Singapore, Sri Lanka, Kenya		Singapore Port
	Decentralized management model: Japan, Australia, Canada, Taiwan(China)		Kaohsiung Port
Port managed by private enterprises	The United Kingdom, Hong Kong(China)		Hong Kong Port

（2）港口管理模式发展趋势

（2）Development Trend of Port Management Model

①港口管理职能分散化

①Decentralization of Port Management Functions

由地方政府或港务局负责行政管理工作,由国有或私有企业负责日常生产经营活动,建立市场化的经营机制和价格体系,提高管理效率和服务质量,增强港口竞争力水平。中国的港口多由港务局负责行政工作,包括拟定规章制度、建设和维护公共设施等,而由港务集团或港务有限公司负责相关的生产经营活动。

The local government or the port authority is responsible for the administrative work, while state-owned or private enterprises provide production and operation activities. Market-oriented operating mechanisms and price systems are established for improving management efficiency and service quality, and enhancing port competitiveness. The administrative work of ports in China is mainly undertaken by port authorities, including outlining and issuing regulations, constructing and maintaining public facilities, etc. Related production and operation activities are provided by Port Group or Port Affairs Co., Ltd.

②港口企业集团化

②Port Collectivization

由一城一港的管理体系向港口集团过渡,打破港口管理中的城市区域限制。例如,各省组建了省港口集团有限公司,在考虑省内多个港口功能定位的基础上,统筹省内交通基础设施的建设和发展,实现多港口之间的优势互补,缓解重复建设和同质化竞争的矛盾。

A gradual transition of the management system from one city with one port to a port group has broken the limits of urban areas in port management. For example, Provincial Port Group Co., Ltd. was set up for coordinated development of transportation infrastructures in the province, taking into account various functions of multiple ports in each province. Complementary advantages of multiple ports could be realized, and duplicate port construction and homogeneous competition would also be alleviated.

③港口私有化

③Port Privatization

由于港口产业是资本密集型产业,港口基础设施投资建设所需资金量大,回收周期较长,投资回报率低。港口管理模式正在由政府机构和国有企业管理的模式,转向由政府机构或国有企业和私营企业共同管理的模式,吸引私有资本以促进港口基础设施的改造升级。

As the port industry is a capital-intensive industry, large-scale investment is required for port infrastructures, which would cause a long payback period and lower return on investment. There is the main trend of the port management model from a model managed by government agencies and state-owned enterprises to a model jointly managed by government agencies or state-owned enterprises and private enterprises. The improvement and upgrading of port infrastructure could be achieved by attracting private capital.

5.1.3 港口物流激励政策介绍
5.1.3 Incentive Policy for Port Logistics

（1）构建高效的口岸物流系统
(1) Establish an Efficient Port Logistics System

从物流系统的角度来看,港口物流链是港口连接经济腹地的纽带,完整的港口物流链的发展对区域经济协调有巨大的推动作用。建设高效经济的口岸物流系统,不仅是港口发展的必然要求,也是港口城市及腹地经济发展的客观需要。优化口岸物流系统结构,将港口功能进一步向港口城市全域和内陆腹地延伸,对提升整个口岸物流系统效率至关重要,也是推动整个航运中心建设的重要方面。港口采取向内陆腹地延伸的战略,构建港口和腹地"无水港"高效衔接的集散网络,共享港口优势,提高各环节协调。此外,无水港与进出口企业、物流企业、海关、商检、政府等多个实体之间发挥联动作用,形成一个以提供物流服务为主的服务型供应链,方便内陆地区企业办理进出口货运业务,搭建起沿海港口和内陆经济腹地的桥梁,从而达到多方共赢的状态。

From the perspective of the logistics system, the port logistics chain connects the port with the economic hinterland, and the development of the whole port logistics chain would promote regional economic coordination. An efficient and economical port logistics system is not only an inevitable requirement for port development, but also an objective need for the development of port cities and hinterlands. The optimization of the port logistics system structure would further extend the port functions to the entire port city and inland hinterland, which is vital to improving the efficiency of the port logistics system and the construction of the entire shipping center. The port adopts the strategy of extending to the inland hinterland to build an efficient distribution network between the port and the hinterland "dry port". The highly efficient distribution network would share the advantages of the port and improve the coordination of all links. In addition, dry ports cooperate with multiple entities such as import and export enterprises, logistics enterprises, customs, commodity inspection, and government to form a service-based supply chain, which facilitates enterprises in inland to handle import and export freight business, builds a bridge between coastal ports and inland economic hinterland and achieves a win-win situation for all parties.

①加强无水港群的基础设施建设

①Strengthen the Infrastructure Construction of Dry Port Clusters

天津港凭借完备的内陆运输体系,与内陆城市开展合作,通过建设"无水港"逐步将港口功能延伸至内陆地区,以港口的区位优势和经济优势带动北方地区的经济协同发展,打破货源增长困局。在东北区域内,以大连港为门户港口,在沈阳、长春和哈尔滨等内陆地区设立内陆无水港,通过联盟形式,构成大连港的东北无水港群,显著提升区域性货源控制力。上海港地处长江东西运输通道与海上南北运输通道的交汇点,辐射川渝及鄂湘赣皖苏等省市,横跨东中西三大经济区,这些地区都直接或间接地担当着上海港无水港的角色。

Tianjin Port cooperates with inland cities by virtue of an effective inland transport system, and port functions are gradually expanded to inland areas through the construction of "dry ports". The geographical and economic advantages of Tianjin Port drive the collaborative development of northern regions, which solves the dilemma of slower transport demands. In the northeast region, Dalian Port is the gateway port, and inland dry ports are established in many areas, such as Changchun, Harbin, Shenyang, etc., which forms a northeast dry port group of Dalian Port. The regional dry port alliance significantly enhances the control of regional transport demands. Shanghai Port is located at the intersection of the east-west transportation channel of the Yangtze River and the north-south transportation channel on the sea. Shanghai Port spans three major economic zones in the east, middle and west and radiates Sichuan, Chongqing, Hubei, Hunan, Jiangxi, Anhui, Jiangsu. These areas directly or indirectly play the role of Shanghai Port's dry ports.

②加强口岸物流链各环节的联系与协调

②Promote Cooperation and Coordination Among Links in the Port Logistics Chain

无水港建设和无水港与海港之间物流通道的建设相辅相成,无水港和沿海港口的衔接性是提升港口口岸物流系统的协调性、提高货物集散效率的重要因素。第一,大力发展内河运输、铁路运输与海运的多式联运模式,完善内支线运输网络,开通铁路集装箱直达班列,加强内支线运输网络与内陆集疏运通道的相互衔接,实现物流服务的整体化和系统化。第二,采取灵活的入港方式,降低集港时间,实现枢纽港口与内陆无水港的无缝衔接,加深便利化程度,节省进出口企业物流、通关成本,缓解港口拥堵。

The construction of dry ports and the construction of related logistics channels between dry ports and seaports complement each other. The effective connection between dry ports and the seaport is an important factor to improve the coordination of the port logistics system and the efficiency of cargo distribution. First, multimodal transport modes of inland water transport, railway transport and maritime transport would be vigorously developed through improving the inland transport network, opening direct railway access to the port terminals, and strengthening the interconnection between the feeder transport network and inland distribution channels. An integrated and systematic logistics services would be achieved. Second, flexible entry modes to port terminals would reduce the time of cargo gathering, achieve the seamless connection between the hub

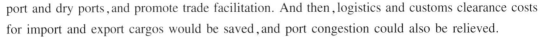

port and dry ports, and promote trade facilitation. And then, logistics and customs clearance costs for import and export cargos would be saved, and port congestion could also be relieved.

③推进口岸"单一窗口"建设,实现口岸通关便利化

③Promote the Construction of a "Single Window" and Facilitate Customs Clearance

建设"单一窗口",实行一站式服务,即通过一个信息平台,企业完成报关、检验检疫、税务、支付结算、保险等业务,监管部门根据企业提供的电子信息和标准化单证,将处理结果通过该平台反馈给企业。口岸"单一窗口"能够加强部门间的业务协作,实现区域贸易便利化,提高企业的运营效率,降低政府各部门的监管成本,促进行政管理的集约化。

The "single window" is built to implement the one-stop service; That is, all related services could be offered through an information platform, including customs declaration, inspection and quarantine, taxation, payment settlement, insurance and other services. Meanwhile, according to the electronic information and standardized documents provided by the enterprise, the supervisory department will feedback the processing results to the enterprise through the platform. The "single window" at the port could strengthen the cooperation between different departments, so that regional trade facilitation would be achieved, and intensive administrative management would also be promoted with higher operational efficiency and lower supervision costs.

(2) 推进港口供应链的建设

(2) Promote the Construction of Port Supply Chain

枢纽港是港口供应链的核心,产业链的配套基础设施和配套政策可以促进港口与物流、贸易和金融服务公司之间的有效联系,最大限度地提高港口供应链整体运营效率。通过考虑各种形式的补贴政策,整合政府部门、托运人、港口、航运公司、物流公司、加工公司、金融服务提供商等,可以实现跨地区、跨行业的合作。通过整合物流、业务流、信息流和资金流,提供全方位的信息服务,形成完整的港口供应链体系。需要激发港口供应链的创新,以提高整个物流链的效率,促进区域国际贸易。

Hub ports are the core of the port supply chain, and the ancillary infrastructure and supporting policies of the industrial chain could promote the effective connection between the port and logistics, trade, and financial service companies, and maximize the overall operational efficiency of the port supply chain. With the consideration of various forms of subsidy policies and the integration of governmental departments, consignors, ports, shipping companies, logistics companies, processing companies, financial service providers, etc., the cross-region and cross-industry cooperation could be achieved. A full range of information services would be provided by integrating logistics, business flow, information flow and capital flow to form a complete port supply chain system. The innovation of the port supply chain needs to be stimulated for improving the efficiency of the entire logistics chain and promoting regional international trade.

◆ 5.2　保税港与自由贸易港
5.2　Bonded Port and Free Trade Port

5.2.1　保税区、出口加工区与保税港区
5.2.1　Bonded Area, Export Processing Zone and Bonded Port Zone

（1）保税区

（1）Bonded Area

保税区，又称保税仓库区，是一国海关设置或经海关批准注册、受海关监督和管理、在海关监管下对外开放的区域，其可较长时间储存商品。保税区功能主要包括保税仓储、出口加工、转口贸易、商品展示等，针对境外进入保税区的部分货物实行免税和保税政策，以保障转口贸易的便利性。针对运送到保税区内的货物，在海关的监管范围内可以进行储存、改装、分类、混合、展览以及加工制造等。外国的商品不用交纳进口关税只需要交纳存储费和少量其他费用即可存入保税区，但是如果进入关境则需要交纳关税。

Bonded area, also known as bonded warehouse area. It is an area set up or approved to be registered, or subjected and managed by a country's customs and open to the outside world under the supervision of the customs, which can store commodities for a long time. The main functions of the bonded area include bonded warehousing, export processing, entrepot trade, commodity display, etc., and implementing duty-free and bonded policies for some goods entering the bonded area from abroad to ensure the convenience of entrepot trade. Goods transported to the bonded area can be stored, modified, classified, mixed, exhibited, processed, and manufactured within the scope of customs supervision. Foreign goods can be deposited in the bonded area without paying import duties and only need to pay storage fees and a small number of other fees and can be deposited into the bonded area, but foreign goods need to pay customs duties if they enter the customs territory.

中国保税区是通过借鉴国际上自由贸易区的通行做法并结合中国国情设立的新型综合性对外开放区域。上海外高桥保税区于1990年6月设立，是中国启动最早的保税区，目前已有上海外高桥保税区、天津港保税区、大连保税区、张家港保税区、宁波保税区、福州保税区、厦门象屿保税区、广州保税区、深圳福田保税区、珠海保税区、汕头保税区等11个保税区。

The bonded area of China is a new type of comprehensive opening-up area established by drawing lessons from the common practices of international bonded area and combining them with China's national conditions. Shanghai Waigaoqiao Bonded Area, which was established in June 1990, is the earliest bonded area in China. At present, there are 11 bonded areas in China, including Shanghai Waigaoqiao Bonded Area, Tianjin Port Bonded Area, Dalian Bonded Area, Zhangjiagang Bonded Area, Ningbo Bonded Area, Fuzhou Bonded Area, Xiamen Xiangyu

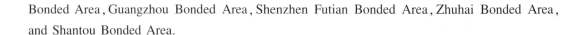

Bonded Area, Guangzhou Bonded Area, Shenzhen Futian Bonded Area, Zhuhai Bonded Area, and Shantou Bonded Area.

（2）出口加工区
（2）Export Processing Zone

出口加工区是一国为了鼓励外贸出口,设置的受海关监管的集研发、制造、加工、装配、储存出口货物等功能于一体的特定区域。在中国境内设立出口加工区只限于现有的经济技术开发区内。出口加工区最初的功能定位仅是单一的产品加工功能,2007 年首次拓展保税物流功能,试点开展研发、检测、维修业务,向整合海关特殊监管区域迈出了第一步。出口加工区的主要特点如下:

The export processing zone is a specific area set up by a country under the supervision of the customs to integrate the functions of research and development, manufacturing, processing, assembly, and storage of export goods, in order to encourage foreign trade export. The establishment of export processing zones in China is limited to existing economic and technological development zones. The initial functional orientation of the export processing zone is only a single product processing function. In 2007, the bonded logistics function was expanded for the first time, and the research and development, testing and maintenance business was carried out on a pilot basis, which took the first step towards the integration of special customs supervision areas. The main features of the export processing zone are as follows:

第一,规划面积相对较小,一般不超过 3 km²。出口加工区最初功能定位较为单一,仅提供出口加工业务,不得经营商业零售、一般贸易、转口贸易等与加工区无关的业务。允许入区的企业只有出口加工企业和为出口加工企业提供服务的仓储、运输企业。

First, the planning area is relatively small, generally no more than 3 square kilometers. The initial functional positioning of the export processing zone is relatively simple, providing only export processing business, and may not engage in commercial retail, general trade, entrepot trade and other businesses that have nothing to do with the processing zone. The only enterprises allowed to enter the zone are export processing enterprises and warehousing and transportation enterprises that provide services for export processing enterprises.

第二,具有较高的物流效率。四通八达的立体交通网络是原材料、零部件、元器件、包装物料、生产所需设施设备和加工产品集散的关键,是保障出口加工业务顺利开展的基础。

Second, it has high logistics efficiency. The three-dimensional transportation network extending in all directions is the key to the collection and distribution of raw materials, spare parts, components, packaging materials, production facilities and equipment, and processing products, and is the basis to ensure the smooth development of the export processing business.

第三,区内产业与区外产业具有较强关联性。出口加工区实施的税赋优惠政策有助于降低区内企业的加工成本,促进加工贸易的发展。区内产业以加工附加值较高的电子信息产品为主,吸引了电子信息行业龙头企业聚集,区外形成了完整的产业链。

Third, there is a strong relationship between the industry within the region and the industry outside the region. The preferential tax policy implemented in the export processing zone helps to reduce the processing costs of enterprises in the area and promote the development of processing trade. The industry in the region mainly processes electronic information products with high added value, which attracts the gathering of leading enterprises in the electronic information industry, and a complete industrial chain has been formed outside the region.

第四,具有多功能化的发展趋势。在中国海关特殊监管区域整合优化的背景下,出口加工区功能在传统的加工制造功能的基础上逐步丰富,推进出口加工区向综合保税区的转型升级。

Fourth, it has a development trend of multi-function. Under the background of regional integration and optimization of special supervision of Chinese customs, the functions of export processing zones are gradually enriched based on traditional processing and manufacturing functions, promoting the transformation and upgrading of export processing zones to comprehensive bonded areas.

(3) 保税港区
(3) Bonded Port Zone

保税港区是指经国务院批准,设立在国家对外开放的口岸港区和与之相连的特定区域内,具有口岸、物流、加工等功能的海关特殊监管区域(中华人民共和国海关总署)。保税港区将港口和陆地区域相结合,具有明显的区位优势,提供最优惠的政策支持,在形式上最接近自由贸易港的运作模式。保税港结合了邻近港区的保税区和港口,具有保税区、出口加工区等多种特殊监管区域的功能的基础上,同时具备码头和港口的功能。保税港区内可开展货物存储、国际转口贸易、国际采购、分销和配送、国际中转、检测和售后服务维修、商品展示、研发、加工、制造、港口作业等业务,并具备国际中转、国际配送、国际采购、转口贸易、出口加工等功能。保税港区的特点如下:

The bonded port zone refers to the special customs supervision area with the functions of port, logistics, and processing, which is established in the port area and the specific area connected with it with the approval of the State Council (General Administration of Customs of the People's Republic of China). The bonded port zone combines the port with the land area, has obvious location advantages, provides the most preferential policy support, and is closest to the operation mode of the free trade port in form. The bonded port combines the bonded area and the port area adjacent to the port area, and has the functions of a bonded area, export processing zones, and other special supervision areas, as well as the functions of wharves and ports. The bonded port area can carry out goods storage, international entrepot trade, international procurement, distribution and distribution, international transit, testing and after-sales service maintenance, commodity display, research and development, processing, manufacturing, port operations, and other services and has the functions of international transit, international distribution, international procurement, entrepot trade, export processing and so on. The characteristics of the bonded port area are as follows:

第一,区港结合,政策统一。保税港由港口和临近的保税区组成,形成"区港合一"的运作模式,港口和临近的保税区实行统一的政策,在行政管理上由一个行政机构统一负责,在监管上由一个海关负责。

First, it combines the area and the port and owns the unity of policies. The bonded port is composed of the port and the adjacent bonded area, which forms the operation mode of "integration of area and port". The port and the neighboring bonded area implement a unified policy, which is uniformly responsible for administrative management by one administrative agency and for supervision by one custom.

第二,功能齐全。保税港是集合了保税区、出口加工区等功能区的海关监管的特殊区域,具有生产、加工、仓储、物流、口岸、保税等多种功能,是一个综合性的对外开放的区域。

Second, it has complete functions. The bonded port is a special area under the customs supervision, which integrates bonded areas, export processing zones, and other functional areas, with production, processing, warehousing, logistics, ports, bonded, and other functions. It is a comprehensive area opening to the outside world.

第三,政策优惠。保税港作为"境内关外"的特殊经济区域,除了享有保税区的"免税、免证"以及国内货物区内退税等优惠政策外,还享有国内各类功能区的优惠政策,是目前我国政策最优惠的对外开放经济区域。

Third, the policy is preferential. As a special economic region outside the customs, the bonded port not only enjoys the preferential policies of "tax exemption and certificate exemption" and the tax rebate in the domestic goods area but also enjoys the preferential policies of various domestic functional areas. At present, it is the most favorable economic area for opening up to the outside world.

第四,通关便利。为简化通关手续,实现快捷通关,提高高效管理及便利化服务,保税港采取了封闭管理保税港,智能管理海关,提升园区管理的信息化程度,提高海关通关效率等措施,做到一次申报、一次查验、一次放行。同时,采用高科技技术,设置高科技的海关监督设施和完善的信息管理系统,从而实现进出口货物的快速流通。

Fourth, customs clearance is convenient. In order to simplify customs clearance procedures, achieve quick customs clearance, improve efficient management and facilitation services, the bonded port has adopted measures such as closed management of the bonded port, intelligent management of the customs, promotion of the informatization of the area management, and improvement of the efficiency of customs clearance, to achieve one declaration, one inspection, and one release. At the same time, the use of high-tech technology, the establishment of high-tech customs supervision facilities, and perfect information management system, to achieve the rapid flow of import and export goods.

第五,产业外向。由于保税港的定位以及特殊的功能,港区内的产业呈现外向的特征,如仓储物流、加工后出口业务、进口分拣业务以及转口贸易业务等,港区的主要功能导向是对外国市场的物流业务、贸易业务等。

Fifth, industry extroversion. Due to the positioning and special functions of the bonded port, the industries in the port area show extroverted characteristics, such as warehousing and logistics, post-processing export business, import sorting business, entrepot trade business and so on. The primary functional orientation of the port area is the logistics business and trade business to foreign markets.

5.2.2　自由贸易试验区与自由贸易港
5.2.2　Free Trade Pilot Zone and Free Trade Port

（1）自由贸易试验区
(1) Free Trade Pilot Zone

自由贸易园区是指在某一国家或地区境内设立的实行优惠税收和特殊监管政策的小块特定区域(中华人民共和国商务部)。自由贸易区地理位置优越,具有自由的交易环境。中国的经济特区、保税区、出口加工区、保税港、经济技术开发区等特殊经济功能区都具有自由贸易区的某些特征,但并不是真正意义上的自由贸易区。

A free trade zone refers to a small particular area established in a country or region with preferential taxation and particular regulatory policies (Ministry of Commerce of the People's Republic of China). The free trade zone has a superior geographical location and an unrestricted trading environment. China's particular economic functional areas, such as special economic zones, bonded areas, export processing zones, bonded ports, economic and technological development zones, all have some characteristics of free trade zone, but they are not free trade areas in the real sense.

自由贸易试验区与自由贸易园区概念相似,是中国探索实践的结果。为提高投资和贸易的便利度、推进金融开放创新、探索改革和开放的新途径,2013 年 9 月中国(上海)自由贸易试验区率先设立,目前已形成"18+1"自由贸易试验区发展格局,实现了沿海省份全覆盖。自由贸易试验区是为深化改革和扩大对外开放提出的一系列创新政策的试验田,在政府职能转变、管理制度改革、贸易监管模式、金融领域等方面取得了突出的制度创新成果,形成了可复制、可推广的经验。

The concept of the free trade pilot zone is similar to that of the free trade zone, which is the result of China's exploration and practice. To improve the convenience of investment and trade, promote financial opening and innovation, and explore new ways of reform and opening up, the China (Shanghai) Free Trade Pilot Zone was first established in September 2013. At present, the development pattern of the "18+1" free trade pilot zone has been formed and achieved full coverage of coastal provinces. The free trade pilot zone is a testing ground for a series of innovative policies put forward to deepen reform and open wider to the outside world. Through the pilot reform of the free trade pilot zone, outstanding institutional innovation achievements have been made in the transformation of government functions, the reform of management system, the mode of trade supervision and the financial field, and the experience that can be replicated and popular-

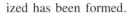

ized has been formed.

自由贸易试验区主要特征为:第一,政府机构的整合。打破了传统部门之间的壁垒,整合职能和业务范围相近的部门,提高行政服务效率。同时,建立以信用监管为核心的事中事后监管体系,推进政府职能的转变。第二,负面清单管理的管理理念。提出外商投资准入特别管理措施(负面清单),列明了不符合国民待遇等原则的特别管理措施,提高了投资贸易的便利性和自由度。第三,明确的功能划分。自由贸易试验区的实施范围较大,由多个片区构成,在自由贸易试验区的建设方案中,充分考虑所在区域地理位置特征及产业结构,针对每一个片区均有明确的功能划分和发展重点。

The main features of the pilot free trade zone are as follows:First,the integration of government agencies. Break down the barriers between traditional departments,integrate departments with similar functions and business scope,and improve the efficiency of administrative services. At the same time,the supervision system after the event with credit supervision as the core should be established to promote the transformation of government functions. Second,the management concept of negative list management. Put forward the special management measures for the access of foreign investment (negative list),clearly list the special management measures that are not in line with the principles of national treatment,and improve the convenience and freedom of investment and trade. Third,a clear division of functions. The implementation scope of the free trade pilot zone is enormous,which is composed of several areas. In the construction plan of the free trade pilot zone,the geographical location characteristics and industrial structure of the region are fully taken into account,and each area has a clear functional division and development focus.

(2)自由贸易港
(2)Free Trade Port

1547年,在意大利热那亚湾建成了世界上第一个自由贸易港雷格亨港,目前较为典型的自由贸易港有新加坡港、中国香港港、荷兰鹿特丹港、迪拜杰贝阿里港等。自由贸易港是设在一国(地区)境内关外,货物、资金和人员进出自由,绝大多数商品免征关税的特定区域,是目前全球开放水平最高的特殊经济功能区。自由贸易港的主要特征:

In 1547,the world's first free trade port,Regehenge,was built in the Gulf of Genoa,Italy. At present,the more typical free trade ports are Singapore Port,Hong Kong Port in China,Rotterdam Port in the Netherlands,and Jebel Ali in Dubai. The free trade trade port is a specific area located outside the customs within the territory of a country (region),free for the entry and exit of goods,capital and personnel,and duty-free for the vast majority of commodities. It is currently a special economic functional area with the highest level of openness in the world. The main features of free trade ports are as follows:

第一,境内关外的管理制度。在港区内可以享受高效率的物流服务,货物流通没有层层申报的限制。第二,港区事务自主管理。自由贸易港内事务的管理由厂商自主管理,脱离了政府管制,降低政府对自由贸易港的介入。第三,港区内货物免征关税。从国外运到港区内进行营运的货物以及港区自用的设备均免征关税。第四,货物流通自由。从国外或国内其他自由贸易港运至港区内的货物,或从港区内运至国外或国内其他自由贸易港的货物,经海关通报、记录备案后即可将货物运送至目的地。第五,产品附加值高。自由贸易港可以进行零部件组装等深层次加工,充分发挥制造高附加值产品的优势,以提高港区物流竞争力。第六,吸引商务活动。自由贸易港简化国际商务人士申请入境的程序,可以方便国际商务人士进入港区从事商务活动。第七,资金流通便捷化。自由贸易港区内允许从事外币汇兑及外汇交易等业务活动,便于资金的流通。第八,行政手续便捷化。港区内的行政管理尽量授权港区内的管理机构自主办理,以提高港区内行政效率。

First, the management system of "inside borders and outside the customs". In the port area, you can enjoy efficient logistics services, and there are no layers of restrictions on the flow of goods. Second, independent management of port affairs. The management of the affairs of the free trade port is managed by the manufacturers themselves, who is divorced from government control and reduces the government's intervention in the free trade port. Third, goods in the port area are exempt from customs duties. Goods shipped from abroad in the port area for operation and equipment for self-use in the port area shall be exempted from customs duties. Fourth, the free flow of goods. Goods shipped from foreign or domestic free trade ports to the port area, or goods shipped from the port area to foreign or domestic free trade ports can be transported to their destination after being notified by the customs and recorded by the customs. Fifth, the product has a high added value. The free trade port carries out in-depth processing such as parts assembly to make the most of the advantages of manufacturing high value-added products and improve the logistics competitiveness of the port area. Sixth, attract business activities. The free trade port simplifies the procedures for international business people to apply for entry and facilitate international business people to enter the port area to engage in business activities. Seventh, the flow of funds is convenient. Free trade port areas can engage in foreign currency exchange and foreign exchange transactions and other business activities to facilitate the flow of funds. Eighth, administrative procedures are convenient. The administrative management in the port area shall authorize the administrative agencies in the port area to handle it independently as far as possible, to improve the administrative efficiency in the port area.

5.2.3 典型案例分析
5.2.3 Typical Case Analysis

(1)洋山保税港区
(1) Yangshan Bonded Port Area

洋山保税港区由上海市和浙江省跨省市合作建设,由小洋山港口区域、东海大桥和上海市南汇区芦潮港陆地区域组成,由海关特殊监管,区内创新性地实行港口和保税区、出口加工区、保税物流园区功能合一的运作模式。

Yangshan bonded port area is jointly built by Shanghai and Zhejiang Province and is composed of the Xiaoyangshan Port area, Donghai Bridge, and Luchao Port Land area of Nanhui District of Shanghai. It is an area under special supervision by the customs. The region creatively implements the operation mode of the integration of port and bonded area, export processing zone, and bonded logistics park.

洋山保税港区主要规划、开发和建设的功能区域包括查验区、港口辅助区、仓储配送区、集拼中转区、加工制造区、商贸展示区等，能够提供国际中转、配送、采购、转口贸易和出口加工等业务，其周围设有配套临港非保税物流园区、铁路中心编组站、集装箱内河转运区、危险品仓储区等物流运作区域。

The main functional areas for the planning, development, and construction of the Yangshan bonded port area include the inspection area, auxiliary port area, warehousing and distribution area, assembly transfer area, processing and manufacturing area, trade exhibition area and so on. It can provide international transit, distribution, procurement, entrepot trade, and export processing services. The port area is equipped with logistics operation areas such as port-adjacent non-bonded logistics park, railway center marshalling yard, container inland river transfer area, dangerous goods storage area, and so on.

与实施"区港联动"的保税物流园区相比，洋山保税港区具有两大政策上的重要突破：第一，洋山保税港区实行的"区港一体"管理模式，将港口和产业园区连成一体，避免在监管上多重设卡的问题，对港口和陆上区域进行统一管理，优化口岸通关环境和效率。第二，洋山保税港区把保税物流园区和出口加工区的政策进行叠加，使其不仅拥有了进区退税的税收优势，还拥有了出口加工功能，使得货物卸船后可以直接进行加工、储存和贸易。

Compared with the bonded logistics park with the implementation of "zone-port linkage", Yangshan bonded port area has two important policy breakthroughs: First, the "district-port integration" management mode implemented in Yangshan bonded port area connects the port and the industrial park into one. It avoids the problem of setting up multiple cards in supervision, unifies the management of the port and the land area, and optimizes the customs clearance environment and efficiency of the port. Second, Yangshan bonded port area overlays the policies of the bonded logistics park and export processing zone so that it not only has the tax advantage of a tax rebate but also has the function of export processing so that the goods can be processed, stored and traded directly after unloading.

（2）中国（上海）自由贸易试验区
（2）China（Shanghai）Free Trade Pilot Zone

中国(上海)自由贸易试验区是国务院率先批准设立的第一个自由贸易试验区，涵盖外高桥保税区、外高桥保税物流园区、洋山保税港和上海浦东机场综合保税区、金桥出口加工区、张江高科技园区和陆家嘴金融贸易区等七个片区。2019 年 7 月，进一步规划中国(上海)自由贸易试验区临港新片区。

China（Shanghai）free trade pilot zone is the first free trade pilot zone approved by the

State Council. It covers seven areas, including Waigaoqiao Bonded Aera, Waigaoqiao Bonded Logistics Park, Yangshan Bonded Port Area, and Shanghai Pudong Airport Comprehensive Bonded Aera, Jinqiao Export Processing Zone, Zhangjiang High-tech Park, and Lujiazui Financial and Trade Zone. In July 2019, the new area of China (Shanghai) Free Trade Pilot Zone near the port will be further planned.

　　自由贸易试验区关键在"试验"。作为中国首个自由贸易试验区,中国(上海)自由贸易试验区先行先试,率先在投资管理、贸易便利化、金融、服务业开放、事后监管等领域开展了外商投资准入负面清单和备案管理、证照分离、单一窗口、利率市场化、分类监管等多项改革措施,获得了可复制、可推广的制度创新成果。

The key to the free trade pilot zone lies in the "experiment". As China's first free trade pilot zone, China (Shanghai) Free Trade Pilot Zone took the lead in carrying out several reform measures such as the negative list of foreign investment access and record management, license separation, single window, interest rate marketization, classified supervision and other areas in the fields of investment management, trade facilitation, finance, service industry liberalization, and post-event supervision, and achieved replicable and popularizing achievements in institutional innovation.

(3) 中国香港自由贸易港
(3) The Free Trade Port of Hong Kong, China

　　香港自由贸易港由香港岛、九龙和新界组成,其范围包括整个香港地区。自 1841 年推行自由贸易政策以来,香港由之前单一的转口贸易港,发展成为现在的经济结构多元化的自由贸易港。香港地处亚太地区的要冲,是欧洲、非洲通往东南亚的航运要道,同时也是中国内地与世界进行经济往来的重要桥梁。香港自由贸易港通过一系列自由化政策,推动了经济跃升,其发展阶段大致可以分为转口贸易型、加工贸易型、服务型和综合型自由贸易港等四个发展阶段。

The free trade port of Hong Kong, China consists of Hong Kong Island, Kowloon, and the New Territories, covering the whole of Hong Kong. Since the implementation of the free trade policy in 1841, Hong Kong has developed from a single entrepot to a free trade port with a diversified economic structure. As Hong Kong is located at the heart of the Asia-Pacific region, it is also a shipping route from Europe and Africa to Southeast Asia, as well as an important bridge for economic exchanges between Chinese mainland and the world. The free trade port of Hong Kong, China has promoted the economic leap through a series of liberalization policies, and its development stage can be divided into four stages: entrepot trade, processing trade, service, and comprehensive free trade port.

　　第一阶段:1841 年至 1949 年,转口贸易型自由贸易港阶段。作为一个通商自由的港口门户,通过允许外国船舶自由进出港口、对进出口货物免征关税等方式,大力发展转口贸易。

The first stage: the stage of entrepot free trade port from 1841 to 1949. As a port portal with free trade, it vigorously develops entrepot trade by allowing foreign ships to enter and leave the

port freely and exempting import and export goods from customs duties.

第二阶段:1950 年至 1978 年,加工贸易型自由贸易港阶段。香港充分运用来自内地以及东南亚国家的大量资金、设备和技术,依仗廉价的劳动力资源和免税优惠条件,大力发展制造产业,弥补了自然资源匮乏、工业基础薄弱、本地市场狭小等短板。

The second stage: the stage of processing trade free trade port from 1950 to 1978. Hong Kong has made full use of a large amount of capital, equipment, and technology from Chinese mainland and Southeast Asian countries, and vigorously developed the manufacturing industry by relying on cheap labor resources and tax-free preferential conditions. It has made up for the shortcomings such as the lack of natural resources, the weak industrial base, and the narrow local market.

第三阶段:1979 年至 1996 年,服务型自由贸易港阶段。自 1978 年,中国内地实行对内改革、对外开放的政策下,保障了香港的服务市场,香港转向了以贸易、金融、物流等服务业为主的服务型经济。

The third stage: the stage of service-oriented free trade port from 1979 to 1996. Since 1978, under the policy of domestic reform and opening up into the outside world, Chinese mainland has protected Hong Kong's service market, and Hong Kong has turned to a service-oriented economy dominated by trade, finance, logistics, and other services.

第四阶段:1997 年至今,综合型自由贸易港阶段。香港作为内地最重要的转口港和离岸集资中心,香港与内地的合作紧密,粤港地区经济一体化发展。香港经济的持续稳定发展、健全的金融法律与法规,以及税收优惠政策,使得香港经济保持扩张态势。

The fourth stage: the stage of a comprehensive free trade port from 1997 to the present. As the most important entrepot and offshore fund-raising center in Chinese mainland, Hong Kong has close cooperation with Chinese mainland, and the economy of Guangdong and Hong Kong has developed into an integrated one. Hong Kong's sustained and stable economic development, sound financial laws and regulations, and preferential tax policies have enabled Hong Kong's economy to maintain its expansion.

(4) 中国海南自由贸易港
(4) Hainan Free Trade Port

2020 年,中共中央、国务院印发了《海南自由贸易港建设总体方案》,聚焦发展旅游业、现代服务业和高新技术产业,力争打造开放层次高、营商环境优、辐射作用强的中国特色自由贸易港,着重加强与东南亚国家交流合作,促进与粤港澳大湾区的联动发展。

In 2020, the Central Committee of the Communist Party of China and the State Council issued the "General Plan for the Construction of Hainan Free Trade Port", focusing on the development of tourism, modern services and high-tech industries. A free trade port with Chinese characteristics at a high level of openness, excellent business environment and strong radiation effect is being worked on. Hainan free trade port focus on strengthening exchanges and cooperation with Southeast Asian countries and promoting the development of linkages with Guangdong,

Hong Kong and Macao in the Greater Bay Area.

以海南岛全岛作为试验区,采用全球最高标准构建开放新格局。以具有成熟制度体系和运作模式的高水平自由贸易港为发展目标,重点任务可概括为"6+1+4",以实现制度集成创新。"6"即贸易自由便利、投资自由便利、跨境资金流动自由便利、人员进出自由便利、运输来往自由便利和数据安全有序流动。"1"即构建现代产业体系。"4"即加强税收、社会治理、法治、风险防控等制度建设。

With the whole island of Hainan as a pilot area, a new pattern of openness would be built according to the highest global standards. With the development goal of a high-level free trade port with a mature institutional system and operational mode, the key tasks could be summarized as "6+1+4" in order to achieve integrated system innovation. "6" that is, free and convenient trade, free and convenient investment, free and convenient cross-border capital flow, free and convenient entry and exit of people, free and convenient transportation and safe and orderly flow of data. "1" is to build a modern industrial system. "4" is to strengthen the system of taxation, social governance, rule of law, risk prevention and control.

参考文献
Reference

［1］杨茅甄. 件杂货港口管理实务［M］. 2 版. 上海：上海人民出版社，2015.

［2］BERESFORD A K C，GARDNER B M，PETTIT S J，et al. The UNCTAD and WORK-PORT models of port development：evolution or revolution？［J］. Maritime Policy & Management，2004，31（2）：93-107.

［3］真虹. 港口管理［M］. 2 版. 北京：人民交通出版社，2009.

［4］汪长江，等. 港口物流：理论、实物与技术［M］. 北京：清华大学出版社，2012.

［5］WANG L. Study on port logistics marketing under the environment of supply chain［J］. International Journal of Business & Management，2011，6（3）：267.

［6］汪长江. 港口物流学［M］. 浙江：浙江大学出版社，2010.

［7］郭子雪，康慧聪，赵婉，等. 京津冀港口物流与区域经济发展的互动关系研究：基于格兰杰因果检验和灰色关联度的分析［J］. 数学的实践与认识，2020，50（5）：32-39.

［8］汪长江. 港口物流研究：浙江舟山群岛新区建设背景下的探讨［M］. 杭州：浙江大学出版社，2014.

［9］顾波军. 港口物流供应链优化研究［M］. 北京：海洋出版社，2014.

［10］张旖，尹传忠. 港口物流［M］. 上海：上海交通大学出版社，2012.

［11］中华人民共和国交通运输部.全国沿海港口布局规划［EB/OL］.（2006-09-12）［2021-06-22］. http：//xxgk.mot.gov.cn/jigou/zhghs/201304/t20130412_2976731.html.

［12］王斌义. 港口物流［M］. 2 版. 北京：机械工业出版社，2018.

［13］胡祥培，孙玉姣，曾庆成. 集装箱码头同贝同步装卸作业的序列优化模型［J］. 系统工程理论与实践，2016，36（3）：623-634.

［14］PAN J，XU Y，ZHANG G. Online integrated allocation of berths and quay cranes in container terminals with 1-lookahead［J］. Journal of Combinatorial Optimization，2018，36：617-636.

［15］IRIS Ç，PACINO D，ROPKE S. Improved formulations and an adaptive large neighborhood search heuristic for the integrated berth allocation and quay crane assignment problem[J]. Transportation Research Part E:Logistics and Transportation Review,2017,105:123-147.

[16] ROBENEK T,UMANG N,BIERLAIRE M,et al. A branch-and-price algorithm to solve the integrated berth allocation and yard assignment problem in bulk ports[J]. European Journal of Operational Research,2014,235(2):399-411.

[17] SHEN Y F,ZHAO N,XIA M J,et al. A deep q-learning network for ship stowage planning problem[J]. Polish Maritime Research,2017,24(S3):102-109.

[18] SALIDO M A,RODRIGUEZ-MOLINS M,BARBER F. A decision support system for managing combinatorial problems in container terminals[J]. Knowledge-Based Systems, 2012,29:63-74.

[19] DE LEÓN A D,LALLA-RUIZ E,MELIÁN-BATISTA B,et al. A machine learning-based system for berth scheduling at bulk terminals[J]. Expert Systems with Applications,2017, 87:170-182.

[20] 刘翠莲. 港口装卸工艺[M]. 大连:大连海事大学出版社,2013.

[21] XIE Y C,HUYNH N. Kernel-based machine learning models for predicting daily truck volume at seaport terminals[J]. Journal of Transportation Engineering,2010,136(12): 1145-1152.

[22] 韩兆燕,杨志嵩."互联网"背景下青岛港建设智慧港口发展模式研究[J].智库时代, 2018(25):259,261.

[23] 罗本成. 智慧港口:探索实践与发展趋势[J].中国远洋海运,2018(6):32-35.

[24] 龙丹.物联网技术在港口信息化建设中的应用研究[J].物流工程与管理,2019,41(5): 84-86.

[25] 耿波.物联网技术在散杂货港口物流运作中的设计与应用[J].物流技术,2014,33 (21):435-437.

[26] 宓翠,袁旭梅.基于物联网技术的港口煤炭作业流程的系统分析与设计[J].物流技术, 2013,32(9):425-428.

[27] 吴达. 天津东方海陆集装箱码头公司"预约集港"研究[D]. 大连:大连海事大学,2014.

[28] 王泽浩. 自动化码头 AGV 实时调度优化方法研究[D].大连:大连海事大学,2019.

[29] 张弛. 多式联运:为港口经济腾飞插上"双翼"[J].中国水运,2017(11):21-22.

[30] 张永坚.仍不应被忽视的《国际货物多式联运公约》[J].中国海商法研究,2018,29(4): 81-86.

[31] 赖菲,张祎.港口多式联运信息平台建设方式分析及阐述[J].中国管理信息化,2016,19 (20):60-61.

[32] 吴昊. 珠海港集装箱海铁联运发展策略研究[D].大连:大连海事大学,2017.

[33] 本刊编辑部.港口多式联运成港口发展新增长点[J].中国港口,2017(4):21-23.

[34] 宋炳良,德兰根. 港口经济、政策与管理[M].上海:格致出版社,上海:上海人民出版社,2009.

[35] 林仲琪.港口管理政企分开的成功尝试:厦门港口管理体制改革纪实[J].中国港口,

1998(5):2-15.

[36] 周哲,申雅君.国际物流[M].北京:清华大学出版社,2007.

[37] 中华人民共和国海关总署.中华人民共和国海关对出口加工区监管的暂行办法[EB/OL].(2000-05-24)[2021-06-22]. http://www.customs.gov.cn/customs/302249/302266/302267/356582/index.html.

[38] 赵倩.长江经济带出口加工区转型发展研究[D].上海:上海工程技术大学,2016.

[39] 薛荣久.国际贸易[M].5版.北京:对外经济贸易大学出版社,2008.

[40] 魏建平,韦梦鹍.浅议我国出口加工区产业发展的特点[J].建设科技,2006(15):66-67.

[41] 陈晓倩.青岛保税港竞争力提升研究[J].中国经济特区研究,2015(0):151-176.

[42] 王晓东,胡瑞娟.现代物流管理[M].2版.北京:对外经济贸易大学出版社,2007.

[43] 国务院办公厅.自由贸易试验区外商投资准入特别管理措施(负面清单)(2017年版)[EB/OL].[2021-06-22]. http://www.gov.cn/zhengce/content/2017-06/16/content_5202973.htm.

[44] 吴蓉,何万篷.中国特色自由贸易港政策制度体系创新的基点与内涵探讨[J].海关与经贸研究,2020,41(1):98-107.

[45] 汪洋.推动形成全面开放新格局[EB/OL].(2017-11-10)[2021-06-22]. http://ydyl.people.com.cn/n1/2017/1110/c411837-29638172.html.